International Political Economy Series

General Editor: **Timothy M. Shaw**, Professor of Political Science and International Development Studies, Dalhousie University, Halifax, Nova Scotia

Titles include:

Leslie Elliott Armijo (*editor*)
FINANCIAL GLOBALIZATION AND DEMOCRACY IN EMERGING MARKETS

Robert Boardman
THE POLITICAL ECONOMY OF NATURE
Environmental Debates and the Social Sciences

Gordon Crawford
FOREIGN AID AND POLITICAL REFORM
A Comparative Analysis of Democracy Assistance and Political Conditionality

Matt Davies
INTERNATIONAL POLITICAL ECONOMY AND MASS COMMUNICATION IN CHILE
National Intellectuals and Transnational Hegemony

Martin Doornbos
INSTITUTIONALIZING DEVELOPMENT POLICIES AND RESOURCE STRATEGIES IN EASTERN AFRICA AND INDIA
Developing Winners and Losers

Fred P. Gale
THE TROPICAL TIMBER TRADE REGIME

Mary Ann Haley
FREEDOM AND FINANCE
Democratization and Institutional Investors in Developing Countries

Keith M. Henderson and O. P. Dwivedi (*editors*)
BUREAUCRACY AND THE ALTERNATIVES IN WORLD PERSPECTIVES

Jomo K. S. and Shyamala Nagaraj (*editors*)
GLOBALIZATION VERSUS DEVELOPMENT

Angela W. Little
LABOURING TO LEARN
Towards a Political Economy of Plantations, People and Education in Sri Lanka

John Loxley (*editor*)
INTERDEPENDENCE, DISEQUILIBRIUM AND GROWTH
Reflections on the Political Economy of North–South Relations at the Turn of the Century

Don D. Marshall
CARIBBEAN POLITICAL ECONOMY AT THE CROSSROADS
NAFTA and Regional Developmentalism

Susan M. McMillan
FOREIGN DIRECT INVESTMENT IN THREE REGIONS OF THE SOUTH AT
THE END OF THE TWENTIETH CENTURY

James H. Mittelman and Mustapha Pasha (*editors*)
OUT FROM UNDERDEVELOPMENT
Prospects for the Third World (Second Edition)

Lars Rudebeck, Olle Törnquist and Virgilio Rojas (*editors*)
DEMOCRATIZATION IN THE THIRD WORLD
Concrete Cases in Comparative and Theoretical Perspective

Howard Stein (*editor*)
ASIAN INDUSTRIALIZATION AND AFRICA
Studies in Policy Alternatives to Structural Adjustment

International Political Economy Series
Series Standing Order ISBN 0–333–71708–2 hardcover
Series Standing Order ISBN 0–333–71110–6 paperback
(*outside North America only*)

You can receive future titles in this series as they are published by placing a standing order.
Please contact your bookseller or, in case of difficulty, write to us at the address below with
your name and address, the title of the series and one of the ISBNs quoted above.

Customer Services Department, Macmillan Distribution Ltd, Houndmills, Basingstoke,
Hampshire RG21 6XS, England

Globalization versus Development

Edited by

Jomo K. S.
Professor
Department of Analytical Economics
Faculty of Economics and Administration
University of Malaya
Kuala Lumpur
Malaysia

and

Shyamala Nagaraj
Professor
Department of Applied Statistics
Faculty of Economics and Administration
University of Malaya
Kuala Lumpur
Malaysia

First published 2001 by
PALGRAVE
Houndmills, Basingstoke, Hampshire RG21 6XS and
175 Fifth Avenue, New York, N. Y. 10010
Companies and representatives throughout the world

PALGRAVE is the new global academic imprint of
St. Martin's Press LLC Scholarly and Reference Division and
Palgrave Publishers Ltd (formerly Macmillan Press Ltd).

ISBN 0–333–91965–3 hardback
ISBN 0–333–91966–1 paperback

This book is printed on paper suitable for recycling and
made from fully managed and sustained forest sources.

A catalogue record for this book is available
from the British Library.

Library of Congress Cataloging-in-Publication Data
Globalization versus development / edited by Jomo K. S. and
Shyamala Nagaraj.
    p. cm. — (International political economy series)
    Rev. papers selected from an international conference on
"Globalisation and development: lessons for the Malaysian
economy" held in mid-Aug. 1996 in Kuala Lumpur.
    Includes bibliographical references and index.
    ISBN 0–333–91965–3
    1. International economic integration. 2. Free trade. 3. International
finance. 4. Globalization—Economic aspects. 5. Economic development.
6. Globalization—Economic aspects—Developing countries. I. Jomo K. S.
(Jomo Kwame Sundaram) II. Nagaraj, Shyamala. III. Series.
    HF1418.5 .G58188 2001
    337—dc21
                                                        2001021728

10   9   8   7   6   5   4   3   2   1
10   09   08   07   06   05   04   03   02   01

Printed in Great Britain by Antony Rowe Ltd, Chippenham, Wiltshire

Contents

List of Tables

List of Charts and Figures

List of Abbreviations

AG	Aktiengesellschaft (Joint-Stock Company)
APEC	Asia Pacific Economic Caucus (Cooperation)
APs	Approval Permits
ASEAN	Association of South East Asian Nations
BAFIA	Banking and Financial Institutions Act
BIS	Bank of International Settlements
BoP	Balance of Payments
CBU	Completely Built-Up
CERES	Coalition for Environmentally Responsible Economies
CFI	Country Futures Indicators
CPI	Consumer Price Index
CVDs	Countervailing Duties
EEC	European Economic Community
EFTS	Electronic Funds Transfer Systems
EMS	Environmental Management Systems
EMU	European Monetary Union
EU	European Union
FDI	Foreign Direct Investment
FRG	Federal Republic of Germany
GATS	General Agreement on Trade in Services
GATT	General Agreement on Tariffs and Trade
GDP	Gross Domestic Product
GNP	Gross National Product
GSP	Generalized System of Preferences
HCLC	Holding Company Liquidation Commission
HDI	United Nations Human Development Index
HPAEs	High Performing Asian Economies
IBJ	Industrial Bank of Japan
IBRD	International Bank for Reconstruction and Development
IFC	International Finance Corporation
ILO	International Labour Organization
IMF	International Monetary Fund
IOSCO	International Organization of Securities Commissions
IPOs	Initial Public Offerings
IPRs	Industrial Property Rights
ITA	Information Technology Agreement

ITO	International Trade Organization
ITU	International Communications Union
LDCs	Less Developed Countries
LETS	Local Exchange Trading Systems
LTCM	The Long Term Capital Management
MAI	Multilateral Agreement on Investment
MFA	Multi-Fibre Arrangement
MFN	Most-Favoured-Nation
MIA	Multilateral Investment Agreement
MITI	Ministry of International Trade and Industry
NAFTA	North America Free Trade Area
NAIRU	Non-Accelerating Inflation Rate of Unemployment
NFPEs	Non-Financial Public Enterprises
NGOs	Non-Governmental Organizations
NICs	Newly Industrializing Countries
NIEs	Newly Industrializing Economies
NTMs	Non-Tariff Measures
OECD	Organization for Economic Cooperation and Development
PPP	Purchasing Power Parity
PQLI	Physical Quality of Life Index
R&D	Research and Development
SADC	Southern African Development Cooperation
SAP	Structural Adjustment Programmes
SCAP	Supreme Commander for the Allied Powers
SDRs	Special Drawing Rights
SEC	US Securities and Exchange Commission
TFP	Total Factor Productivity
TNCs	Transnational Corporations
TOT	Terms-of-Trade
TRIMs	Trade-Related Investment Measures
TRIPs	Trade-Related Intellectual Property Rights
UK	United Kingdom
UN	United Nations
UNCTAD	United Nations Conference on Trade and Development
UNCTC	United Nations Centre on Transnational Corporations
UNDP	United Nations Development Program
UNSNA	United Nations System of National Accounts
UR	Uruguay Round
US(A)	United States of America
WBCSD	World Business Council on Sustainable Development
WIPO	World Intellectual Property Organization

WTO   World Trade Organization
WTP   Willingness to Pay

Notes on the Contributors

Mohamed Aslam, Lecturer, Department of Analytical Economics, Faculty of Economics and Administration, University of Malaya, Kuala Lumpur, Malaysia.

Chin Kok Fay, Lecturer, Faculty of Development Sciences, National University of Malaysia, Bangi, Selangor, Malaysia.

Jayati Ghosh, Associate Professor, Centre for Economic Studies, Jawaharlal Nehru University, New Delhi, India.

Hazel Henderson, Commissioner of the Global Commission to Fund the United Nations (GCFUN), Florida, USA.

Jomo K. S., Professor, Department of Applied Economics, Faculty of Economics and Administration, University of Malaya, Kuala Lumpur, Malaysia.

Martin Khor, Director, Third World Network, Penang, Malaysia.

Shyamala Nagaraj, Professor, Department of Applied Statistics, Faculty of Economics and Administration, University of Malaya, Kuala Lumpur, Malaysia.

Deepak Nayyar, Professor, Centre for Economic Studies, Jawaharlal Nehru University, New Delhi, India.

Robert Rowthorn, Professor, Faculty of Economics and Politics, Cambridge University, United Kingdom.

Ajit Singh, Professor, Faculty of Economics and Politics, Cambridge University, United Kingdom.

Acknowledgements

In mid-August 1996, the Faculty of Economics and Administration of the University of Malaya in Kuala Lumpur celebrated the thirtieth anniversary of its establishment by hosting an international conference on 'Globalization and Development: Lessons for the Malaysian Economy' at which about 30 papers were presented.

Some of the papers will be published elsewhere, including about a dozen in a volume considering challenges for Malaysia as it enters the twenty-first century and new millennium. Some of the chapters in this volume have been revised from papers selected on the basis of their likely interest to those desiring to draw broader lessons about the likely consequences of globalization and economic liberalization, especially for available economic development options in these times.

An extended version of the Henderson chapter and an earlier version of the Ghosh chapter were presented at the conference on 'Economic Sovereignty in a Globalizing World: Creating People- Centred Economics for the 21st Century'. The conference was held 23–26 March 1999 at Chulalongkorn University, Bangkok, Thailand. It was organized by Focus on the Global South, a policy research and advocacy non-government organization based in Bangkok. Unedited versions of all papers presented at this conference are available on the website http://focus web.org. An edited collection of some other papers can be found in Bello, Bullard and Malhotra (2000). Finally, the three chapters by Nayyar, Khor, and Jomo were specifically solicited to ensure the definitive nature of this volume.

Foo AL Hiang provided consistent and meticulous assistance in preparing this volume for publication for which we are most appreciative.

Introduction

Jomo K. S.

Like the proverbial elephant and the blind man, both development and globalization mean different things to different people. While there is no consensus, development is usually invoked in reference to economic growth, structural change and improved living standards; often the term carries a certain normative connotation implying human progress, lacking in the use of the term 'growth' for example. In this volume, globalization refers primarily to the accelerated increase in international economic relations in the recent period, usually associated with greater economic liberalization, both internationally as well as within national economies, from the 1980s. In much of the literature, both by those approving of globalization as well as those who are critical, there is a sense of the phenomenon emanating from, and largely determined by, the centres of world capital, advanced technology and, it is often presumed, human civilization. In a sense then, globalization is seen as the latest, accelerated and – very importantly – most intensely transnationalized stage of the process identified with development and modernization with which earlier generations have been concerned. The information revolution as well as the reduced costs, greater ease and consequent intensification of communications, including transportation, are generally believed to have facilitated and furthered these processes.

Many of those favouring globalization have been ideologically inspired by liberal, neo-liberal, market and other pro-business ideologies. In this sense, globalization is not simply an analytical concept, but also expresses particular views of what are considered inevitable or desirable. For many such proponents, globalization refers primarily to the extension and deepening of global markets. It is further maintained that national governments have consequently lost much of their power, with this often seen as desirable for enhancing economic efficiency and even human welfare.

Many analysts portray the contemporary globalization experience as without precedent, but also as natural and desirable. In fact, the process of international economic integration from the last third of the nineteenth century until the outbreak of the First World War surpassed many of the contemporary indices of globalization, albeit perhaps not at the same pace; interestingly, globalization from the late nineteenth century involved far more trans-border labour flows, involving greater human migration, than currently allowed by most national governments. This is not to suggest that there is nothing new about contemporary globalization; such an attitude would only blind us to the significance of the monumental changes currently taking place.

The centrality of technological change for contemporary globalization cannot be over-emphasised, and the full potential and implications of recent, current and future technological developments can hardly be fully anticipated. Yet, while there undoubtedly are many aspects of the current globalization which have been made possible by recent technological developments, particularly in communications, transport and information technology, many of these aspects of contemporary globalization are certainly not inevitable consequences of such technical changes. They are more often due to the historical circumstances of the economic, social and political control and deployment of such technology.

And, as many have argued, globalization and its implications are quite complex, often uneven and even contradictory, and certainly not unambiguously desirable in their totality. While opening up new possibilities and opportunities, it has also closed off many others. At the very moment when so much more is possible due to technological progress, so much more is also denied by the simultaneously growing ownership and control of new technology, with the strengthening of intellectual property rights and the means for their enforcement.

Globalization then is often associated with the emergence, since the eighties, of a new transnational regime characterized by weaker national, including state, sovereignty as well as local, including community, autonomy. In retrospect, it appears that the early eighties debt crises, induced by the US-led deflationary policies, provided a critical opportunity for Washington to try to impose a succession of new international economic policy regimes through the Bretton Woods institutions and more recently, through the World Trade Organization (WTO). While the International Monetary Fund (IMF) imposed short-term macroeconomic stabilization policies forcing indebted governments to open up their national economies to imports and capital from the North, the World Bank (International Bank for Reconstruction and Development, or IRBD) followed through with complementary medium-term policies for structural adjustment. The policies associated with this 'Washington Consensus' – of US political leadership, the IMF and the World Bank – have had mixed consequences, and have usually not proven to be the panaceas they were touted to be. Nevertheless, there has been a clearly discernible trend towards global economic liberalization, with at least some 'freeing' of most markets dominated by the North (goods, services, capital, etc.) except, of course, for international labour migration, and the strengthening and protection of intellectual property rights.

There has been a strong presumption in much of the recent economic literature that economic nationalism and government intervention have undermined market forces and property rights, with adverse implications for economic growth, welfare, equity and efficiency, particularly in terms of resource allocation. Economic liberalization, including globalization, it is argued, will undermine all this, with generally benevolent consequences on balance. The collapse of the Soviet bloc, the crises of the European welfare states and the development failure of much of the rest of the South are invoked as evidence of the failure of Keynesianism, dirigism, economic nationalism, socialism and all other projects involving state intervention.

However, the sustained rapid growth and late industrialization of East Asia associated with industrial policy has posed awkward challenges for the neo-liberal orthodoxy identified with the 'Washington Consensus'. In the nineties, the literature acknowledging the importance of good governance has grown, thus letting the state back in. Meanwhile, even the World Bank (1993) has acknowledged the significant contribution of 'directed credit' in financing late industrialization in East Asia, though it claims that there is no evidence of successful selective industrial policy associated with trade interventions. Instead, it argues that the second-generation Southeast Asian Newly Industrializing Countries (NICs), notably Malaysia and Indonesia, performed best after abandoning industrial policy intervention in the mid-eighties. Although the evidence is hardly conclusive (Jomo *et al.* 1997), the Bank goes on to suggest that the second-generation Southeast Asian NICs are therefore the more appropriate models for emulation for the rest of the developing world compared to the first-generation East Asian NICs of South Korea, Taiwan, Singapore and Hong Kong. Ironically, in the aftermath of the currency meltdowns and financial crises in Southeast Asia since mid-1977, pundits are arguing precisely the opposite, that is that Southeast Asia's recent problems have been due to emulating Japan and South Korea, and not liberalizing enough.

Much of the contemporary interest in globalizing economic liberalization has focused on the international trade in goods and services on the one hand, and the flows of international capital (direct foreign investment, portfolio equity investment, debt, etc.) on the other, though the two are often closely related. The changes in transnational economic governance since the 1980s have largely been along lines acceptable to and promoted by the Washington Consensus, now greatly enhanced by the establishment of the WTO with the conclusion of the Uruguay Round of the General Agreement on Tariffs and Trade (GATT) negotiations in 1993, as well as the greatly strengthened intellectual property rights of the last decade. These have raised the costs of technology acquisition, thus further frustrating late industrialization efforts. Resistance by various national governments and others – especially in the face of the protracted global economic slowdown since the end of the post-war Keynesian 'Golden Age' – as well as increasingly intense rivalries among the US, the European Union (EU) and Japan, have rendered the process uneven and the consequences quite mixed. Perhaps most importantly, the actual consequences of global liberalization have been much more adverse than they were widely expected to be, thus undermining the case for further liberalization. However, despite the inevitable hesitancy this record has brought about, in contrast to the often arrogant and over-confident predictions and promises of the 1980s, the liberalizing juggernaut lumbers on, with a momentum sustained by the apparent absence of viable alternatives while the new ideological hegemony defines the terms and scope of permissible discourse and debate, as Paul Krugman (1995) reminds us. However, the issues implicit in the Bank's influential prescriptions are hardly settled, and provide the context in which this book was organized.

The chapters in this volume address the central question of the implications of recent globalization for economic development prospects in the South generally, sometimes with reference to the relatively more open economies of Southeast Asia, especially Malaysia. The first three chapters are premised on a critical perspective on the effects of trade liberalization. The opening chapter by Nayyar surveys the major consequences of contemporary globalization for economic development, emphasizing both the new constraints as well as possible corrective measures. Aslam and Jomo's discussion of the post-Uruguay Round international economic regime highlights some ominous implications of increased global economic liberalization for economies of the South as well as for national governments' developmentalist efforts by highlighting some aspects of the Malaysian experience. Khor draws attention to the nature of the new international economic governance emerging under the aegis of the WTO, focusing on the new issues and their dire consequences for the South.

The next two chapters critically explore some challenges for economic development in the face of globalization. Rowthorn reminds us of the exceptional nature of the East Asian Newly Industrializing Economies' (NIEs) experiences with foreign direct investment (FDI) and manufactured exports, underscoring the difficulties of replicating the Malaysian experience, for example, on a much larger scale. Henderson places developments associated with international financial liberalization within the larger context of globalization, financial disintermediation and the ascendance of the multi-national corporate, and argues strongly for improved measures of development The following three chapters focus on financial liberalization and its likely implications for sustaining economic development. Chin and Jomo argue that much of Malaysian government intervention in the financial sector has been for the purpose of interethnic redistribution, that is 'affirmative action', with little support for industrial policy. Singh emphasizes the great dangers posed by recent economic, especially financial, liberalization for sustained economic development, both for the North as well as for the South. Jomo critically considers the adverse implications of international financial liberalization for late industrialization and the developmentalist state in the aftermath of the East Asian financial crisis.

Finally, Ghosh provides almost an epilogue to the discussions of the earlier chapters. She ponders on the relevance in the global economy today of Keynesian economics, which had such a crucial role in economic policy making for much of the twentieth century. The following summaries offer a more detailed feel for the texture of the chapters in this volume.

Globalization

Deepak Nayyar's review of the implications of globalization for development surveys the process and nature of integration into the contemporary world economy, reviews the main underlying forces, and examines their implications for development prospects in the South. He begins with a brief survey of the nature of contemporary globalization, highlighting the underlying forces at work as well as the ostensible economic arguments in favour of the process. Nayyar then compares the contemporary process with the historical experience of the late nineteenth century, emphasizing that the current developments have had important precedents, which were more extensive and hence different in significant ways. After drawing attention to some important implications of the contemporary globalization processes for development, he suggests some corrective measures which might reduce some of their more non-egalitarian consequences. Nayyar's historically-informed overview anticipates many of the themes explored and elaborated in subsequent chapters.

Impact of the GATT Uruguay Round

Mohamed Aslam and Jomo K. S. are concerned that the conclusion of the Uruguay Round of GATT negotiations in December 1993 may cause net losses to Malaysia's open economy as the adverse aspects exceed the gains from further international economic liberalization. Besides considering the consequences of the envisaged further trade liberalization, which will also reduce the scope for trade policy as an instrument of selective industrial policy, they highlight some major consequences of the new non-merchandise trade-related provisions of the Uruguay Round, namely the General Agreement on Trade in Services (GATS), TRIMs (Trade-related Investment Measures) and Trade-related Intellectual Property Rights (TRIPs) as well as the establishment of the WTO to supersede GATT. Aslam and Jomo show a significant deterioration in Malaysia's terms of trade by almost half in the last three and a half decades from 1.43 in 1960 to 0.75 in 1995, and offer some estimates of its implications for Malaysia's very open economy. They also demonstrate how Malaysia's services and current accounts have been adversely affected by growing investment income flows and other services as well as patents, copyright and related payments abroad, which are likely to worsen with liberalization of investment regulation and services, as well as with the strengthening of intellectual property rights. As the following chapter by Khor argues, further liberalization will also have untold adverse consequences in terms of undermining previously available government industrial policy instruments and the related potential for long-term economic growth, industrialization and structural change.

WTO: the new global economic governance

A prominent campaigner against the emerging global economic governance, Martin Khor critically examines developments involving the establishment and rapid expansion of the scope of the WTO, initially conceived as the successor to the General Agreement on Tariffs and Trade. Beginning with an analysis of trade agreements as new instruments shaping the emerging global economic governance, he demonstrates how the WTO has become the major instrument for this purpose with the proliferation of ostensibly trade-related issues being brought to the negotiating table to redefine the relevant rules of the game. In line with Aslam and Jomo's findings in the previous chapter, Khor also argues that the conclusion of the Uruguay Round of GATT negotiations was generally unfavourable to the South, and challenges neo-liberal claims by showing how the Uruguay Round has only been selectively liberal, with greater protectionism in areas such as intellectual property rights and labour mobility. Despite its ostensibly more democratic structure compared to, say, the Bretton Woods institutions, the conduct of the Singapore WTO Ministerial Conference in late 1996 suggests that, in fact, the WTO is already dominated by the North in practice, aided by deliberate manipulation, limited transparency and the failure of the South to get its act together. Although efforts to introduce labour and the environment for protectionist purposes have not succeeded thus far, Khor warns that new, supposedly fair initiatives 'to level the investment playing field', ensure competition and limit discretionary use of government procurement for public policy purposes, are likely to prove much more difficult to rebuff.

Limits to NIC replication

Robert Rowthorn raises the question of the possibility and feasibility of replication of the East Asian NIEs' experiences, particularly on a greater scale. While replication is probably still possible for certain relatively small developing countries, replication on a large scale would increase exports, flood markets and drive prices down. It has been suggested that the terms of trade have already begun to shift against manufactured exports from the South, reviving the spectre of unequal exchange, a concern of the two preceding chapters by Aslam and Jomo, and Khor. Rowthorn notes that the case has been exaggerated by including non-ferrous metals (mainly copper), and that after excluding this category, the decline has not been very large. However, if the supply of manufactured goods from the South were to rapidly increase, in excess of the absorptive capacity of foreign, especially Northern markets, Southern export prices could be depressed dramatically. Rowthorn illustrates his argument about the fallacy of composition by examining the example of clothing exports, currently still partially regulated by the Multi-Fibre Arrangement (MFA) due to be phased out in a few years. Following the pioneering work by William Cline (1982), Rowthorn considers the significance of demography and income levels, emphasizing that China and India are unlikely to ever become as external trade dependent as the much smaller East Asian NIEs. He also emphasizes that it would be impossible for other developing countries as a whole to be able to attract as much foreign direct investment as Malaysia (and Singapore) have. However, Rowthorn suggests that these constraints may be partially overcome with appropriate sequencing by late industrializers, greater diversification of the manufactured export mix, increased South–South trade and more restrictions on consumer good imports into the South.

Global financial casino

Futurist Hazel Henderson's chapter locates recent developments associated with international financial liberalization within the larger context of globalization, financial disintermediation and the ascendance of the financial sphere over the real economy (Wall Street over Main Street). She notes the adverse consequences of economic liberalization and globalization for economic volatility, hence her title 'The Global Financial Casino'. She suggests that contrary to the claims of its advocates, deregulation has adversely affected economic growth and the quality of life by encouraging a 'race to the bottom'. Nevertheless, she insists, governments are far from being completely powerless, and in fact, in democratic and accountable societies, have great responsibility for protecting the interests and welfare of the people. She doubts much of the hype about a 'new economy' based on more extensive and intensive usage of information and communication technologies. In the face of such new challenges, she believes that new forms of global intervention are desperately needed to create new conditions for raising the ethical floor for the new global economy.

'Financial restraint' for late industrialization?

Chin Kok Fay and Jomo K. S. examine industrial financing options for Malaysia. Drawing on the work of Stiglitz and others as well as historical experiences reviewed by Lazonick and O'Sullivan, they suggest that 'financial restraint' – understood as a set of policies intended to create rents to induce agents in the financial sector to engage in particular publicly desired activities – is more desirable than either 'financial repression' or *laissez faire* policies. Distinguishing between banks and market based financial systems, Chin and Jomo briefly review the relative contribution of bank credit as well as stock markets to economic growth and structural change in terms of economic theory and empirical evidence before focusing on finance-industry relations in Japan, Korea and Germany. They then argue that financial restraint has been practised in Malaysia primarily to ensure bank profitability, especially with increasing ethnic *Bumiputera* (indigenes, mostly Malay) dominance of Malaysian banks from the 1970s. Though utilised to support interethnic redistribution and other public policies, financial restraint in Malaysia has not done very much to favour long-term productive investments, especially in non-resource-based export-oriented manufacturing, which continues to be dominated by FDI. Instead, the handsome banking margins have fostered wasteful competition (such as too many bank branches competing for limited business in particular locales). Emphasis on loan security has encouraged loans to the real property sector, for share purchases and for consumption, rather than production. The successful promotion of the stock market in recent years has been accompanied by a significant shift in financial intermediation from the banking system to the security market, though corporate savings continue to account for most corporate financing. Imminent financial liberalization is expected to exacerbate most of these trends, and to further reduce the financial sector's support of productive long-term investments.

Financial liberalization's adverse consequences

Ajit Singh queries the alleged virtues of financial liberalization and integration of international capital and currency markets for the world economy as a whole, and for developing countries in particular. He argues that financial liberalization and global integration of capital markets in the last decade and a half in the advanced economies has had largely uninspiring consequences for the real economy, and the situation is unlikely to improve in the foreseeable future – findings taken up in Jomo's final chapter. Besides adverse trends in growth, productivity and unemployment, Singh acknowledges that inflation trends provide the only silver lining on an otherwise gloomy picture. In line with Lazonick and O'Sullivan's findings, he proceeds to consider and reject other plausible explanations for this poor economic performance, and to assess why the confident predictions of orthodox liberal economic models have not been realised. Singh argues that the apparent consensus can only be understood in terms of the sociology of the foundation of conventional wisdom, but warns that the spectre of mass unemployment and/or low real wages is likely to encourage the jingoist protectionism, particularly against the South. He then critically assesses the arguments for, as well as the consequences of, the recent rapid expansion of stock markets in the developing countries, drawing conclusions corroborated by Chin and Jomo's earlier chapter. Singh also argues that despite greater share price volatility in emerging markets, there has been a huge increase in corporate growth as developing country firms have been raising considerable capital through emerging market listings and activity. In his view, this has mainly been due to proactive government roles as well as the relative lower cost of equity capital (compared to loan capital) in recent years, rather than simply in response to market forces. There is little evidence, however, that this has led to increased aggregate savings and investments, or raised productivity of investments. Singh argues that further financial liberalization will hinder, rather than accelerate industrialization, long-term economic growth and structural change in these economies. However, in so far as share markets are here to stay, Singh argues for restriction of portfolio capital flows and warns against the emergence of an Anglo-American type of market for corporate control.

International financial liberalization versus development

Jomo argues that the failure to recognise the nature of accumulation and growth in the region prevented the design and implementation of a more appropriate pro-active financial strategy for development in much of Southeast Asia as recommended in the preceding chapters by Henderson, Chin and Jomo, and Singh. Nevertheless, with rising savings rates, national financial systems generated enough funds to support rapid capital accumulation. While international financial liberalization has generally failed to move much funds from capital-rich to capital-poor economies, East Asia was the exception for most of the nineties before mid-1997. The availability of such cheap funds encouraged financial reforms which weakened existing prudential regulations while encouraging full capital account convertibility, inadvertently creating the conditions for asset price bubbles, and then regional financial panic. Financial liberalization in the region saw massive capital inflows from foreign borrowings as well as investments in securities. There is little serious disagreement now that the East Asian economic crises since mid-1997 began as currency and liquidity crises. The currency and financial crises became crises of the 'real economy' mainly due to inappropriate government and IMF policy responses. The crises were due to panic after the undermining of effective financial governance at both international and national levels. 'Irrational' herd behaviour greatly exaggerated the impact of speculative market behaviour to gain advantage from some unintended consequences of the region's currency appreciations. The over-valued regional currencies had emerged from partial financial liberalization, which also created the conditions for the asset price inflationary bubble that burst with devastating consequences for the region.

Relevance of Keynesian ideas in the global economy

Jayati Ghosh discusses the relevance and limitation of Keynesian Economics in the global economy today. She notes that for about three decades, macroeconomic management was heavily influenced by Keynes' ideas and, for the subsequent three decades, Keynesian economics was seen as not just outmoded but wrong. She argues that Keynes' essential ideas – the principle of effective demand, the possibility of unemployment equilibrium, the working of the multiplier, the role of the state, and the concept of liquidity preference and monetary instability – retain their relevance in the face of globalization. The task is to translate these insights into practical policy alternatives that serve the needs of national economic development in a global economy where financial markets remain open and capital can move across borders in response to policy changes or expectations.

Taken together then, this volume offers a nuanced and subtle assessment of the implications of economic globalization for development prospects in the South. It offers important lessons from the recent 'economic miracle' in the East, including Southeast Asia, and particularly from Malaysia, while fully acknowledging some of its exceptional features. While generally critical of the single-minded free market dogmatism currently popular among neo-liberals, it does not endorse its opposite, namely dogmatic state dirigism, which unwittingly has provided the opportunity for the current neo-liberal ideological hegemony. Instead, the authors in this volume are all fully appreciative of the market's strength as an information economiser, but also recognise that – to paraphrase the late Professor Sukhamoy Chakravarthy – while the market may be an efficient servant, it can be a terrible master.

1
Globalization: What Does It Mean for Development?[1]

Deepak Nayyar

Globalization means different things to different people. It can be defined, simply, as the expansion of economic activities across the political boundaries of nation states. More importantly, perhaps, it refers to a process of deepening economic integration, increasing economic openness and growing economic interdependence between countries in the world economy. It is associated not only with a phenomenal spread and volume of cross-border economic transactions, but also with an organization of economic activities which straddles national boundaries. This process is driven by the lure of profit and the threat of competition in the market.

The word globalization can be used in two different contexts, and is thereby a source of confusion and a cause of controversy. It is used in a *positive* sense to *describe* a process of increasing integration into the world economy: the characterization of this process is by no means uniform. It is used in a *normative* sense to *prescribe* a strategy of development based on rapid integration with the world economy: some see this as salvation, while others see it as damnation.

The object of this chapter is to sketch the contours of the process of integration in the contemporary world economy, explore the underlying factors, and analyse its implications for development. The next section outlines the dimensions and characteristics of globalization in our times. The following section examines the economic factors, the political conjuncture and the intellectual rationale underlying globalization. The fourth section considers the historical origins of globalization through a comparison with the late nineteenth century. The penultimate section analyses the implications of globalization for development to suggest that the benefits are likely to be distributed in an uneven and unequal manner. The concluding section sets out some

1

correctives that might make globalization conducive to more egalitarian economic and social development.

Dimensions and characteristics

The world economy has experienced progressive international economic integration since 1950. However, there was a marked acceleration in this process of globalization during the last quarter of the twentieth century. The fundamental attribute of globalization is the increasing degree of openness in most countries. There are, at present, three dimensions of this phenomenon: international trade, international investment, and international finance. It needs to be said that openness is not simply confined to trade flows, investment flows, and financial flows. It also extends to flows of services, technology, information, ideas, and people across national boundaries. There can be no doubt, however, that trade, investment, and finance constitute the cutting edge of globalization.

The second half of the twentieth century witnessed a phenomenal expansion in international trade flows. World exports increased from US$61 billion in 1950 to US$315 billion in 1970 and US$3,447 billion in 1990.[2] Throughout this period, the growth in world trade was significantly higher than the growth in world output, although the gap narrowed after the early 1970s.[3] Consequently, an increasing proportion of world output entered into world trade. The share of world exports in world gross domestic product (GDP) rose from about 6 per cent in 1950 to 12 per cent in 1973 and 16 per cent in 1992. For the industrialized countries, this proportion increased from 12 per cent in 1973 to 17 per cent in 1992.

During the period 1950–70, inter-industry trade in manufactures, based on differences in factor endowments, labour productivity, or technological leads and lags, constituted an increasing proportion of international trade. During the period 1970–90, intra-industry trade in manufactures, based on scale economies and product differentiation, constituted a growing proportion of international trade. In this context, it is important to note that an increasing proportion of these trade flows is made up of intra-firm trade, across national boundaries but between affiliates of the same firm. In the early 1970s, such intra-firm trade accounted for about one-fifth of world trade, but by the early 1990s this proportion was one-third of world trade.[4] More importantly, the composition of intra-firm trade has changed: there has been a steady decline in the importance of primary commodities, and a sharp increase in the importance of manufactured goods and intermediate products.

The story is similar for international investment flows. The stock of direct foreign investment in the world economy increased from US$68 billion in 1960 to US$502 billion in 1980 and US$1,948 billion in 1992. The flows of direct foreign investment in the world economy increased from less than US$5 billion in 1960 to US$52 billion in 1980 and US$171 billion in 1992.[5] Consequently, the stock of direct foreign investment in the world as a proportion of world output increased from 4.4 per cent in 1960 to 4.8 per cent in 1980 and 8.4 per cent in 1992.[6] Over the same period, world direct foreign investment inflows as a proportion of world gross fixed capital formation rose from 1.1 per cent in 1960 to 2.0 per cent in 1980 and 3.7 per cent in 1992.[7]

The geographical destination and the sectoral distribution of investment flows is worth noting. During the 1980s, industrialized countries absorbed about 80 per cent of the investment flows of direct foreign investment in the world economy, whereas the developing countries received only 20 per cent.[8] Similarly, in 1992, 78 per cent of the stock of direct foreign investment in the world economy was in the industrialized countries, while the remaining 22 per cent was in the developing countries.[9] In the same year, the primary sector accounted for less than 10 per cent of the stock of direct foreign investment, while the manufacturing sector accounted for about 40 per cent, and the services sector for the remaining 50 per cent.[10] There is evidence to suggest that the significance of developing countries as a destination for, and the importance of the services sector as a recipient of, direct foreign investment has registered an increase in the 1990s.

The past two decades have witnessed an explosive growth in international finance. The movement of finance across national boundaries is enormous. So much so that, in terms of magnitude, trade, and investment are now dwarfed by finance. This internationalization of financial markets has four dimensions: foreign exchange, bank lending, financial assets, and government bonds. Let us consider each in turn.

In foreign exchange markets, trading was a modest US$15 billion per day in 1973. It rose to US$60 billion per day in 1983, and soared to US$900 billion per day in 1992.[11] Consequently, the ratio of world-wide transactions in foreign exchange to world trade rose from 9:1 in 1973 to 12:1 in 1983 and 90:1 in 1992.[12] Some absolute numbers would help situate these magnitudes in perspective. In 1992, for example, world GDP was US$64 billion per day while world exports were US$10 billion per day, compared with global foreign exchange transactions of US$900 billion per day.[13] It is also worth noting that daily foreign exchange transactions in the world economy were larger than the foreign exchange reserves of all central banks put together, which were US$693 billion in 1992.[14]

The expansion of international banking is also phenomenal. As a proportion of world output, net international bank loans rose from 0.7 per cent in 1964 to 8.0 per cent in 1980 and 16.3 per cent in 1991. As a proportion of world trade, net international bank loans rose from 7.5 per cent in 1964 to 42.6 per cent in 1980 and 104.6 per cent in 1991. As a proportion of world gross fixed domestic investment, net international bank loans rose from 6.2 per cent in 1964 to 51.1 per cent in 1980 and 131.4 per cent in 1991.[15]

The international market for financial assets experienced a similar growth starting somewhat later. Between 1980 and 1993, gross sales and purchases of bonds and equities transacted between domestic and foreign residents rose from less than 10 per cent of GDP in the United States, Germany and Japan to 135 per cent of GDP in the United States, 170 per cent of GDP in Germany and 80 per cent of GDP in Japan.[16] In the UK, the value of such transactions was more than ten times that of the GDP in 1993. Similarly, between 1980 and 1993, the share of foreign bonds and equities in pension-fund assets rose from 10 per cent to 20 per cent in the UK, from 0.7 per cent to 6 per cent in the United States, and from 0.5 per cent to 9 per cent in Japan. IMF estimates suggest that in 1992, total cross-border ownership of tradable securities was US$2,500 billion.

Government debt has also become tradable in the global market for financial assets. There is a growing international market for government bonds. Between 1980 and 1992, the proportion of government bonds held by foreigners rose from less than one per cent to 43 per cent in France, from 9 per cent to 17 per cent in the UK, from 10 per cent to 27 per cent in Germany, but it remained steady at about 20 per cent in the United States.[17]

The characteristics of such financial flows are implicit in the destinations, objects, intermediaries, and instruments. These flows are destined mostly for the industrialized countries that have high deficits and high interest rates to finance public consumption and transfer payments rather than productive investment. Such financial flows are constituted mostly of short-term capital movements that are sensitive to exchange rates and interest rates and in search of capital gains. Institutional investors, such as pension-funds and mutual-funds, are more important than banks as intermediaries. The latter continue to act as intermediaries, but now borrow short to lend long, thus resulting in a maturity mismatch. Consequently, the financial instruments need to be far more sophisticated and diversified. There has also been an enormous amount of financial innovation through the introduction of derivatives: futures, swaps, and options. These derivatives are a means of managing the financial risks associated with international investment. This is essential to compensate for the maturity mismatch and to provide effective securitization. International financial markets have simply developed the instruments to meet the needs of the times.[18]

Origins and foundations

The origins of globalization need to be analysed in terms of the economic factors underlying the process, the political conjuncture which has enabled it to gather momentum, and the intellectual rationale that is now almost prescriptive. Let us consider each in turn.

The economic factors that have made globalization possible are the dismantling of barriers to international economic transactions, the development of enabling technologies, and emerging forms of industrial organization.

Globalization has followed the sequence of deregulation in the world economy. Trade liberalization came first, and led to an unprecedented expansion of international trade between 1950 and 1970. The liberalization of regimes for foreign investment came next. There was a surge in international investment which began in the late 1960s. Financial liberalization came last, starting in the early 1980s. This had two dimensions: the deregulation of the domestic financial sector in the industrialized countries and the introduction of convertibility on capital account in the balance of payments. The latter was not simultaneous. The United States, Canada, Germany, and Switzerland removed restrictions on capital movements in 1973, Britain in 1979, Japan in 1980, while France and Italy made the transition as late as 1990. The globalization of finance, at a scorching pace since the mid-1980s, is not unrelated to the dismantling of regulations and controls.

The technological revolution in transport and communications has been a crucial factor. The second half of the twentieth century witnessed the advent of jet aircraft, computers and satellites. The synthesis of communications technology, which is concerned with the transmission of information, and computer technology, which is concerned with the processing of information, has created information technology, which is remarkable in both reach and speed. These technological developments have had a dramatic impact on reducing geographical barriers. The time needed is a tiny fraction of what it was earlier. The cost incurred has come down sharply.

New forms of industrial organization have played a role in making globalization possible. The emerging flexible production system, shaped by the nature of technical progress, changing output mix and the organizational characteristics (based on Japanese management systems) is forcing firms constantly to choose between trade and investment in their drive to expand activities across borders. The declining share of wages in production costs, the increasing importance of proximity between producers and consumers, and the growing externalization of services, is exercising a strong influence on the strategies and the behaviour of firms in the process of globalization.[19]

The politics of hegemony or dominance is conducive to the economics of globalization. The process of globalization beginning in the early 1970s has coincided with the political dominance of the United States as the superpower. This political dominance has grown stronger with the collapse of communism and the triumph of capitalism. So much so that this has been described by a contemporary historian as 'the end of history' (Fukuyama 1989). The political conjuncture has transformed the concept of globalization into a virtual ideology of our times. Dominance in the realm of politics is associated with an important attribute in the sphere of economics. Globalization requires a dominant economic power with a national currency which is accepted as the equivalent of international money: as a unit of account, a medium of exchange and a store of value. In the early twenty-first century, this role is being performed by the US dollar, ironically enough after the collapse of the Bretton Woods system when its statutory role as a reserve currency came to an end.

Economic theorizing often follows in the footsteps of political reality. It should come as no surprise, then, that recent years have witnessed the formulation of an intellectual rationale for globalization. It is perceived as a means to ensure not only efficiency and equity, but also growth and development in the world economy.

The analytical foundations of this world view are provided by the neo-liberal model. Orthodox neo-classical economics suggests that intervention in markets is inefficient. Neo-liberal political economy argues that governments are incapable of intervening efficiently. The essence of the neo-liberal model, then, can be stated as follows. First, the government should be rolled back wherever possible so that it approximates to the ideal of a minimalist state. Second, the market is not only a substitute for the state, but also the preferred alternative, because it performs better. Third, resource allocation and resource utilization must be based on market prices which should conform as closely as possible to international prices. Fourth, national political objectives, domestic economic concerns or even national boundaries should not act as constraints. It is suggested that such policy regimes would provide the foundations for a global economic system characterized by free trade, unrestricted capital mobility, open markets and harmonized institutions. The ideologues believe that such globalization promises economic prosperity for countries that join the system and economic deprivation for countries that do not (see, for example, Sachs and Warner 1995).

Historical parallel

There is a common presumption that the present conjuncture, when globalization is changing the character of the world economy, is altogether new and represents a fundamental departure from the past. But this presumption is not correct. Globalization is nothing new. There was a similar phase of globalization which began a century earlier, *circa* 1870, and gathered momentum until 1914 when it came to an abrupt end.

The four decades from 1870 to 1914 were the age of *laissez faire*. There was almost no restriction on the movement of goods, capital and labour across national boundaries. Government intervention in economic activity was minimal. The gold standard, strictly adhered to by most countries, imparted stability to the system. Keynes believed that a virtuous circle of rapid economic growth and international economic integration in this era created the core of a global economy (Keynes 1921).

In many ways, the world economy in the early twenty-first century resembles the world economy in the late nineteenth century. The parallels between the two periods are striking and suggest that the historical origins of globalization need to be recognized.[20]

The period from 1870 to 1913 witnessed an expansion in international trade flows that was faster than the growth in world output.[21] For 16 major industrialized countries, now in the Organization for Economic Cooperation and Development (OECD), the share of exports in GDP rose from 18.2 per cent in 1900 to 21.2 per cent in 1913. It would seem that the integration of the world economy through international trade at the turn of the nineteenth century was about the same as it is at the turn of the twentieth century.[22]

The stock of direct foreign investment in the world economy as a proportion of world output was 9 per cent in 1913. The total stock of long-term foreign investment in the world reached US\$44 billion by 1914, of which US\$14 billion, about one-third, was direct foreign investment.[23] At 1980 prices, total foreign investment in the world economy in 1914 was US\$347 billion compared with the actual stock of direct foreign investment in 1980 at US\$448 billion.[24] The stock of foreign investment, direct and portfolio, in developing countries rose from US\$5.3 billion in 1870 to US\$11.4 billion in 1900 and US\$22.7 billion in 1914 (Maddison 1989: 29–30). Such foreign investment in the developing world was large in both relative and absolute terms. For one, it was probably equal to about one-fourth of the GDP of developing countries at the turn of the century (Maddison 1989: 29–30). For another, it was substantial even by contemporary standards. The stock of foreign investment in developing countries in 1914, at 1980 prices, was US\$179 billion which was almost double the stock of direct foreign investment in developing countries in 1980 at US\$96 billion.[25]

There was also a significant integration of international financial markets in the late nineteenth century and early twentieth century. The only dimension missing was international transactions in foreign exchange which were determined entirely by trade flows and capital flows, given the regime of fixed exchange rates under the gold standard. The cross-national ownership of securities, including government bonds, reached very high levels during this period. In 1913, for example, foreign securities constituted 59 per cent of all securities traded in London. Similarly, in 1908, the corresponding proportion was 53 per cent in Paris.[26] There was also an established market for government bonds. In 1920, for instance, Moody's rated bonds were issued by 50 governments. As late as 1985, only 15 governments were borrowing in the capital market of the United States. The number reached 50, once again, in the 1990s. International bank lending was substantial. Both governments and private investors floated long-term bonds directly in the financial markets of London, Paris, and New York. Merchant banks or investment banks were the intermediaries in facilitating these capital flows from private individuals and financial institutions in these industrialized countries in search of long-term investments to firms or governments mostly in the industrializing countries or the underdeveloped countries which issued long-term liabilities.[27] In relative terms, net international capital flows then were much bigger than now. During the period from 1880 to 1913, Britain ran an average current account surplus in its balance of payments which was the equivalent of 5 per cent of GDP (Panic 1992). In some years, this was as much as 8 per cent of GDP. In contrast, since 1950, the current account surplus of the United States to begin with, or Germany and Japan in subsequent years, did not exceed 3 per cent of GDP.

It is not sufficient to focus on these dimensions alone. There are both similarities and differences between these two phases of globalization in the world economy. The similarities are in underlying factors which made globalization possible then and now. The differences are in the form, nature and depth of the globalization process during these two periods.

There are four similarities of the previous period with the current one that I would like to highlight. First, there were almost no restrictions on the movement of goods, capital and labour across national boundaries, so that there was no need for dismantling barriers or liberalizing regimes for international economic transactions. Second, the advent of the steamship, the railway, and the telegraph brought about a revolution in transport and communications. This led to an enormous reduction in the time needed, as also the cost incurred, in traversing geographical distances.[28] Third, emerging forms of industrial organization performed a critical role. The advent of mass production realized economies of scale and led to huge cost reductions compared with craft manufacturing.[29] Fourth, this phase of globalization coincided with what has been described as 'the age of empire', when Britain more or less ruled the world.[30] Apart from dominance in the realm of politics, Pax Britannica provided a reserve currency, the pound sterling, which was the equivalent of international money.

There are also important differences between the two phases of globalization. I would like to highlight four such differences: in trade flows, in investment flows, in financial flows, and most importantly, perhaps, in labour flows.

There are differences in the composition of trade and in the channels of trade. During the period from 1870 to 1913, an overwhelming proportion of international trade was constituted by inter-sectoral trade, where primary commodities were exchanged for manufactured goods. The trade was, to a significant extent, based on absolute advantage derived from natural resources or climatic conditions. Although trade flows were in the domain of large international firms, it was not intra-firm trade. There are differences in the geographical destination and the sectoral-distribution of investment flows. In 1914, the stock of long-term foreign investment in the world economy was distributed as follows: 55 per cent in the industrialized world (30 per cent in Europe, 25 per cent in the United States) and 45 per cent in the underdeveloped world (20 per cent in Latin America and 25 per cent in Asia and Africa).[31] It is clear that developing countries are now far less central to the process. In 1913, the primary sector accounted for 55 per cent of long-term foreign investment in the world, while transport, trade and distribution accounted for another 30 per cent; the manufacturing sector accounted for only 10 per cent, and much of this was concentrated in North America or Europe (Dunning 1983: 89). The primary sector is now far less important while the manufacturing sector is much more important. In financial flows, there are significant differences in the destinations, objects, intermediaries and instruments. In the last quarter of the nineteenth century, capital flows were a means of transferring investible resources to underdeveloped countries or newly industrializing countries with the most attractive growth opportunities. The object was to find avenues for long-term investments in search of profits. Banks were the only intermediaries between lenders and borrowers in the form of bonds with very long maturities. Securitization of long-term bonds with sovereign guarantees was provided by the imperial powers or the governments in the borrowing countries.

The fundamental difference between the two phases of globalization, however, is in the sphere of labour flows. In the late nineteenth century, there were no restrictions on the mobility of people across national boundaries. Passports were seldom needed. Immigrants were granted citizenship with ease. Between 1870 and 1914, international labour migration was enormous. During this period, about 50 million people left Europe, of whom two-thirds went to the United States while the remaining one-third went to Canada, Australia, New Zealand, South Africa, Argentina, and Brazil (Lewis 1977). This mass emigration from Europe amounted to one-eighth of its population in 1900.[32] But that was not all. Beginning somewhat earlier, following the abolition of slavery in the British Empire, about 50 million people left India and China to work as indentured labour on mines and plantations and in construction in Latin America, the Caribbean, Southern Africa, Southeast Asia, and other distant lands (Tinker 1974, Lewis 1978). The destinations were mostly British, Dutch, French, and German colonies. In the second half of the twentieth century, there was a limited amount of international labour migration from the developing countries to the industrialized world during the period 1950–70.[33] Since then, however, international migration has been reduced to a trickle because of draconian immigration laws and restrictive consular practices.[34] The present phase of globalization has found substitutes for labour mobility in the form of trade flows and investment flows. For one, industrialized countries now import manufactured goods that embody scarce labour. For another, industrialized countries export capital which employs scarce labour abroad to provide such goods.

Uneven development

A comparison of globalization in the late twentieth and early twenty-first centuries with globalization in the nineteenth century suggests that the game is similar, though not quite the same. The players of the game are new and the rules of the game are very different.

The process of globalization was then dominated by imperial nation states, not only in the realm of politics, but also in the sphere of economics. There can be no doubt that these imperial nation states were the key players in the game. The process of globalization has now placed new players centre-stage. There are two main sets of players in this game: transnational corporations which dominate investment, production, and trade in the world economy, and international banks or financial intermediaries which control the world of finance. It would seem that the present conjuncture represents the final frontier in the global reach of capitalism to organize production, trade, investment and finance on a world scale without any fetters except, of course, for tight controls on labour mobility.

It is not surprising that the advent of international capital has meant significant political adjustments in the contemporary world. It has induced a strategic withdrawal on the part of the nation state in some important spheres. Thus, nation states are not the key players that they were in the late nineteenth century during the first incarnation of globalization. They remain the main political players, but are no longer the main economic players. We live in an era where the old fashioned autonomy of the nation state is being eroded by international industrial capital and international finance capital everywhere, both in the industrialized world and in the developing world. It needs to be stressed, however, that there is a qualitative difference in the relationship between international capital and the nation state, when we compare the industrialized world with the developing world. The nation state in the former has far more room for manoeuvre than the nation state in the latter. In the industrialized countries, the political interests of the nation state often coincide with the economic interests of international capital. This is not so for developing countries from which very few transnational corporations or international banks originate. In spite of the profound changes unleashed by the present phase of globalization, however, it would be naive to write off the nation state, for it remains a crucial player in political and strategic terms. Even today, only nation states have the authority to set the rules of the game. The nation states in the industrialized world provide international capital with the means to set new rules for the game of globalization. The nation states in the developing world provide these countries and their people with the means of finding degrees of freedom *vis-à-vis* international capital in the pursuit of development. Transnational corporations and international banks or financial intermediaries wish to set new rules of the game which would enable them to manage the risks associated with globalization. In this task, the nation states of the industrialized world provide the much needed political clout and support. The multilateral framework of the World Trade Organization (WTO), the International Monetary Fund (IMF) and the World Bank is, perhaps, the most important medium.

The Uruguay Round of multilateral trade negotiations was different from its predecessor rounds in a fundamental sense. The differences are much wider and deeper than its enlarged scope. The General Agreement on Tariffs and Trade (GATT) type rules and principles, with provision for dispute settlement, compensation and retaliation, are sought to be extended beyond trade in goods to international flows of capital, technology, information, services and personnel. The multilateral regimes for trade-related investment measures, trade-related intellectual property rights and trade in services, now created in the WTO, coincide closely with the interests of transnational corporations which are capital-exporters, technology-leaders and service-providers in the world economy.

The international regime of discipline that is being created is asymmetrical in almost every dimension. The liberalization of the international trade in goods is selective, for the discipline on non-tariff barriers is not binding, just as there are important exclusions. In the sphere of textiles, the dismantling of the Multi-Fibre Arrangement (MFA) remains a distant promise, and in substantive terms, trade liberalization will only begin in the twenty-first century. The pressure from the industrialized countries to introduce a 'social clause' and an 'environment clause' on the agenda for the world trading system are simply pretexts for circumventing the rules of trade liberalization wherever necessary. In the General Agreement on Trade in Services (GATS), there is almost nothing on labour mobility which would allow developing countries to exploit their comparative advantage in services. In sharp contrast, it caters to the

interests of the industrialized countries, which have a revealed comparative advantage in capital-intensive or technology-intensive services,
even if this implies changes in investment laws or technology policies
of developing countries. The Uruguay Round did not yield significant
results on trade-related investment measures, but there is a new attempt
to create a multilateral regime for international investment in the WTO,
which seeks free access and national treatment for foreign investors,
combined with provisions to enforce commitments and obligations to
foreign investors. While liberalization and guarantees are sought for
investment flows, the international regime of discipline for technology
flows embodies protection with guarantees. The WTO regime for the
protection of intellectual property rights is both restrictive and protec-
tive. The inequality is obvious. It seeks to protect monopoly profits or
quasi-rents of transnational corporations but ignores the implications
for developing countries.[35]

It would seem that the institutional framework for globalization is
characterized by a striking asymmetry. National boundaries should not
matter for trade flows and capital flows, but should be clearly demar-
cated for technology flows and labour flows. It follows that developing
countries would provide access to their markets without corresponding
access to technology, and would accept capital mobility without a corresponding provision for labour mobility. This asymmetry, particularly
that between the free movement of capital and the non-free movement
of labour across national boundaries lies at the heart of the inequality in
the rules of the game for globalization as we move into the twenty-first
century. These new rules, which serve the interests of transnational
corporations in the process of globalization, are explicit as an integral
part of a multilateral regime of discipline.

The rules of the game, which would serve the interests of international banks or financial intermediaries in the process of globalization,
are in part implicit and in part unwritten. Even here, there is an asymmetry as there are rules for some but not for others. There are no rules for
surplus countries, or even deficit countries, in the industrialized world
which do not borrow from the multilateral financial institutions. But
the IMF and the World Bank set rules for borrowers in the developing
world and the erstwhile socialist bloc. The conditionality is meant in
principle to ensure repayment, but in practice, it imposes conditions or
invokes rules to serve the interests of international banks which lend
to the same countries. The Bretton Woods institutions, then, act as
watchdogs for moneylenders in international capital markets. This has
been so for some time. But there is more to it now. IMF programmes of

stabilization and World Bank programmes of structural adjustment, in developing countries and in the erstwhile communist countries, impose conditions that stipulate a structural reform of policy regimes. The object is to increase the degree of openness of these economies and to reduce the role of the state, so that market forces shape economic decisions. In this manner, the Bretton Woods institutions seek to harmonize policies and institutions across countries to meet the needs of globalization.

The ideologues believe that globalization led to rapid industrialization and economic convergence in the world economy during the late nineteenth century. In their view, the promise of the emerging global capitalist system was wasted for more than half a century, to begin with by three decades of conflict and autarchy that followed the First World War, and subsequently for another three decades, by the socialist path and statist worldviews (see, for example, Sachs and Warner 1995). The return of globalization in the late twentieth century was thus seen as the road to salvation, particularly for the developing countries and the former communist countries where governments are urged or pushed into adopting a comprehensive agenda of privatization (to minimize the role of the state) and liberalization (of trade flows, capital flows and financial flows). It needs to be stressed that this normative and prescriptive view of globalization is driven in part by ideology and in part by hope. Facts tell a different story. It should be obvious that the process of globalization will not reproduce or replicate the United States everywhere, just as it did not reproduce or replicate Britain everywhere a century earlier. It was associated with uneven development then, and is bound to produce uneven development now, not only between countries, but also within countries.

This is a lesson that emerges from history. The economic consequences of globalization in the late nineteenth century were, to say the least, asymmetrical. Most of the gains from the international economic integration of this era accrued to the imperial countries which exported capital and imported commodities. There were a few countries such as the United States and Canada – new lands with temperate climates and white settlers – which also derived some benefits. In these countries, the pre-conditions for industrialization were already being created, and international economic integration strengthened this process. Direct foreign investment in manufacturing activities, stimulated by rising tariff barriers, combined with technological and managerial flows, reinforced the process (Lewis 1978, Panic 1992). The outcome was industrialization and development. But this did not happen everywhere. Development was uneven in the industrial world.

Much of southern and eastern Europe lagged behind.[36] Countries in Asia, Africa, and Latin America, which were also a part of this process of globalization, were even less fortunate. Indeed, during the same period of rapid international economic integration, some of the most open economies in this phase of globalization – India, China, and Indonesia – experienced de-industrialization and underdevelopment. We need to remind ourselves that, in the period from 1870 to 1914, these three countries practised free trade as much as the United Kingdom and the Netherlands, where average tariff levels were close to negligible (3–5 per cent); in contrast, tariff levels in Germany, Japan, and France were significantly higher (12–14 per cent) and in the United States were very much higher (33 per cent) (Maddison 1989, Bairoch 1993). Furthermore, these three countries were also among the largest recipients of foreign investment (Maddison 1989). However, their globalization did not lead to development. The outcome was similar elsewhere, in Asia, Africa and Latin America. Between 1860 and 1913, the share of developing countries in world manufacturing output declined from over one-third to under one-tenth (Bairoch 1982). Export-oriented production in mines, plantations and cash-crop agriculture created enclaves in these economies which were integrated with the world economy in a vertical division of labour. But there were almost no backward linkages. Productivity levels outside the export enclaves stagnated at low levels. They simply created dualist economic structures where the benefits of globalization accrued mostly to the outside world and in small part to local elites.

The process of globalization was uneven then, and is also uneven now. Less than a dozen developing countries were an integral part of globalization at the end of twentieth century: Argentina, Brazil and Mexico in Latin America, and Korea, Hong Kong, Taiwan, Singapore, China, Indonesia, Malaysia, and Thailand in Asia. These eleven countries accounted for about 30 per cent of total exports from developing countries during the period 1970–80. This share rose to 59 per cent in 1990 and 66 per cent in 1992.[37] The same countries, excluding Korea, were also the main recipients of direct foreign investment in the developing world, accounting for 66 per cent of the average annual inflows during the period 1981–91.[38] There are no firm data on the distribution of portfolio investment, but it is almost certain that the same countries, described as 'emerging markets', were the destinations for an overwhelming proportion of portfolio investment flows to the developing world. This evidence suggests that globalization is most uneven in its spread, and that there is exclusion in the process. Sub-Saharan Africa, West Asia, Central

Asia, and South Asia are simply not in the picture, apart from many countries in Latin America, Asia, and the Pacific which are left out altogether.

The process of globalization has been uneven both over time and across space. The inequalities and the asymmetries implicit in the process which led to uneven development in the late nineteenth century, mostly for political reasons, were bound to create uneven development in the late twentieth century, mostly for economic reasons. There is a real danger that some countries may experience exclusion from this process of globalization, just as many people within these countries would experience exclusion from prosperity. Such exclusion from the process of development would increase the economic distance between nations and widen the income disparities between the peoples of the world. This would be difficult to sustain in a world where demonstration effects are strong and are reinforced by globalization which creates strong aspirations for certain consumption patterns or life styles. Economic deprivation could accentuate social divides and political alienation. If globalization turns into a secession of the successful, it could have an analogue in terms of a secession of the deprived.

Some correctives

As the twenty-first century begins, the facts of life in the world economy are clear. Globalization is the name of the game from which no country, whether Brazil, China, India, Mexico, Russia, South Africa, or Vietnam, wishes to be excluded. Not even large countries can afford to opt out. Is it possible, then, to modify the current process of integration to include more political equality and more partnership? A candid answer can only be in the negative. For the world is made up of unequal partners with conflicting interests. However, it is possible to contemplate correctives that would make the market-driven process of globalization conducive to a more egalitarian economic development and a more broad-based social development. The object of such a design should be to provide more countries with opportunities to improve their development prospects and more people within these countries with opportunities to improve their living conditions. In other words, even if we cannot create a world economy for the benefit of *all*, it can be shaped to benefit *many*, rather than just a *few*.

Globalization has reduced the autonomy of the nation state in economic, if not political matters, but there remain some degrees of freedom which must be exploited in the pursuit of industrialization and development. The object of any sensible strategy of development in a world of liberalization and globalization should be to create economic space for the pursuit of national interests and development objectives. In this task, there is a strategic role for the nation state.

Clearly, it is necessary to redefine the economic role of the state *vis-à-vis* the market in the present conjuncture. Such a redefinition should be based on two basic propositions.[39] First, the state and the market cannot be substitutes for each other, but must complement each other. Second, the relationship between the state and the market cannot be specified once and for all in any dogmatic manner, for the two institutions must adapt to one another in a cooperative manner over time. The ideology of globalization seeks to harmonize not only policy regimes but also institutions, including the economic role of the state, across the world. This is a mistake because the role of the state in an economy depends on its level of income and stage of development. What is more, the state is the only institution that can create room for introducing correctives.

In fact, during the twentieth century, success at economic development was observed mostly in cases where the state performed a strategic role *vis-à-vis* international capital and also created the pre-conditions for industrialization. This is evident if we consider, for example, the development experience of industrial capitalism in Japan after the Meiji Restoration in 1868, or the emergence of market socialism in China after the modernization and reform programme was launched in 1978. The economic role of the state has been just as crucial in South Korea, Taiwan and even Singapore (Amsden 1989, Wade 1991).

The pursuit of development in the context of globalization necessitates a role for the nation state in the domestic economic sphere and in economic or political interaction with the outside world. In the national context, the state must endeavour to create the pre-conditions for more equitable development, bargain with international capital to improve the distribution of gains from cross-border economic transactions, practice prudence in the macro management of the economy so as to reduce vulnerability, and intervene to minimize the social costs associated with globalization. In the international context, the state should attempt to reduce the asymmetries and the inequalities in the rules of the game, build strategic alliances among developing countries for this purpose and, wherever possible, seek out areas of convergence with the state in industrialized countries in terms of realpolitik or geo-political interests. It is worth considering these possibilities in turn, but it is important to stress that the discussion is meant to be illustrative rather than exhaustive.

Let me begin with the national context. First, in the earlier stages of industrialization, the state must create the conditions for the development of industrial capitalism. This requires the creation of a physical infrastructure through government investment. This implies investing in the development of human resources through education, catalysing institutional change, say, through agrarian reform, using strategic industrial policy for the development of technological and managerial capabilities at a micro-level, and establishing institutions that would regulate, govern and facilitate the functioning of markets. In each of these pursuits, strategic forms of state intervention are essential, and such state intervention has been crucial for development among late industrializers, particularly the success stories in East Asia that are now perceived as role models. It must be emphasized that the benefits of integration with the world economy through globalization would accrue only to those countries which have laid such requisite foundations for industrialization and development. Similarly, economic development would be more equitable and social development more broad-based in countries which have created these pre-conditions. Both propositions are borne out by the East Asian development experience.

Second, the state must bargain with large international firms, not only to improve the distribution of gains from economic transactions with them, but also to ensure that their activities are conducive to development. The reason is simple. Transnational corporations are in the business of profit while governments are in the business of development. Unilateral trade liberalization, which reduces tariffs across the board, opens up the market for foreign goods. Uniform investment liberalization, irrespective of country-of-origin or sector-of-destination, opens up the economy to foreign firms. This is obviously in the interest of large international firms. But it may not be in the interest of developing countries. Transnational corporations want access to domestic markets of large countries such as India and China, or access to natural resources in countries with such endowments. Governments in thesehost countries should, therefore, drive a bargain on a reciprocal basis: to improve terms of trade, to obtain market access for exports, to facilitate transfer of technology, or to establish manufacturing capacities in ancillaries, components or downstream activities. Such examples can be multiplied. This means strategic negotiations in the sphere of trade and investment, which can only be done by governments, and not by individuals or firms. Hence, governments must possess the minimal determination to negotiate, rather than to surrender from a perceived position of weakness or to give concessions without reciprocity, in keeping with the rhetoric of unilateral liberalization.

Third, the state must ensure prudent macro-management of the economy, particularly in the sphere of government finances. This is important for two reasons. For one, it saves governments from being forced into stabilization and adjustment programmes that come with high conditionality in terms of a prescribed policy regime which, in turn, reduces degrees of freedom in the pursuit of development objectives. For another, it reduces the vulnerability associated with rapid integration into international financial markets which often begins with a reliance on portfolio investment to finance current account deficits in the balance of payments. The object of reducing fiscal deficits in the government sector often squeezes public investment in infrastructure and public expenditure on social sectors, while contractionary monetary policies, implemented through tight credit and high interest rates, squeeze domestic investment. An economy also needs these high interest rates, together with a strong exchange rate regime, to sustain portfolio investment inflows in terms of both profitability and confidence. This erodes the competitiveness of exports over time and enlarges the trade deficit. It is important to recognize the macroeconomic implications. Larger trade deficits and current account deficits require larger portfolio investment inflows which, beyond a point, undermine confidence and create adverse expectations even if the government keeps the exchange rate pegged. But when a stifling of exports does ultimately force an exchange rate depreciation, confidence may simply collapse and lead to capital flight. These problems have indeed surfaced in several Latin American economies, most recently in Mexico. The problem is, in fact, much deeper and larger. Exchange rates can no longer be used as a strategic device to provide an entry into the world market for differentiated manufactured goods, just as interest rates can no longer be used as a strategic instrument for guiding the allocation of scarce investible resources in a market economy. What is more, countries that are integrated into the world monetary system are constrained in using autonomous management of demand to maintain levels of output and employment. Expansionary fiscal and monetary policies – large government deficits to stimulate aggregate demand or low interest rates to encourage domestic investment – can no longer be used because of an overwhelming fear that such measures could lead to speculative capital flight and a run on the national currency. The moral of the story is that prudent macro-management of the economy can enable a country to avoid some of the costs of integration through globalization, particularly those associated with vulnerability, and, at the same time, to capture some benefits by retaining the freedom to create the necessary conditions.

Fourth, from the perspective of social progress and human development, active state intervention is an important means of minimizing the social costs or the negative externalities associated with the process of globalization. It is possible to cite several examples: unbridled consumerism, industrial pollution, environmental degradation, sex tourism, stringent labour laws, and so on. The necessity for such intervention is greater in developing countries where absolute poverty is widespread, environmental concerns are minimal and the rights of citizens are not assured. The process of globalization often also relocates the production of goods and services, in whole or in part, to avoid laws and regulations in the industrialized world or the home countries of transnational corporations.

In the international context, nation states must endeavour to influence the rules of the game so that the playing field is less uneven, even if it is not level, and the outcome is more equitable. There is need for greater symmetry in the rules of the international trading system. If developing countries provide access to their markets, it should be matched with a corresponding access to technology. This, in turn, requires that the regime for the protection of intellectual property rights should recognize that the interests of technology-followers and technology-importers is just as important as the interests of technology-leaders and technology-exporters. Similarly, if there is almost complete freedom for capital mobility across national boundaries, the draconian restrictions on labour mobility across national boundaries should at least be reduced, if not eliminated. It needs to be recognized that any provisions for the commercial presence of corporate entities (capital) should correspond to provisions for the temporary migration of workers (labour), just as the right-of-establishment for corporate entities (capital) has an analogue in the right-of-residence for persons (labour).[40] The need for symmetry extends beyond the rules of the international trading system. There is a need to influence and reshape the rules of the multilateral financial institutions, in particular, the IMF and the World Bank. Stabilization programmes and structural adjustment programmes need to be flexible in terms of conditionalities, particularly where these are not consistent with national development objectives in the long term. It is possible to cite many examples. The fetish about reducing fiscal deficits might reduce the benefits of integration through globalization if it reduces public investment in infrastructure or public expenditure on social sectors. The insistence on high interest rates might squeeze domestic investment and constrain growth. Import liberalization supported by portfolio investment inflows may simply not be sustainable. Liberal entry for foreign firms and easy access to foreign technology might stifle the development of domestic managerial and technological capabilities. It is inevitable that moneylenders have their rates, but the imposition of a standardized package of policies, which is inflexible, on borrowers creates many difficulties. In sum, there is need to reduce asymmetries and inequalities in the rules of the game.

How is this to be done? In the multilateral institutions, whether the WTO, the IMF, or the World Bank, developing countries and transitional economies must ensure that their voices are heard. This is easier said than done, but groups of countries with mutual interests are more likely to be heard than single countries by themselves. For this purpose, it is essential to find common causes in a world where there are many conflicts and contradictions. There are two means of creating such country-groupings: regional and sub-regional economic initiatives (such as the Association of Southeast Asian Nations or ASEAN), or strategic alliances between countries across regions (say, China, India, Iran, South Africa, and Brazil). Such arrangements can succeed and be sustained only if member countries recognize that trade-offs are a necessary condition. In other words, there must be a willingness and an ability to accept some compromise, in respect of national political sovereignty, within the grouping, to acquire greater economic influence or stronger bargaining power in the international context. The more discerning and farsighted might even be willing to accept some erosion of national autonomy in the short term to improve economic performance in the medium term on the premise that, ultimately, it is economic strength which provides nation states with political clout in the international community.

Regional arrangements or strategic alliances may also straddle countries at different levels of development. We have a concrete example of the former in the North America Free Trade Area (NAFTA) and a potential example of the latter in the Asia Pacific Economic Caucus (APEC). The dynamics of economic competition and political rivalry among nation states may lead to the formation of trade blocs as strategic alliances or strategic responses. However, there might be more to it than meets the eye. For a wide range of reasons, nation states in the industrialized world may also wish to create economic space or degrees of freedom *vis-à-vis* international capital. The European Community, after all, is not simply a counterpoint to the United States as an economic or political bloc. Globalization, particularly in the realm of finance, has almost certainly eroded the ability of governments everywhere to tax, to print money, and to borrow. Monetary and fiscal policy are blunted. Macroeconomic management in the pursuit of internal and external balances is much more difficult. International financial markets are much too powerful for governments that may wish to maintain an exchange rate. Governments are concerned about the high levels of unemployment in the industrialized world, even if it is not part of the objective function that large international firms seek to maximize, because governments need legitimacy and support in domestic political constituencies. Europeans, particularly the French, are concerned about the preservation of culture given the advent of globalization which seeks to reproduce American culture everywhere. There may thus be some willingness on the part of nation states in the industrialized world to set rules that introduce a modicum of discipline on the forces of globalization.

It is essential to stress that these strategic alliances, whether among developing countries, among industrialized countries, or between developing countries and industrialized countries, must be based on a coincidence of mutual interests. Unless they constitute an integral part of the pursuit of national interest, such alliances or arrangements cannot sustain themselves, let alone provide a real solution. This is, perhaps, the most important lesson that we must learn from the failed quest for a new international economic order during the 1970s. If the North–South dialogue was a dialogue of the deaf, South–South cooperation was a search of the blind. We must learn from this experience. An appeal to the enlightened self interest of the rich, which was the spirit of the North–South dialogue, or the rhetoric of solidarity among the poor, which was the spirit of South-South cooperation, cannot suffice. The impetus can only come from material interests in the sphere of economics and national interests in the realm of politics. There will always be conflict and contradiction. But there would also be areas where it is possible to find common cause and accept trade-offs.

In conclusion, it is important to stress two limitations of this entire exercise. First, nation states are not Plato's guardians. Thus, governments do not always act in the interests of people at large. Indeed, governments are frequently sectarian in their actions and interventionist as they seek to promote or to protect the interests of the classes, or groups, that they represent. Sometimes, if not often, they may manipulate on behalf of groups which can exercise influence. The correctives suggested in this chapter are based on the presumption that the nation state can be persuaded to act in the interest of its people. This may be easier wherever democratic political systems provide the necessary checks and balances. However, even authoritarian regimes need some political legitimacy from their people. But there can be no doubt that correctives would be most effective in situations where people are at the centre of economic development, not only as its beneficiaries, but also as the main actors. Second, the world is made up of unequal partners: the rich and the poor, or the strong and the weak. Such economic and political inequalities between countries are nothing new and are bound to persist. It is only the incurable romantic who contemplates a world where countries are equal partners and people are equal citizens. It would be naive to believe that a fundamental change in international economic relations is feasible. It is not. But it should be possible to think of correctives in our search for a modified alternative such that the outcome of globalization is more equitable.

Notes

1 An earlier version of this chapter was first presented at a Copenhagen Seminar on 'Conditions for Social Progress: A World Economy for the Benefit of All' in September 1996. It also draws upon some earlier work of the author (Nayyar 1995a and 1997).

2 United Nations, *Yearbook of International Trade Statistics*, various issues.

3 For a comparison of growth in world trade and world output, see Maddison (1991). The export-GDP ratios in this paragraph, however, are calculated from data on exports in UNCTAD, *Handbook of International Trade and Development Statistics* (various issues) and data on GDP in World Bank, *World Development Report* (various issues) and United Nations, *Yearbook of National Accounts Statistics* (various issues).

4 UNCTAD, *World Investment Report, 1994*: 143.

5 For data on stocks and flows of direct foreign investment cited here, see United Nations, *Transnational Corporations in World Development*, various surveys, and UNCTAD, *World Investment Report*, various issues.

6 UNCTAD, *World Investment Report, 1994*: 130.

7 *ibid.*

8 UNCTAD, *World Investment Report, 1993*: 243–7.

9 UNCTAD, *World Investment Report, 1994*: 19.

10 *ibid.*

11 Bank of International Settlements (BIS), *Survey of Foreign Exchange Market Activity*, various issues.

12 Calculated from BIS data on trading in foreign exchange markets and United Nations data on world trade.

13 The values of world GDP and world exports in 1992, reported by the United Nations, have been converted into average daily figures for the purpose of this comparison.

14 International Monetary Fund, *Annual Report, 1993*: 105.

15 The figures on the increasing significance of net international bank loans, cited in this paragraph, are obtained from UNCTAD, *World Investment Report, 1994*: 128.

16 These proportions, as also the others cited in this paragraph, are estimated from data compiled by the BIS and the IMF, and are reported in 'A Survey of the World Economy', *The Economist*, London, 7 October 1995.

17 These proportions, as also the others cited in this paragraph, are estimated from data compiled by the BIS and the IMF, and are reported in 'A Survey of the World Economy', *The Economist*, London, 7 October 1995.

18 It is paradoxical that such derivatives, which have been introduced to counter risk may, in effect, increase the risk associated with international financial flows by increasing the volatility of short-term capital movements.

19 For a detailed discussion, see Oman (1994).

20 The discussion that follows in this section of the chapter, draws upon earlier work of the author. For a detailed analysis of the historical parallel, see Nayyar (1995a).

21 Maizels (1963) and Bairoch (1982). For estimates of the share of exports in GDP during this period, cited in this paragraph, see Maddison (1989).

22 It is striking that the average tariff rates on imports of manufactured goods in these industrialized countries, with the exception of the United Kingdom at that time, were in the range of 20 to 40 per cent, compared with an average tariff rate of about 5 per cent in 1990 (Bairoch 1993). Tariffs were much higher then, but non-tariff barriers are stronger now.

23 See *World Investment Report, 1994*: 120–1 and 130.

24 The deflator used is the US consumer price index.

25 The figure for the stock of direct foreign investment in developing countries in 1980 is obtained from UNCTAD, *World Investment Report, 1993*: 248, while the estimate of the stock of foreign capital in developing countries in 1914, at 1980 prices, is obtained from Maddison (1989: 30).

26 For a discussion and evidence, see Morgenstern (1959).

27 This intermediation is described and analysed in Kregel (1994).

28 For example, the substitution of steam for sails, and of iron for wooden hulls in ships, reduced ocean freight by two-thirds between 1870 and 1900 (Lewis 1977).

29 The production of perfectly interchangeable parts, the introduction of the moving assembly line developed by Ford, and methods of management evolved by Taylor, provided the foundations for this new form of industrial organization (see Oman 1994).

30 For a succinct and perceptive historical analysis of this period, see Hobsbawm (1987).

31 These estimates are reported by UNCTAD in *World Investment Report, 1994*.

32 For some countries, such as the United Kingdom, Italy, Spain and Portugal, such migration constituted 20 to 40 per cent of their populations (Stalker 1994).

33 This was largely attributable to the post-war labour shortages in Europe and the post-colonial ties often embedded in a common language (Nayyar 1994).

34 The only significant evidence of labour mobility during the last quarter of the twentieth century is the temporary migration of workers to Europe, the Middle East, and East Asia.

35 For a discussion on the implications of the new intellectual property rights regime for developing countries, see Nayyar (1993).

36 See Bairoch and Kozul-Wright (1996). The authors provide a lucid discussion of how globalization in the period 1870–1913 led to uneven development in the world economy, which meant divergence, rather than convergence, between countries in terms of industrialization and growth.

37 These proportions have been calculated from UNCTAD, *Handbook of International Trade and Development Statistics*, various issues.

38 See UNCTAD, *World Investment Report, 1994.*

39 For a detailed discussion, see Bhaduri and Nayyar (1996).

40 For a further discussion of this issue, see Nayyar (1989).

2
Implications of the GATT Uruguay Round for Development: the Malaysian Case

Mohamed Aslam and Jomo K. S.

After the Second World War, plans were drawn up for an International Trade Organization (ITO) to set the rules for international trade. Fifty-three governments drew up and signed a charter at Havana in Cuba for establishing this organization, which would serve as the counterpart for the field of trade to the International Monetary Fund (IMF) and the International Bank for Reconstruction and Development (IBRD, or World Bank). The three organizations were considered essential for sustained growth of the post-war global economy. However, although the IMF and the IBRD had been set up by the historic 1944 Bretton Woods conference, the ITO charter faced heavy opposition; and when the US Congress declined to approve the ITO, it was dropped. The demise of the ITO, however, did not eliminate the need for an international organization to deal with negotiations for reducing tariff and non-tariff barriers to international trade (Akhtar 1994). Twenty-three nations agreed to continue extensive negotiations for trade and tariff concessions at Geneva. These were incorporated in a General Agreement on Tariffs and Trade (GATT), signed in October 1947, which came into effect in January 1948. From this unlikely beginning, the GATT emerged as a more modest counterpart to the IMF and the IBRD. By 1993, 117 nations had signed the GATT multilateral treaty as contracting parties.

The GATT provided a more or less permanent forum and agency for reducing trade barriers. The main objective of the GATT was to achieve freer trade through reduction of tariff and non-tariff barriers on the basis of non-discrimination, reciprocity, and national treatment. It also provided safeguards against unexpected situations, binding tariff levels among member countries, and establishing a framework for resolving disputes among members over its rules, such as those regarding dumping. Generally, the GATT succeeded in facilitating freer trade, even if only gradually. Since the first trade talks in 1947, tariff rates around the world have declined, with weighted-average tariff levels lowered to below 5 per cent in the major industrialized countries (Lawrence 1993). Prior to the Uruguay Round concluded in 1993, the GATT had successfully held seven rounds of trade negotiations:

1) Geneva in 1947: the 23 countries that founded the GATT decided to exchange 45 000 tariff concessions worth US$10 billion.
2) Annecy (France) in 1949: the 13 countries participating in this Round proposed 5,000 additional tariff reductions.
3) Torquay (Britain) in 1950–51: the 38 countries involved adopted 8,700 tariff reductions, equivalent to 25 per cent of the 1948 level.
4) Geneva in 1955–56: the 26 participating countries decided to further cut customs tariffs by US$2.5 billion.
5) The Dillon Round held in Geneva in 1960–62: the 26 participating countries decided to cut customs tariffs on 4,400 items, equivalent to US$4.9 billion.
6) The Kennedy Round in Geneva in 1964–67: signed by 50 participating countries accounting for 75 per cent of world trade. For the first time, tariffs were cut by whole sectors instead of by products. Aiming for a 50 per cent tariff cut target, cuts of about US$40 billion were achieved.
7) The Tokyo Round began in 1973 in Tokyo and ended in 1979 in Geneva. The 99 participating countries (including many newly independent developing countries) decided on tariff reductions averaging 20 to 30 per cent, involving US$300 billion in trade, and signed agreements on subsidies, technical barriers to trade, government procurement, meat, dairy products, and civil aircraft. They also signed the Multi-Fibre Arrangement (MFA) in 1974 to regulate the liberalization of textile exports.

The Uruguay Round (UR) was the eighth, lengthiest, and most comprehensive round in the series of GATT multilateral trade negotiations. Involving 125 countries, it started at Punta Del Este (Uruguay) in 1986 and was completed on 15 December 1993 in Geneva. The most important new institutional development to come out of the Uruguay Round has been the establishment of the World Trade Organization (WTO) to take over from, and expand the role of, the GATT.

Some of the main Uruguay Round achievements in terms of 'market access' are:

a) developed countries agreeing to lower average tariff rates on industrial products by about 40 per cent;
b) in agriculture, the contracting parties agreeing to replace various border taxes with tariffs (known as 'tariffication'), to lower tariffs, and to reduce domestic and export subsidies;
c) in textiles and apparel, the contracting parties agreeing to integrate the MFA into the WTO in ten years.

Besides tightening rules on dispute settlements, anti-dumping regulations, clarification of subsidies, and safeguard measures, new agreements were also concluded. The General Agreement on Trade in Services (GATS) contains provisions for most-favoured-nation (MFN) treatment (the same treatment to be given to all member countries), national treatment (no discrimination against services by firms of other countries), and abolition of restrictions on market access (no adoption of measures such as those which restrict the number of service suppliers). Agreements were also concluded on Trade-Related Intellectual Property Rights (TRIPs), and Trade-Related Investment Measures (TRIMs); for example, local content requirements specifying that foreign enterprises must procure a certain percentage of their component parts locally have been prohibited.

The Uruguay Round has required the economies of developing countries to be more open to industrial countries for trade, capital/investment, and technology. Countries will be obliged to agree to increased foreign firm domination with the new intellectual property, services, and investment rules. They also face tougher punitive measures and regulations, for example, the national rules of origin requirements to avoid charges of dumping. In general, the sovereignty of developing country governments will be greatly eroded. Developing countries stand to lose preferential treatment from industrial nations under the Generalized System of Preferences (GSP). Such treatment will be gradually removed, and will be increasingly tied to obligations to implement and enforce TRIMs, TRIPs, GATS, and probably social, labour, and environmental standards, besides generally ensuring greater foreign access to national economies.

Malaysia ratified the Final Act of the Uruguay Round in September 1994 and agreed to the setting up of the WTO. In line with TRIPs, the government has tightened the law by introducing amendments to the Copyright and Trademarks Act (Patents 1983) in 1994. Malaysia also agreed to the GATS on 28 July 1995, and has offered to liberalize 14 of 16 service areas, including banking, insurance, and other financial services.

The two sectors that the government did not agree to liberalize are settlement and clearing services, and transfer of financial information services.

As a small open economy, Malaysia is closely linked to the world through trade ties, investment flows, and monetary links. More than most other developing countries, including the East Asian newly industrializing countries but not including the cities of Hong Kong and Singapore, its economic growth depends heavily on trade and investment flows. Thus, further liberalizing trade will make the country's economic growth even more vulnerable to external instability. In the long run, the TRIMs and TRIPs provisions will retard the development of local industry and technology. Opening up the country's services to foreigners will further worsen the services account deficit. This chapter offers a preliminary assessment of some implications of the Uruguay Round for the Malaysian economy by considering the likely impact of various relevant provisions of the agreement.

Trade liberalization

Malaysia is committed to import liberalization, but also hopes to gain greater market access under the Uruguay Round. One estimate is that with the reduced tariff rates under the Uruguay Round, Malaysia will gain about US$0.7 billion per annum in the short-run and US$2.6 billion in the long-run (Harrison 1995). The country expects to gain from the 45 per cent (weighted average) of tariff reduction in its major markets, which should benefit its manufactured exports. The average tariff reductions offered by some of its main trading partners to Malaysia were as follows: the United States of America (USA) 53.0 per cent, European Union (EU) 35.0 per cent, Japan 83.6 per cent, Canada 48.5 per cent, Australia 43.1 per cent, New Zealand 68.0 per cent, South Korea 57.0 per cent, Sweden 23.0 per cent, Switzerland 36.0 per cent, Brazil 51.2 per cent, Chile 28.6 per cent, and Thailand 15.1 per cent. The Malaysian manufacturing sub-sectors that should gain most include: electrical machinery (40 per cent tariff cut by developed countries), and wood, pulp, paper, and furniture (65 per cent tariff cut).

The Uruguay Round promises to ensure that non-tariff measures (NTMs) can no longer be used as disguised forms of protection. The NTMs erected by member countries of the Organization for Economic Cooperation and Development (OECD) affect a notably higher share of imports from developing countries than imports from other industrial countries. Approximately 18 per cent of developing countries' non-oil exports face NTMs in OECD countries. However, protectionism, in the form of NTMs and tariff escalation, may linger on after the agreed deadline (2005); and even as NTMs and tariff escalation are phased out, anti-dumping laws, countervailing duties (CVDs), and safeguard clauses may be used even more arbitrarily than is currently the case (Smeets 1995). In the immediate future, companies seeking protection will attempt to make far greater use of anti-dumping laws and CVDs. Such protection has increased significantly in recent years, and the trend is likely to accelerate. Meanwhile, government procurement may continue to exclude foreign suppliers. Beyond that and over the longer run, governments and firms will probably invent new measures to circumvent the new rules (Kreinen 1995). In the long run, particularly after the elimination of NTMs, the industrialized nations may face strong competition from developing countries, threatening their industries and even causing macroeconomic instability.

In recent years, several export products from Malaysia have been subject to new NTMs in Australia, the EU, and the US. Such countries are increasingly employing stronger market defence mechanisms, including safeguard clauses, anti-dumping and countervailing measures, as well as stricter interpretation of rules of origin, subsidies, and dumping provisions in their domestic laws (MITI 1995: 157). In response, Malaysia introduced a Countervailing and Anti-Dumping Act in 1993, enforced from April 1994, to safeguard Malaysian industries from unfair trade practices by foreign exporters.

Malaysia offered to reduce tariffs on 7,218 items, including industrial and agricultural products worth RM80.1 billion or 79 per cent of imports in 1992 (*Business Times*, 17 December 1993). From just one per cent before the Uruguay Round, 65 per cent of Malaysia's tariff lines would now be 'bound', that is, subject to ceilings on import duty increases. As a result, Malaysia's trade weighted-average tariff rate for industrial products was reduced to 8.9 per cent from 10.2 per cent, which was lower than the rates for a number of developed and developing countries.

Besides reducing tariffs, the government has also dismantled and converted non-tariff measures into tariffs, mainly affecting import licensing involving approval permits (APs) (that is, import quotas with tariffs) to protect and preserve local markets from foreign goods. The number of items requiring import APs increased from 223 in 1973 to 1,135 in 1990, before being reduced slightly to 1,124 in 1994. Finished manufactured goods that are subject to APs include completely-built-up (CBU) vehicles, electrical consumer durables, textiles and apparel

(Aslam 1997). Although the Malaysian government has shown a commitment to NTM tariffication, it is difficult to set a tariff level comparable in effect to a particular AP. This may encourage 'dirty tariffication' in the conversion process, with the government deliberately imposing higher tariff rates than should be the case to protect local producers.

Reduced tariff levels will increase domestic market access for foreign goods bringing in more imports. Tougher competition between domestic and foreign producers should emerge, improving consumer welfare, but also undermining the expansion of indigenous industrial capability and capacity. The economy will be more susceptible to external shocks, which will adversely affect the country's economic stability. While exports will be further enhanced, payments for imports will also increase. As shown in Table 2.1, the shares of both exports and imports to gross domestic product (GDP) have been rising; the index of trade liberalization has been moving downward, indicating that the economy is becoming more liberalized.[1]

Terms-of-trade losses

If the terms-of-trade (TOT) for a country deteriorate, more trade will disproportionately favour its trading partners. Trade liberalization increases trading, exacerbating losses due to the terms-of-trade deterioration. Thus, the Uruguay Round is likely to worsen such losses to the Malaysian economy.

As with much of the rest of the South, Malaysia's terms-of-trade declined sharply in the 1980s. The import price index increased greatly, while the export price index worsened (Table 2.2), significantly affecting the country's trade performance. As Table 2.3 shows, for the period between 1960 and 1997, the volume of exports rose 2,987 per cent, much more than the 1,998 per cent increase in import volume. However, import prices rose 378 per cent, while export prices rose by 97 per cent, resulting in a 52 per cent fall in the terms-of-trade. Thus, while the income from exports rose by 5,981 per cent, the foreign exchange needed to pay for imports rose by 7,830 per cent. To pay for the same unit of imports obtainable with one unit of exports in 1960, Malaysia had to export 1.29 units of exports in 1997 because of the terms-of-trade decline. Thus, to finance the 1,998 per cent rise in import volume, export volume would have had to rise by 3,910 per cent if the 1960 trade surplus equivalent of 23 per cent of export value was to be preserved. But there was only a far lower 2,987 per cent increase in volume of exports, meaning that the value of exports rose far slower than the

Table 2.1   Malaysia: Shares of Exports and Imports to Gross Domestic Product and Trade Liberalization Index, 1960–97

Year	Exports/GDP (%)	Imports/GDP (%)	Degree of Openness (X+M)/GDP	Index of Trade Liberalization
1960	55	42	0.97	0.27
1961	47	41	0.88	0.12
1962	45	42	0.88	0.32
1963	43	42	0.85	0.25
1964	41	39	0.80	0.17
1965	42	37	0.79	0.27
1966	40	35	0.75	0.29
1967	38	34	0.72	0.41
1968	39	34	0.74	0.31
1969	44	31	0.75	0.36
1970	41	34	0.76	0.26
1971	39	34	0.73	0.20
1972	35	32	0.67	0.18
1973	41	33	0.74	0.19
1974	47	45	0.92	0.13
1975	42	38	0.80	0.12
1976	48	35	0.82	0.10
1977	46	35	0.81	0.10
1978	47	38	0.85	0.09
1979	54	38	0.92	0.08
1980	53	44	0.97	0.09
1981	47	46	0.93	0.08
1982	45	46	0.91	0.09
1983	47	44	0.91	0.10
1984	49	41	0.90	0.11
1985	49	39	0.88	0.11
1986	49	39	0.88	0.15
1987	57	40	0.98	0.14
1988	61	48	1.09	0.16
1989	67	60	1.27	0.12
1990	69	69	1.38	0.09
1991	71	70	1.41	0.09
1992	69	63	1.32	0.09
1993	73	68	1.41	0.08
1994	78	76	1.54	0.08
1995	82	82	1.64	0.08
1996	77	73	1.50	0.08
1997	79	75	1.54	0.08

Sources: Aslam 1993: pp. 59, 149; Ministry of Finance, Malaysia, *Economic Report 1998/1999.*

Table 2.2 Malaysia: Terms-of-Trade, 1960–97 (1960 = 1.00)

Year	Export Price Index	Import Price Index	Terms-of-Trade
1960	1.00	1.00	1.00
1961	0.80	1.00	0.80
1962	0.80	0.98	0.82
1963	0.78	1.00	0.78
1964	0.80	1.01	0.79
1965	0.84	1.00	0.84
1966	0.80	1.02	0.78
1967	0.73	1.00	0.73
1968	0.70	1.04	0.67
1969	0.80	1.05	0.76
1970	0.77	1.05	0.73
1971	0.71	1.13	0.63
1972	0.67	1.17	0.57
1973	0.88	1.36	0.65
1974	1.17	1.93	0.61
1975	1.02	2.05	0.50
1976	1.23	2.08	0.59
1977	1.44	2.13	0.68
1978	1.54	2.18	0.71
1979	1.78	2.34	0.76
1980	1.96	2.81	0.70
1981	1.84	3.21	0.57
1982	1.65	3.19	0.52
1983	1.74	3.06	0.57
1984	1.75	2.97	0.59
1985	1.63	2.94	0.55
1986	1.34	2.83	0.47
1987	1.53	2.84	0.54
1988	1.63	3.04	0.54
1989	1.80	3.23	0.56
1990	1.60	3.31	0.48
1991	1.66	3.40	0.49
1992	1.71	3.42	0.50
1993	1.77	3.49	0.51
1994	1.83	3.62	0.51
1995	1.94	3.69	0.53
1996	1.94	3.67	0.53
1997	1.97	3.78	0.52

Sources: Bank Negara Malaysia, *Quarterly Economic Bulletin*, various issues; Bank Negara Malaysia, *Annual Report 1992, 1994, 1996, 1997*; International Monetary Fund, *International Financial Statistics*, various years.

Table 2.3 Malaysia: Terms of Trade Effects on Imports and Exports, 1960–97

			Exports	Imports
(a)	*Changes between 1960 and 1997*			
	1960:	Current value	RM3,632.6 mil.	RM2,786.0 mil.
		Volume increase	2,986.7%	1,997.9%
		Price increase	97.0%	378.0%
		Value increase	5,980.8%	7,830.2%
	1997:	Current value	RM220,890.5 mil.	RM220,935.5 mil.
(b)	*Changes between 1960 and 1975*			
	1960:	Current value	RM3,632.6 mil.	RM2,786.4 mil.
		Volume increase	149.4%	49.4%
		Price increase	44.0%	205.0%
		Value increase	154.1%	206.1%
	1975:	Current value	RM9,230.9 mil.	RM8,530.4 mil.
(c)	*Changes between 1975 and 1994*			
	1975:	Current value	RM9,230.9 mil.	RM8,530.4 mil.
		Volume increase	1,137.9%	1,304.6%
		Price increase	36.8%	84.4%
		Value increase	2,292.9%	2,490.0%
	1997:	Current value	RM220,890.5 mil.	RM220,935.5 mil.

Sources: Bank Negara Malaysia, *Quarterly Economic Bulletin*, various issues; Bank Negara Malaysia, *Annual Report 1997*; International Monetary Fund, *International Financial Statistics*, various years.

value of imports. As a result, Malaysia suffered severe trading losses. The losses rose from RM809 million in 1961 to RM53, 691 million in 1997 (Table 2.4).

The two possible outcomes of a decline in the terms-of-trade are as follows: (a) a big fall in the terms-of-trade would mean that the country suffers a large loss, either in terms of lower import volume, or a much lower rate of real import growth, if the trade balance is maintained; (b) alternatively, if the country's imports grow at or near the same rate as its exports despite the big terms-of-trade decline, then it would suffer a severe deterioration in its trade balance. In either case, the terms-of-trade decline seriously reduces the import-purchasing capacity of the country's exports (that is, the exports' purchasing power) and thus greatly reduces the quantity of imports into the economy (Khor 1983: 98). These developments seem to have been exacerbated by the secular decline in the primary commodity terms-of-trade in the early and mid-1980s and possibly by a similar decline in the terms-of-trade for manufactured products as well (see Chapter 4).

Table 2.4 Malaysia: Trading Losses, 1960–97

Year	Gross exports at current prices (RM mil.) (1)	Export price index (1960=1.00) (2)	Import price index (1960=1.00) (3)	Export purchasing power (RM mil.) (1)/(3) (4)	Real exports at constant 1960 prices (1)/(2) (5)	Trading gain or loss at 1960 prices (4) – (5)	Trading gain or loss of GDP (%)
1960	3 632.6	1.00	1.00	3 632.6	3 632.6	0.0	0.0
1961	3 238.3	0.80	1.00	3 238.3	4 047.5	–809.2	11.8
1962	3 259.6	0.80	0.98	3 324.0	4 074.1	–750.1	10.4
1963	3 330.0	0.78	1.00	3 330.0	4 263.5	–933.5	12.2
1964	3 381.9	0.80	1.01	3 349.0	4 227.0	–878.0	10.7
1965	3 782.5	0.84	1.00	3 782.5	4 513.0	–730.5	8.1
1966	3 845.8	0.80	1.02	3 772.8	4 806.8	–1 034.0	10.7
1967	3 723.7	0.73	1.00	3 723.7	5 077.5	–1 353.8	13.8
1968	4 122.6	0.70	1.04	3 968.9	5 929.1	–1 960.2	19.0
1969	5 063.1	0.80	1.05	4 820.7	6 317.8	–1 497.1	12.9
1970	5 163.1	0.77	1.05	4 924.1	6 692.9	–1 768.8	14.1
1971	5 016.8	0.71	1.13	4 454.4	7 023.0	–2 568.6	20.0
1972	4 854.0	0.67	1.17	4 131.8	7 177.5	–3 045.7	21.7
1973	7 372.1	0.88	1.36	5 424.1	8 413.7	–2 989.6	16.5
1974	10 194.7	1.17	1.93	5 276.5	8 702.5	–3 426.0	15.7
1975	9 230.9	1.02	2.05	4 506.1	9 058.5	–4 552.4	20.5
1976	13 442.0	1.23	2.08	6 469.6	10 941.2	–4 471.6	15.9
1977	14 959.2	1.44	2.13	7 035.4	10 402.1	–3 366.7	10.4
1978	17 073.9	1.54	2.18	7 816.5	11 066.3	–3 249.8	9.0
1979	24 222.0	1.78	2.34	10 352.2	13 599.7	–3 247.5	7.2
1980	28 171.6	1.96	2.81	10 040.4	14 359.1	–4 318.7	8.1

36

Table 2.4 (continued)

Year	Gross exports at current prices (RM mil.) (1)	Export price index (1960=1.00) (2)	Import price index (1960=1.00) (3)	Export purchasing power (RM mil.) (1)/(3) (4)	Real exports at constant 1960 prices (1)/(2) (5)	Trading gain or loss at 1960 prices (4) – (5)	Trading gain or loss of GDP (%)
1981	27 109.4	1.84	3.21	8 436.0	14 748.3	−6 312.2	11.0
1982	28 108.2	1.65	3.19	8 799.9	17 059.7	−8 259.8	13.2
1983	32 771.2	1.74	3.06	10 715.3	18 803.9	−8 088.6	11.6
1984	38 646.9	1.75	2.97	13 008.8	22 130.5	−9 121.7	11.5
1985	38 016.7	1.63	2.94	12 923.7	23 343.1	−10 419.4	13.4
1986	35 318.6	1.34	2.83	12 501.3	26 299.3	−13 798.0	19.2
1987	45 224.9	1.53	2.84	15 898.8	29 492.2	−13 593.4	17.2
1988	55 260.0	1.63	3.04	18 185.3	33 930.9	−15 745.6	17.3
1989	67 824.5	1.80	3.23	20 983.2	37 723.9	−16 740.7	16.5
1990	79 646.4	1.60	3.31	24 035.6	49 902.6	−25 867.0	22.6
1991	94 496.6	1.66	3.40	27 794.5	57 428.1	−29 633.6	22.9
1992	103 656.7	1.71	3.42	30 276.4	60 575.3	−30 298.9	20.5
1993	121 237.5	1.77	3.49	34 717.2	68 516.2	−33 799.0	20.7
1994	153 921.2	1.83	3.62	42 545.0	84 286.3	−41 741.3	23.0
1995	184 986.5	1.94	3.69	50 128.6	95 297.8	−45 169.2	22.2
1996	197 026.1	1.94	3.67	53 685.6	101 559.8	−47 874.2	19.2
1997	220 890.5	1.97	3.78	58 436.6	112 127.2	−53 690.6	19.5

Sources: Bank Negara Malaysia, *Quarterly Economic Bulletin,* December 1996; Bank Negara Malaysia, *Annual Report 1992, 1994, 1996* and *1997.*

Agricultural markets

Under the Uruguay Round, developed countries are required to reduce tariffs by at least 36 per cent, and developing countries by 24 per cent.[2] Some of Malaysia's major agricultural markets are reducing tariffs by 35 per cent. Malaysian products which stand to benefit include palm oil, palm oil products, cocoa products, pepper, tropical fruits, fish, and fish products. On the other hand, Malaysia has offered to bind or reduce tariffs for all agricultural items by 28 per cent on a simple average basis, and to convert all non-tariff import regulatory measures in the agriculture sector to tariffs. Products offered for tariffication include wheat flour, refined sugar, chicken, chicken wings, pork, ham, eggs, liquid milk, coffee beans, and cabbages (*Business Times*, 17 December 1993). Malaysia is expected to thus gain US$1.2 billion (Harrison 1995). However, for other products such as meat, dairy products, cereals (mainly wheat, rice, and maize), vegetables, fruits, sugar, and feed for animals, Malaysia may experience heavy losses. Exports of meat in 1980 were RM2.2 million, compared to imports of RM94.8 million, whereas in 1994, imports had increased to RM339.7 compared to exports of RM64.3 million. Imports of dairy products increased from RM266.2 million in 1980 to RM726.5 million in 1994, while cereal imports increased from RM710.6 million in 1980 to RM1,648.9 in 1994. As mentioned above, the Uruguay Round will probably increase the volume of these imports, thus adversely affecting the merchandise trade balance.

Tariff escalation – involving higher duties for more processed products – is still evident in many developed countries, such as the European Union and Japan, even in the post-Uruguay Round tariff regimes. Tariff escalation discourages the downstream processing and export of processed products instead of primary commodities. For example, in the European Union, tariffs on crude palm oil will be reduced from 4.0 per cent to zero under the Uruguay Round, while tariffs for processed palm oil products will still be maintained at 9 per cent for refined palm oil, 9.6 per cent for non-crude palm kernel oil, and 5.1 per cent for stearic acid (*Business Times*, 12 December 1994).

Unlike agricultural exports, Malaysia probably obtained a better deal in terms of improved access to markets for manufactured exports. Exports of manufactures from Malaysia have increased rapidly since the 1970s. Such goods accounted for about only 11.9 per cent of exports in 1970, increasing to 21.6 per cent in 1980 before reaching 78.2 per cent in 1994. The manufacturing sector has been the leading growth sector since the 1960s, and has contributed 48.9 per cent of GDP in 1995 compared to 23.2 per cent in 1970.

Multi-Fibre Arrangement (MFA)

Since 1974, the Multi-Fibre Arrangement (MFA) has placed quotas on Third World exports of textiles and clothing to the North. The MFA was originally conceived as a 'temporary measure' to enable industrial countries to adjust to the competitiveness of Third World imports. Before the conclusion of the Uruguay Round, international trade in textiles and clothing had been conducted under the MFA IV, signed in June 1986. With the Uruguay Round accord, the MFA will be phased out by 2006, by using elevated growth rates in MFA quotas, and through the sequential elimination of products covered by MFA quota restrictions. At the same time, a new system of selective safeguards – whose operational details have yet to be defined – will accompany this process. This is a source of concern to some developing country exporters who fear this regime could prove to be more restrictive than the MFA that it will replace (Hamilton & Whalley 1995).

The elimination of the MFA could adversely affect Malaysian exports of textiles and clothing, with Malaysia losing markets, mainly in the industrialized countries. Currently, most firms in Malaysia producing apparel are contract manufacturers to major overseas buying houses located in Hong Kong and Singapore (MITI, Malaysia 1995: 152). The industry is the second most important sub-sector in manufacturing after the electrical/electronic sub-sector. Out of 1,230 companies in the textiles and apparel sector in 1990, 1,000 or 81.3 per cent were in the apparel sub-sector (MITI, Malaysia 1995: 153). However, most of these apparel companies were very small with limited production capacities, and thus contributed only 31.9 per cent of the output of the whole sub-sector. Also, the textile and apparel sub-sector is the second largest contributor to Malaysia's manufactured exports. Exports of these products have increased tremendously from RM31.7 million in 1970 to RM806.3 million in 1980 and RM6.1 billion in 1994 (apparel accounted for over 68 per cent in the period 1992–94). Most of Malaysia's textile and apparel exports benefited from the quota system under the MFA. The USA, the EU and Canada – which regulate their textile and clothing imports under the MFA through bilateral textile agreements with exporting countries – accounted for almost 70 per cent of Malaysia's external textile market (MITI, Malaysia 1994: 48). Exports to major non-quota markets – such as Singapore, Hong Kong and Japan – were valued at RM1,160 million in 1993, or 17.2 per cent of total exports of textiles and clothing. Malaysia's textile industry is very dependent on exports, particularly in MFA-protected markets. Currently, Malaysia has five bilateral textile agreements – with the USA, EU, Canada, Norway, and Finland. Thus, after the MFA is phased out by the year 2006, multi-fibre export markets will be more competitive. Since Malaysian textile exports currently depend largely on foreign import quotas, Malaysia may no longer be able to compete with lower cost producers.

Trade-Related Investment Measures (TRIMs)

Malaysia's investment policies will have to be modified to conform with the Uruguay Round agreements. Certain 'investment conditions' have been prohibited; for example, all local content requirements related to investments would have to be phased out. Subsidies to local industry to encourage the use of domestic over imported inputs must be phased out by all developing countries, other than the least developed countries. Export subsidies will have to be eliminated under the TRIMs agreement. However, suggested provisions requiring that governments must grant entry to all intending foreign investors, and accord them 'national treatment' – that is equal to local companies – have not yet been included.

Under the guise of 'levelling the playing field', concerted efforts to eliminate all forms of discrimination in favour of domestically-owned industry have continued after the conclusion of the Uruguay Round as the compromises in the TRIMs agreement were not satisfactory to interests in the North. The Organization for Economic Cooperation and Development (OECD) has been working on a Multilateral Agreement on Investment (MAI). Once this is accepted by the industrialized country member governments of OECD and endorsed by other governments desperate to attract foreign investment, the MAI will shape and determine the Multilateral Investment Agreement (MIA) being prepared by the WTO. Meanwhile, specific agreements – such as the Information Technology Agreement (ITA) – have been pushed through by the US to strengthen and advance the interests of the mainly US companies which dominate the industry.

The main consequence of such elements in the new international economic governance under WTO auspices will be the strengthening of the interests and leverage of transnational corporations (TNCs), mainly based in the North. This development will be primarily at the expense of national economic sovereignty, including the ability of developmentalist governments to effectively deploy industrial policy instruments to accelerate growth and structural transformation. Host governments are increasingly required to extend 'national treatment' to foreign investors, thus diminishing the availability of policy instruments to promote the development of new national industrial capabilities.

Foreign direct investment (FDI) has been relatively more important in Malaysia than in most other countries. In the period 1971–79, manufacturing FDI in Malaysia came to RM1,880.6 million, increasing to RM22,326.5 million in 1980–89 before receiving RM80,870.4 million from 1990 until July 1994. Most of the FDI has been concentrated in labour-intensive export-oriented industries, mainly electronic/electrical products, textiles and apparel, chemicals and related products, and wood and related products. Foreign ownership has always been important, growing in import-substituting industries in the 1960s and in non-resource-based export-oriented manufacturing since then, especially since the late 1980s. The foreign share of gross fixed manufacturing assets increased from 19 per cent in 1985 to 40 per cent in 1991. Electric/electronic, beverage and tobacco, and some other manufactured products (mainly scientific instruments and toys) continue to be strongly dominated by foreign capital, which accounts for more than 60 per cent of such investments. Textiles and garments have been more than 50 per cent foreign owned, while foreign capital has also owned more than 40 per cent of fixed assets in rubber products, transport equipment and machinery (Rasiah 1995). Japan's share of foreign-owned fixed manufacturing assets in 1993 was 33.6 per cent, followed by Singapore's 14.8 per cent, the USA's 10.0 per cent, Taiwan's 6.9 per cent, the United Kingdom's 6.3 per cent and Hong Kong's 5.0 per cent (Athukorala and Menon 1996). Foreign establishments increased from 7.6 per cent of all firms in 1985 to 16.2 per cent in 1991, while industrial output from foreign firms increased from 34.6 per cent in 1985 to 47.1 per cent in 1991 (Rasiah 1995).

Foreign ownership of corporate equity at par value increased by an average of 12.6 per cent per annum during the Sixth Malaysian Plan period (1991–95), reaching RM49.8 billion, or 27.7 per cent of total equity in 1995 compared to RM27.5 billion, or 25.4 per cent in 1990 (Malaysia 1996: 86). This is not surprising as ownership regulations were relaxed from the mid-1980s to revive foreign direct investment, accelerate growth, particularly of the manufacturing sector, and obtain the technology to upgrade the skills and quality of the Malaysian labour force (Malaysia 1996: 86).

The heavy influx of FDI into the country has resulted in huge imports of investment and intermediate goods. Imports of intermediate and capital goods – closely associated with foreign investment in the country – have contributed much to the growing import bill and trade deficit. The proportion of investment goods in total imports increased very significantly from 25.2 per cent in 1970 to 41.4 per cent in 1994; machinery has been a major component of imports, accounting for 30 per cent on average. Likewise, the proportion of intermediate goods has also increased from 35.3 per cent in 1970 to 43.5 per cent in 1994, with goods for manufacturing purposes being the major component, accounting for more than 70 per cent by the late 1980s. For example, the electrical and electronic industry has relied heavily on imports of electronic parts and components. In 1994, the imports cost RM28.2 billion compared to RM18.2 billion in 1993 – a 55 per cent increment in one year. Imports of electronic components, such as semiconductors, integrated circuits, thermionic valves and photocells, constituted 66.5 per cent of total imports for the electronics sub-sector in 1994 (MITI, Malaysia 1995: 149). The main sources of imports were the USA, Japan and Taiwan, also the major investors in the manufacturing sector. Weak linkages and low value-added have meant that the share of imported inputs in the gross export value of manufactured exports is as high as 75 per cent (Athukorala and Menon 1996). In addition, there are other 'leakages' such as profit remittances, salaries of expatriates, and interest payments on foreign loans.[3] Internationalized production offers possibilities for tax evasion or minimization through transfer pricing so that profits are largely recorded where tax rates are lowest; such transfer pricing possibilities may either exaggerate or underestimate actual value-added in the Malaysian economy (Athukorala and Menon 1996).

The impact of foreign direct investment on income outflows in terms of profits and dividends is reflected in Tables 2.5 and 2.6. Total FDI rose from RM10,598 million in 1966–80 to RM118,795 million in 1981–98, whereas total income outflows abroad in the same period increased from RM12,113 million to RM127,560 million, and net profits of foreign firms increased from RM14,666 million in 1967–80 to RM80,731 million in 1981–95 (Table 2.5). However, in percentage terms, the average profit rate decreased from 48 per cent to 29 per cent (Table 2.7). In contrast, net fixed assets of foreign firms increased, on average, from 36 per cent (RM5,724 million) to 47 per cent (RM44,457 million) in the same periods, while the average reinvestment rate increased from 46 to 54 per cent. These recent developments, especially from the mid-1980s, differ from the longer term trends for FDI inflows and income outflows.

In the 1980s, the share of profits accruing to foreign-controlled companies was reduced to about 30 per cent. However, this was still

Table 2.5   Malaysia: Foreign Capital Inflows and Outflows, 1966–98 (RM mil.)

Year	Foreign[1] Capital Inflow	% of Private Capital Formation	Gross[2] Revenue	Net Profit[2]	Investment Income Outflow
1966	170	18.8	4 669.4	n.a.	268
1967	130	12.9	5 331.0	251	144
1968	93	9.5	6 280.9	250	154
1969	245	25.8	7 730.7	380	334
1970	287	19.7	8 207.1	414	355
1971	306	18.3	8 168.6	449	363
1972	320	15.6	9 115.8	616	378
1973	420	14.4	11 561.2	1 095	659
1974	1 374	33.1	15 989.0	1 216	997
1975	839	24.0	14 806.5	787	727
1976	969	26.2	19 425.3	1 241	931
1977	999	23.0	19 767.6	1 423	1 276
1978	1 158	17.7	22 351.4	1 875	1 716
1979	1 255	18.5	25 782.2	2 353	1 991
1980	2 033	22.4	32 717.9	2 316	1 820
1981	2 914	28.3	36 368.1	2 317	1 836
1982	3 263	29.4	36 257.4	2 382	1 679
1983	2 926	23.1	39 302.2	3 007	4 208
1984	1 869	14.0	41 329.7	3 121	5 255
1985	1 725	14.1	38 403.0	2 586	5 434
1986	1 262	12.3	32 415.0	1 837	4 597
1987	1 065	9.7	36 931.1	2 597	4 824
1988	1 884	13.5	45 110.0	3 505	5 019
1989	4 518	23.8	57 219.6	4 675	5 935
1990	6 309	26.1	72 473.3	5 733	5 072
1991	10 996	35.0	88 850.2	6 811	6 735
1992	13 204	41.3	101 532.0	7 439	7 920
1993	12 885	32.8	116 716.7	8 354	8 174
1994	10 798	20.9	144 201.3	11 045	9 449
1995	10 464	15.7	175 382.4	15 342	10 338
1996	12 777	16.6	n.a.	n.a.	11 629
1997	14 450	16.8	n.a.	n.a.	14 639
1998	8 490	21.1	n.a.	n.a.	14 817

Notes: [1] Approved foreign direct investment.
[2] Figures from *Financial Survey of Limited Companies*, Department of Statistics. n.a. – not available.
Sources: Bank Negara Malaysia, *Quarterly Economic Bulletin*, various issues; Ministry of Finance, *Economic Report*, various years.

Table 2.6 Malaysia: Inflows and Outflows of Capital, 1970–98

	1970	1975	1978	1979	1980	1981	1982	1983	1984	1985	1986	1987	1988	1989	1990	1991	1992	1993	1994	1995	1996	1997	1998
1. Investment income to abroad	-355	-727	-1571	-1797	-1820	-1836	-2679	-4208	-5255	-5434	-4597	-4824	-5019	-5935	-5072	-6109	-6419	-8174	-9448	-10338	-11629	-14639	-14817
2. Net Transfers	-180	-79	-82	-119	-45	-78	-75	-21	-90	-14	-96	+348	+395	+219	+147	+102	+337	+513	-2225	-2515	-2943	-3345	-9876
3. Current Account Movements (1+2)	-535	-806	-1653	-1916	-1865	-1914	-2754	-4229	-5345	-5448	-4693	-4476	-4624	-5716	-4925	-6007	-6082	-7661	-11673	-12853	-14572	-17984	-24693
4. Private Financial Capital (short-term)	-10	-83	-349	-1579	902	97	+326	-263	-288	+870	-47	-2491	-2914	1562	1356	5135	11957	13931	-8484	-2529	10317	-12913	-20633
5. Errors and Omissions	-260	-397	-1034	2247	-1493	-1488	-963	-885	-2043	-368	1322	147	287	-988	3019	-395	81	9370	3333	-1896	-6371	-1254	13513
6. Inflows of long-term capital	294	1780	1718	2238	2245	5856	8740	9357	7421	4026	2893	-1366	-3192	1849	3458	10362	10423	14028	11795	16599	13442	19133	10670
(a) Public-sector borrowing	2	936	542	703	352	2942	5477	6431	5552	2301	1631	-2431	-5076	-2669	-2851	-634	-2781	1143	997	6135	665	4683	2180
(b) Private capital	287	862	1258	1448	2033	2914	3263	2926	1869	1725	1262	1065	1884	4518	6309	10996	13204	12885	10798	10464	12777	14450	8490
7. Capital Account Movement (4+5+6)	24	1300	335	2906	1654	4465	8103	8209	5090	4528	4168	-3710	-5819	2423	7833	15102	22461	37329	6644	17232	17388	4966	3550
8. Total Movement of Funds (3+7)	-511	494	-1318	990	-211	2551	5349	3980	-255	-920	-525	-8186	-10443	-3293	2908	9095	16379	29668	-5029	4379	2816	-13018	21143
9. Total Outflows (1+2+4+5)	-805	-1286	-3036	-4660	-2456	-3305	-3391	-5377	-7676	-4946	-3418	-6820	-7251	-5142	-550	-1267	5956	15640	-16824	-12220	-10626	-32151	-31813
10. Total Inflows (6)	294	1780	1718	2238	2245	5856	8740	9357	7421	4026	2893	-1366	-3192	1849	3458	10362	10423	14028	11795	16599	13442	19133	10670

Note: Errors and omissions are mainly unrecorded short term capital outflows.

Sources: Bank Negara, *Quarterly Economic Bulletin*, various issues; Khor Kok Peng, 1983: 196–7.

Table 2.7 Malaysia: Rates of Reinvestment, Local and Foreign Companies, 1970–95

	1970	1975	1977	1978	1979	1980	1981	1982	1983	1984	1985	1986	1987	1988	1989	1990	1991	1992	1993	1994	1995
1. NET PROFITS	590	1458	3091	4021	6293	6948	6957	7337	7973	10696	7558	4457	7471	9377	15509	20246	24262	27793	35983	45681	51735
Local (RM mil.)	176	670	1668	2147	3941	4632	4637	4955	4966	7575	4971	2619	4874	5872	10835	14513	17451	20354	27629	34656	40201
Foreign subsidiary (RM mil.)	164	574	683	800	957	1186	1241	1127	1298	1315	876	934	1304	1960	2539	2965	4122	4443	4496	6780	7932
Foreign branch (RM mil.)	250	313	740	1075	1396	1130	1076	1255	1709	1806	1710	903	1293	1545	2136	2768	2689	2996	3858	4245	3602
Foreign share (%)	70	54	46	47	37	33	33	32	38	29	34	41	35	37	30	28	28	27	23	24	22
2. INCREASE IN NET FIXED ASSETS	407	1512	1574	2258	2553	3053	4582	5650	2958	4172	3176	848	284	1945	5024	8587	17291	19101	22109	26504	28483
Local (RM mil.)	236	877	1165	1565	1672	2237	2756	2820	1882	3412	2896	443	-356	819	2952	4612	11328	13609	15364	21432	22284
Foreign subsidiary (RM mil.)	120	469	108	331	309	487	1022	924	583	676	96	412	533	956	1752	3364	5208	4614	6240	4861	5992
Foreign branch (RM mil.)	51	167	301	362	572	329	804	1906	492	83	183	-7	107	170	320	611	755	878	505	211	206
Foreign share (%)	42	53	26	31	35	27	40	50	36	18	9	48	225	58	41	46	34	29	31	19	22
3. REINVESTMENT RATE (%)																					
Local	134	131	70	73	42	48	59	57	38	45	58	17	-7	14	27	32	65	67	56	62	55
Foreign subsidiary	73	99	16	41	32	41	82	82	45	51	11	44	41	49	69	113	126	104	139	76	72
Foreign branch	20	53	41	34	41	29	75	152	29	5	11	-1	8	11	15	22	28	20	13	6	5
All foreign companies	41	81	29	37	37	35	79	119	36	24	11	22	25	32	44	69	88	74	81	54	46

Source: Malaysia, Department of Statistics, *Financial Survey of Limited Companies*, various issues.

proportionally larger than their share of equity capital in limited companies in the country, which was 25.1 per cent in 1990 (Malaysia 1991). In fact, throughout most of the 1980s, the foreign share of corporate assets continued to decline until late in the decade, when the government liberalized equity conditions for foreign direct investment, particularly for manufacturing export-oriented investments. Profit repatriation was largely offset by new FDI, and was thus not perceived as a cause of the balance of payments deficit. However, external private corporate debt servicing has become more problematic with higher interest rates in Malaysia just as public foreign debt servicing has declined in significance.

Trade-Related Intellectual Property Rights (TRIPs)

Another key development under the Uruguay Round is the standardization and enforcement of intellectual property rights, copyright, trademarks, and other such proprietary claims to monopolistic rents. For the South as a whole, the greatest collective loss – both real as well as potential – in the Uruguay Round may be due to TRIPs. Most countries have exempted agriculture, medicines and other products as well as processes from their respective national patent laws, but with the passage of TRIPs, almost everything will be subject to strict international intellectual property protection, unless explicitly exempted in the agreement. In Third World countries that now have national pharmaceutical industries, the prices of medicines will rise significantly as foreign pharmaceuticals make deep inroads. New developments in biotechnology will mean that new seed types will be patented by international agribusinesses so that, in future, small farmers may increasingly have to buy new seeds instead of using their own seed supplies. At present, there is little patent protection in most poor countries, where people are often unable to afford expensive royalty payments. Now, Third World governments will have to introduce, strengthen and enforce laws to protect international patents and their owners, mainly foreign TNCs.

Many fear that developing countries will suffer under the tougher rules, since firms in rich countries hold the bulk of registered patents. Nevertheless, since drafting the agreement, the United States has already pressed developing countries to comply with the TRIPs agreement more quickly than was agreed to in the Uruguay Round (*Business Times*, 29 August 1994). The US may well be able to impose its will. Every year, the US publishes a list of countries it accuses of failing to protect US firms' intellectual property. The list currently runs to 37, including the

EU and Japan, as well as poorer countries. If countries do not reform, they risk US trade sanctions. Top of the list is China, which the US successfully blocked from becoming a founder member of the WTO.

The scope of patentability has been greatly enhanced under the new patent regime. Patents will be available for any invention, whether products or processes, in all fields of industrial technology. Protection will be extended from manufactures and pharmaceuticals to micro-organisms, non-biological and micro-biological processes and plant varieties. In other words, the industrial, agricultural and bio-technology sectors will be covered.

The principles underlying the patent system have also been changed. Importing a patented product was not previously regarded as 'working' the patent. The patent-holders had the obligation actually to work the patent in the country granting patent rights. The new patent regime provides that imports will be considered as working a patent right. This means patents can not only establish a manufacturing monopoly, but also an import monopoly, which may pre-empt the possibility of manu-facturing locally. The patent holder will thus have no obligation, for example, to promote manufacturing locally to the national govern-ments which confer the patent rights. There can also be no restrictions on the imports of patented goods, which can be sold at high transfer prices since no price controls can be applied to them.

It is clear that the industrial countries, led by the US, made TRIPs a part of the GATT agenda to tighten their firms' monopolies over tech-nology, thus restricting, frustrating, and raising the costs of technology transfer to the South. While the GATT and the Uruguay Round are supposed to promote liberalization and free trade flows, the TRIPs agree-ment is clearly a form of protectionism for firms, further constraining the already limited flows of technology, thus enhancing the North's technological advantage and further constrains the emergence of new industrial rivals, thus consolidating existing monopolies. Developing countries are very likely to incur considerable welfare losses as they adopt the standards set in the TRIPs provisions of the WTO agreement. The benefits of improved protection of foreigners' intellectual property rights in the South under the TRIPs agreement of the WTO are modest in comparison (*Business Times*, 29 August 1994).

The main impact of TRIPs on the pharmaceutical industry will be on the prices of medicines,[4] which may go up so much as to make it extremely difficult for many people to afford them (Keayla 1994). In Malaysia, prices of drugs have increased between 6 to 110 per cent since the government privatized the Medical Store to Southern Task Sdn Bhd in late 1994 (Alaigal 1995). With the enforcement of TRIPs, the prices of pharmaceutical drugs will be much higher, and would increase by more than 700 per cent (Correa 1995) since most drugs in the country are imported.

A second impact will be on availability. Availability of new drugs and medicines from indigenous sources can hardly be said to exist (Keayla 1994). Most drugs are imported, and dependence on imported medicines will go up. Also, TRIPs will have an impact on domestic research and development activity. Owing to the paucity of funds, particularly in the drugs and pharmaceuticals field, research in both the public and the private sectors has mainly concentrated on process technologies. Also, research efforts will be severely affected as there would be no takers for process technologies in the new patent regime. On the other hand, like most other developing countries, Malaysia does not have the funds or the infrastructure to match the TNCs for basic research.

Malaysian intellectual property laws have undergone fairly extensive and significant changes in the last two decades, and the laws are more or less in conformity with Western and TNC-set 'world standards', largely defined by the Paris Convention of 1989 and the Berne Convention of 1990. The existing legislation is largely 'TRIPs-consistent', hence requiring little further legislative reform. The Malaysian government presented new amendments to the Copyright and Trademark Acts (Patents Act 1983) to Parliament in 1994. This legislation is expected to benefit foreign firms much more than Malaysian firms. Only five per cent of the over 18 000 applications for patents in the country since 1986 came from Malaysian manufacturers and inventors. The largest number of applications came from US manufacturers, who accounted for 38 per cent of total applications in 1993, followed by Japan, the United Kingdom and Germany. TRIPs will enable foreign firms to penetrate and dominate global markets more easily.

Since foreign direct investment will be able to move more freely into developing countries, and will be granted greater protection under TRIPs, technology transfer to host countries might be curtailed rather than enhanced.[5] Most TNCs are reluctant to transfer technology in Malaysia. Registered technology transfer agreements, increased from 403 in 1975–80 to 1,303 in 1986–93; the total number of such technology transfers during 1975–93 was 2,285. It is quite difficult to make an assessment of the impact and relevance of technology transfer to developing indigenous technology in host countries. There are few efforts by foreign firms to develop technology in Malaysia because foreign firms hardly conduct research and development (R&D) in the country except when necessitated by local conditions. On the other hand, the role of government in promoting technology development is minimal. Allocation of funds for R&D in the country during the Sixth Malaysian Plan (1991–95) period was about 1.1 per cent of GDP, an increase from the Fifth Malaysian Plan (1986–90) period's 0.8 per cent, that is, much lower than South Korea's and Taiwan's averages of more than three per cent in 1993.

General Agreement on Trade in Services (GATS)

Like the GATT, the GATS provides the legal basis on which to negotiate the multilateral elimination of barriers that discriminate against foreign service providers, and otherwise deny them market access. However, the GATS differs from the GATT in several respects. Perhaps the most important differences are that the principles of national treatment (that is, non-discrimination) and market access (that is, freedom of entry and exit) are provided automatically under the GATT, but are negotiated rights and obligations under the GATS. The negotiations on national treatment and market access for services under the GATS have been comparable to tariff negotiations for goods under the GATT. As is well known, restrictions on international transactions in services are embodied in a country's laws, regulations and other policy measures. Under the GATS, these restrictions will have to be liberalized, thus creating services for a regime comparable to a duty-free regime for goods.

In Malaysia, the contribution of the services sector to economic growth has been about 40 to 45 per cent of GDP for more than three decades. In 1995, its contribution to GDP amounted to about 44 per cent. The distributive trade sub-sector has been the single largest sub-sector in the services sector since the 1960s with its contribution to GDP in 1995 at 12.1 per cent. The finance, insurance, real estate, and business services sub-sector has been second, with its contribution to GDP at 10.7 per cent in 1995. The transport, storage, and communications sub-sector accounted for about 7.3 per cent of the GDP in 1995. Overall, the final services sub-sector collectively accounted for 26.2 per cent of the GDP, while intermediate services accounted for another 18.0 per cent in 1995. However, Malaysia's ability to export services is still limited, as is evident in the persistent deficit in the services account of the balance of payments. Even though foreign exchange earnings in the travel and government sub-sectors have increased, this has been more than offset by the outflow for foreign non-factor services, particularly freight and insurance.

The inclusion of the GATS in the Uruguay Round agreement will pose new challenges for services. During 1982–92, world exports of services grew annually at an average rate of 9.5 per cent *vis-à-vis* merchandise export growth of only 7.1 per cent (Harmsen 1995). Most of this international trade in services is dominated by the major industrialized nations. It is evident that financial liberalization is the major thrust of the GATS agreement. The GATS Committee on Trade in Financial Services completed its negotiations on 28 July 1995. Twenty-nine members of the World Trade Organization, including Malaysia and the European Union, agreed to begin implementing the new schedules of commitment by 30 July 1996. The accord covers almost 90 per cent of the global trade in financial services. As noted earlier in this chapter, Malaysia has agreed to liberalize 14 of the 16 areas, including banking, insurance, and other financial services. The two sectors not committed by the government are settlement and clearing services, and provision and transfer of financial information services.

Under the agreement, signatory countries will extend 'most-favoured nation' (MFN) treatment, market access and 'national treatment' to all countries based on provisions under the National Schedule of Commitments. 'National treatment' here refers to treatment accorded to foreign suppliers being no less favourable than to domestic suppliers. The Malaysian government will now have to permit foreign suppliers to deliver financial services via four modes: cross-border supply, consumption abroad, commercial presence, and the movement of natural persons (personnel).

Malaysia has agreed to new entries in offshore banking, insurance and re-insurance, the charge card business, and stockbroking services. Aggregate foreign shareholdings in financial leasing companies and stockbroking companies can be increased to 49 per cent, effective 1 July 2000. In insurance, seven new general re-insurance licences have been bound. Furthermore, Malaysia will relax its equity restrictions by allowing aggregate foreign shareholdings of up to 49 per cent for existing branches of foreign insurers which incorporate locally, as well as foreign-owned locally incorporated companies which restructure to have an aggregate foreign shareholding of not more than 49 per cent by 30 July 1998. Malaysia has also agreed to allow foreign-owned locally incorporated commercial banks accept foreign currency deposits from residents effective 1 July 1996. Under the National Schedule of Commitments, Malaysia's new liberalizing commitments extend to financial leasing, direct insurance, money and foreign exchange brokerage services, underwriting and asset management.

As liberalization proceeds, local suppliers must quickly increase their levels of efficiency and productivity to compete with foreign services. In services, Malaysia is already committed to opening up 64 sectors and sub-sectors to foreign participation. Substantial offers and commitments have been made to liberalize the financial sector, professional services, computer services, audio-visual services, maritime and aviation transportation services, consultancy, and a wide range of business services. Under the GATS, Malaysia is committed to further negotiations on progressive liberalization every five years from the time the WTO came into effect in 1995. However, opening up services to foreign participation will adversely affect Malaysia's current account position. The country's continuing rapid economic expansion in the mid-1990s involved further deterioration in the services account of the balance of payments. The services deficit rose to RM22.3 billion in 1998 (Table 2.8), as gross service payments rose to RM73 billion in 1995, while gross receipts grew to RM49 billion (Bank Negara 1999: 52). Net investment income payment continued to be the largest contributor to the services deficit in 1998, with a share of 66 per cent, compared to 52 per cent in 1990 and 38 per cent in 1980 (Table 2.8).

Malaysia has also experienced rising freight costs. In Table 2.9, net payments for freight and insurance services are compared with merchandise exports for the period 1970–98. Net freight and insurance payments have been rising rapidly from an average of RM774 million in 1970–80 to RM4,086 million in 1981–97 and RM8,435 million in 1998. This is partly due to the rising volume and value of trade, but is also partly attributable to rising freight and insurance rates.

Malaysia has offered to bind nearly all financial services to underscore its commitment to the GATT. Malaysia's offers were based on a 'standstill' of policies, which meant binding existing rules and regulations. Market access will now be on a 'national treatment' basis, except for branching and loans to non-resident companies. Malaysia's offer is significant, given the already high foreign presence in the financial sector. For example, almost half of the entire trade financing business is handled by foreign banks located in Malaysia, while the foreign share of insurance is even more dominant. In the banking sector, of the 37 commercial banks operating in Malaysia, 16 are foreign banks, while 4 out of 41 finance companies are 100 per cent foreign-owned. In addition, foreigners have equity participation in 12 domestic banks, 7 finance companies and one merchant bank. The foreigners' share of net working funds/paid-up capital in the banking system was RM4.4 billion, or 21.6 per cent, at the end of 1995. Foreigners accounted for

Table 2.8 Malaysia: Net Services Balance, 1965–98 (RM mil.)

Year	Freight & Insurance	Other Transportation	Travel	Investment Income	Government Transactions	Other Services	Services Balance
1965	−162	−16	−80	−255	225	−53	−341
1966	−165	−11	−78	−268	189	−74	−407
1967	−170	−9	−69	−144	132	−91	−351
1968	−186	−12	−73	−154	125	−100	−400
1969	−247	−14	−96	−334	105	−116	−702
1970	−304	−21	−105	−355	68	−145	−862
1971	−322	−34	−106	−363	52	−105	−878
1972	−309	−35	−101	−378	25	−108	−906
1973	−420	49	−94	−659	29	−102	−1 197
1974	−714	82	−39	−997	43	−94	−1 719
1975	−621	98	−105	−727	47	−402	−1 710
1976	−726	94	−151	−985	36	−288	−2 020
1977	−883	158	−196	−1 272	22	−344	−2 515
1978	−1 072	110	−308	−1 571	27	−372	−3 186
1979	−1 362	70	−455	−1 797	25	−656	−4 175
1980	−1 934	−11	−521	−1 954	36	−792	−5 176
1981	−2 008	7	−672	−1 836	7	−810	−5 312
1982	−2 158	154	−775	−2 679	29	−1 151	−6 576
1983	−2 132	53	−1 104	−4 208	35	−1 742	−9 098
1984	−2 120	−99	−1 249	−5 255	23	−2 113	−10 813
1985	−1 852	64	−1 332	−5 434	−31	−1 806	−10 391
1986	−1 306	149	−1 368	−4 597	−190	−1 478	−8 790
1987	−1 185	45	−1 327	−4 824	−193	−925	−8 409
1988	−2 072	−44	−1 403	−5 019	−217	−1 425	−10 180
1989	−3 027	−5	−891	−5 935	−261	−1 273	−11 392
1990	−3 837	−25	632	−5 072	−3	−1 418	−9 723
1991	−4 847	−10	547	−6 735	−55	−2 095	−13 195
1992	−4 265	−355	657	−7 920	54	−2 739	−14 568
1993	−4 890	−196	906	−8 174	−72	−4 244	−16 670
1994	−7 367	441	3 603	−9 448	−36	−4 198	−17 005
1995	−9 028	737	4 143	−10 338	−23	−4 720	−19 227
1996	−8 203	1 725	4 801	−11 629	−27	−5 038	−18 371
1997	−9 162	1 747	3 252	−14 639	−150	−3 796	−22 748
1998	−8 435	2 268	3 070	−14 817	−215	−4 209	−22 338

Source: Bank Negara Malaysia, *Quarterly Economic Bulletin*, various issues.

RM42.3 billion, or 21.5 per cent of total deposits mobilized by the banking system, RM44.2 billion, or 24.3 per cent of total loans (Bank Negara Malaysia 1996a: 121), and RM6.3 billion, or 46 per cent of total trade financing in 1993 (Bank Negara Malaysia 1994: 184).

Table 2.9   Malaysia: Freight and Insurance Payments, 1970–98 (RM mil.)

Year	Net payments for freight & insurance	Exports of goods (fob)	Freight & insurance as % of exports
1970	304	5020	6.1
1971	322	4884	6.6
1972	309	4736	6.5
1973	420	7263	5.8
1974	714	10022	7.1
1975	621	9057	6.9
1976	726	13330	5.4
1977	883	14861	5.9
1978	1072	16925	6.3
1979	1362	23977	5.7
1980	1781	28013	6.4
1981	2008	26900	7.5
1982	2154	27946	7.7
1983	2132	31762	6.7
1984	2120	38452	5.5
1985	1852	37576	4.9
1986	1306	34970	3.7
1987	1185	44733	2.6
1988	2072	54607	3.8
1989	3027	66727	4.5
1990	3837	77458	4.9
1991	4847	92220	5.2
1992	4265	100910	4.5
1993	4890	118383	4.1
1994	7367	148506	5.0
1995	9028	179491	5.0
1996	8203	193363	4.2
1997	9162	217712	4.2
1998	8435	281947	3.0

Note: fob – free on board.
Source: Bank Negara Malaysia, *Quarterly Economic Bulletin*, various issues.

The government announced in April 1996 that it will not allow more foreign financial institutions to operate in the country as their presence is already substantial, though the government will nominally allow new foreign banks under the proposed amendments to the Banking and Financial Institutions Act, 1989 (BAFIA). Proposed amendments to BAFIA will, among other things, allow banks controlled and run by foreign governments to operate in the country (*Business Times*, 19

April 1996). Compared to other developing countries, Malaysia is 'already quite liberal' in allowing foreign financial institutions a substantial presence in the industry.

Liberalization is forcing Malaysian financial institutions to be more aggressive, bigger, and more competitive. In 1994, there were eleven 100 per cent foreign-owned companies in insurance, while another eight had foreign equity exceeding 50 per cent (Bank Negara Malaysia 1996b: 72). Foreign equity ownership amounted to RM659.9 million, or 42 per cent of capital funds in the industry. Foreign companies accounted for RM3.6 billion, or 41 per cent of total gross premiums, and RM12 billion, or 52 per cent of total assets (Bank Negara Malaysia 1996b: 72). In the securities industry, foreigners had interests in 11 of the 59 stockbroking firms (Bank Negara Malaysia 1994: 184).

For business services such as accounting, auditing and book-keeping, taxation, computer and related services, advertising, and management consulting services, the Malaysian government has only allowed foreign participation through locally incorporated joint-ventures with Malaysian individuals or at least 30 per cent Malaysian-equity in joint-ventures. Communication services require a locally incorporated joint-venture with Malaysian individuals or Malaysian-controlled corporations, with aggregate foreign shareholdings not exceeding 30 per cent. For the time being, foreign legal services can only be offered through a corporation incorporated in the Federal Territory of Labuan to offshore corporations established there, though further liberalization is envisaged.

The World Trade Organization (WTO)

All members of the GATT, including Malaysia, ratified the establishment of the WTO on 6 September 1994 to replace the GATT from 1 January 1995. Members of the WTO agreed to appoint Renato Ruggiero, the former Italian Trade Minister, as the first Director General of the organization.

The WTO has defined the institutions and procedures structure for the effective implementation and facilitation of the substantive rules that were negotiated in the Uruguay Round. The WTO should essentially continue the GATT's institutional role, with many of its practices made more transparent and better understood by the public, media, government officials and lawyers. The WTO structure includes some important innovations to facilitate the effective implementation of the Uruguay Round (Jackson 1995).

The WTO is also expected to be a more conducive institutional frame-work for the new matters negotiated in the Uruguay Round, particularly services and intellectual property. Without some kind of legal institu-tion such as the WTO, this extension would have been difficult since the GATT only applied to merchandise trade. The WTO Charter offers scope for the future development of an institutional structure for more com-prehensive international economic co-operation and regulation (Jack-son 1995). This structure is complemented by a more effective enforcement mechanism to establish an international economic order ensuring greater freedom of operation for transnational corporations, under which intervention by governments, particularly of the South, will be progressively minimized.

Inevitably, of course, this raises the question of the role of the WTO as part of a new 'Bretton Woods System', as a partner to the International Monetary Fund (IMF), and the World Bank (IBRD). However, unlike the IMF and the World Bank, in the WTO each country will have one vote. But since the WTO will depend on the USA and the other G-7 countries for the bulk of its finances, that democratic advantage will probably be seriously compromised, if not altogether lost (Sen 1994). As these coun-tries also dominate world trade, accounting for two-thirds of such trade, they are likely to be able to exercise disproportionate influence in the WTO. The major powers will certainly try to use the WTO for their own interests. Already, the G-7, led by the United States, is trying to draft policies and direct the WTO in ways favourable to them, as evident at the United Nations and other international fora, especially in recent years. Thus, developing countries fear that the big trading powers who dominate the system will still be able to wield power unilaterally through anti-dumping and other measures to their own advantage.

Several European and Asian countries have also warned against some powers using unilateral measures to resolve bilateral trade disputes, an obvious reference to the US use of its Super 301 law against Japan in February 1994 after conclusion of the Uruguay Round in December 1993. This was also clear in late 1994, with the US-led rejection of the application of China – which had quit the GATT (denouncing it as a 'capitalist cartel') after the 1949 communist take-over – to join the WTO. Washington has also threatened punitive tariffs on US$2.8 billion in imports from China on the grounds that Beijing has not done enough to curb widespread piracy of US copyrights, trademarks, and patents (*Business Times*, 2 January 1995). Such retaliation and trade sanctions are measures resorted to by Washington in settling its trade disputes with other countries. Such actions – sometimes seen as part of a 'managed trade' strategy – clearly threaten the Uruguay Round agreement, but neither the GATT nor the WTO have condemned Washington's actions.

Most WTO members are already finding it difficult to adjust to the Uruguay Round agreements which require major changes to many domestic laws and policies. Some of these changes have had, and will have, negative social and economic effects. Nevertheless, the industrialized countries seem determined to continue introducing new issues such as foreign investment, labour standards, the environment, and competition policy, to the agenda for negotiation.

The first issue to face considerable opposition from many developing country governments has been the attempts at the inclusion of 'social clauses' – such as minimum wage rates, human and labour rights issues, and environmental measures – in the framework of the WTO. Although the US has said that a global minimum wage is not part of the social clause agenda, it has appeared keen to introduce certain international labour standards as part of the WTO agenda. This proposal has been vehemently opposed by most official spokesmen of the developing world who claim that developing countries are already seriously disadvantaged by the WTO. According to them, the major advantage that developing countries have is their relatively lower labour costs. The move to link international labour standards with trade, it is argued, will be tantamount to undermining the one comparative advantage that developing countries have.

Another issue proposed by the European Union recently is to strengthen TRIMs. Investment is seen by many as the single most important new item for the WTO, and industrialized countries grouped in the OECD (Organization for Economic Cooperation and Development), especially from the EU, seem to agree that the issue should be brought on to the WTO agenda. They have proposed setting up a multilateral agreement on investments in the WTO that would give foreign companies the right to enter and establish themselves in any sector of the economy in all member countries of the WTO. Foreign companies must be given 'national treatment', meaning that there cannot be any measures that favour local firms or discriminate against foreign companies, for instance in opening branches, buying property, or limiting equity ownership and profit repatriation. Thus, the WTO would no longer be just a 'trade organization', but an organization regulating investments as well. This would, of course, be a very major extension of the WTO's powers, and would also mean the extension and application of WTO principles and its system of dispute settlement (including the use of trade sanctions and trade retaliation) to investment policy.

The above propositions would have profound effects on the behaviour and operations of foreign investments world-wide, and on each country. Transnational companies would have greater freedom and the right to conduct business almost anywhere in the world, free from the many government regulations they now face. Governments would no longer have the right or power to draw up and enforce their own policies or laws regulating the entry, behaviour and operations of foreign enterprises in their economies. Existing national laws and policies that now impose restrictions on foreigners would have to be cancelled or altered in line with the new multilateral investment treaty. This would, of course, have serious implications since most developing countries now have policies that seek to promote domestic companies and to prevent excessive control of national economies by foreign firms.

The developing countries must give closer attention to the industrialized countries' moves on the issue to prevent establishment of such a treaty. It is not simply a 'technical trade issue' to be left to trade officials to negotiate. Rather, the issue is one of political significance, as it will have an important bearing on economic sovereignty, ownership patterns, the survival of local enterprises, businesses and firms, employment prospects, as well as social and cultural life.

As for market access, the European Union has begun discussing plans to achieve global tariff-free trade by 2020, and has been pushing – so far, without success – for a new round of trade talks towards this end (Islam 1996). This will certainly test economic solidarity in the South, especially Asia, as some Asian exporters clearly relish the prospect of global free trade. However, without tariff protection, much of the agricultural, manufacturing and services sectors in the South will crumble in the face of foreign competition.

The WTO is more powerful than GATT in regulating the new international economic order, covering not only trade in manufactures and agriculture, but also services, intellectual property as well as investment regulation. The WTO is committed to an integrated dispute settlement system, which in effect means that if a country does not fulfil its obligations in one area (say, enforcing intellectual property rights), sanctions can be applied against it in another area which hurts it most (for example, its exports of primary produce) (Khor 1994). The WTO is also likely to co-ordinate its programmes and policies with the World Bank and the International Monetary Fund, and the result is likely to be 'cross-institutional conditionality'. This might entail World Bank loans only being released if the WTO vouches that prospective borrowers have adhered to WTO rules. In these and other ways, the WTO is likely to discipline governments of the South according to the interests of, and guidelines set by, the major economic powers. However, recent experience suggests that it is unlikely to enforce its rules when flouted by its most powerful members. Thus, the United States and Europe can use the WTO as they choose to. Hence, the WTO is a threat to developing countries' sovereignty, both politically and economically. Not surprisingly then, the conclusion of the Uruguay Round of the GATT and the establishment of the WTO have been seen by many in the South as the dawn of a new era of re-colonization.

Notes

1   The degree of openness is calculated as ([exports + imports] / GDP). The index of trade liberalization (also known as the implicit tariff rate) is calculated with the following formula:

$$1 + t = \frac{PimpD/PexpD}{PimpF/PexpF}$$

$$\text{where} \quad PimpD = PimpF(1 + t)e$$

$$PexpD = PexpF(1 + s)e$$

t is the *ad valorem* import tariff, s is the *ad valorem* export subsidy (assumed to be zero for Malaysia), e the exchange rate (units of domestic currency per US dollar), PimpD (PimpF) the domestic (foreign) price levels for importable goods, and PexpD (PexpF) the domestic (foreign) price levels for exportable goods. This index rises with increased trade restrictions, and vice versa (see Favaro and Spiller 1991).

2   The Cairns Group, a coalition of developed and developing countries exporting agricultural products, comprises of Australia, Argentina, Brazil, Canada, Chile, Colombia, Hungary, Indonesia, Malaysia, New Zealand, the Philippines, Thailand, and Uruguay.

3   In Malaysia, exchange controls for capital transactions were loosened in 1973 and 1978. Capital and profits could be freely repatriated abroad. No restrictions were imposed on the remittance of funds by residents, provided they served the purpose of direct or portfolio investment. Similarly, inflows of foreign funds for the purpose of direct or portfolio investment were also free (see Claassen, 1992).

4   Many developing countries did not offer pharmaceutical patent protection prior to the WTO; price levels were closely monitored and regulated in line with domestic health policies.

5   It is quite difficult to prove that there is genuine technology transfer from the home countries to the host countries. Even if there is, it might involve a backward technology or one unsuitable for the industrial environment of the host country.

3
The World Trade Organization and the South: Implications of the Emerging Global Economic Governance for Development

Martin Khor

The newest and perhaps most important phenomenon in the globalization process is the emergence of trade agreements as key instruments of economic liberalization and as mechanisms used by the major countries to have disciplines and rules placed on developing countries in a wide range of issues. Trade agreements that are legally-binding and have strong enforcement capability have become the most important vehicles for disseminating and implementing economic and social policies across the world, policies that have been planned by the few developed countries for developing countries to follow. The World Trade Organization (WTO), which is the organization of the multilateral trading system, has in fact become the main vehicle of choice of industrialized countries for organizing and enforcing global economic governance.

At the regional level, trade agreements are also proliferating. The North American Free Trade Area (NAFTA) is a prototype of a regional legally-binding agreement involving North and South countries, and its model may be extended to South America; the Asia Pacific Economic Cooperation (APEC) is another model, with both North and South countries, but without being ruled by a legally-binding agreement; the European Community is, of course, the main example of a legally-binding regional agreement among developed countries. Regional trade arrangements among developing countries (such as Southeast Asia's ASEAN, Southern Africa's SADC, or Latin America's Mercosur) have also emerged or are also evolving.

The WTO and trade agreements

The WTO is by far the most important institution for evolving and implementing trade agreements. The Uruguay Round vastly expanded the scope of the multilateral trade system so that it no longer deals only with the conduct of trade in manufactures. The scope was expanded to cover trade in agriculture, trade and investment in services, and beyond trade issues into intellectual property rights (IPRs) and investment measures. Moreover, the Uruguay Round directed that the new issue of trade and environment be discussed at committee level in the WTO.

The change from the General Agreement on Tariffs and Trade (GATT) to the WTO, with its expanded powers and jurisdiction, marked the arrival of the age of trade agreements in a new phase of the globalization of policy making. Due to the extension of issues beyond trade into other areas such as intellectual property, investment, and the environment, the WTO is no longer only a 'trade' organization. 'Trade' in the context of the multilateral system has become a code-word to include all issues that have come or may come under the purview of the WTO. Moreover, the WTO agreements have significant implications for non-economic matters; for example, the WTO services agreement and the specific agreements on communications and information technology will have far-reaching effects on the culture of countries around the world. The vastly increased scope of 'trade agreements' through the Uruguay Round, and now beyond it to the current negotiations in the WTO on a new package of issues, has tremendous significance for the shaping of national economic and social policies, for the scope of development options, concerns over equity and marginalization, and national sovereignty. It is thus crucial to understand the meaning and mechanics of this new era of trade agreements.

The conclusion of the Uruguay Round was heralded in the mainstream global media as a major triumph for the international economy and a boon for all countries. It is clear, however, that the results are, at best, mixed for some developing countries, and for many others (especially the poorer countries), the Uruguay Round is likely to have an overall negative effect that will further drain their economic resources. For all South countries, the Uruguay Round will also foreclose a wide range of development options. In a sense, the Uruguay Round complements what structural adjustment programmes (SAP) are achieving. The Uruguay Round will lead to a very significant external liberalization of many sectors and facets of the domestic economy of all the developing country members of the WTO. Structural adjustment affects about 80 indebted developing countries facing repayment problems. Should some of these countries get out of their debt crisis and no longer require SAP loans, or should there be a change of government or government policies, the SAP policies can be changed or reversed.

However, once a country's government has signed on to the Uruguay Round agreements and enters the WTO, that country is obliged to follow the WTO rules. Domestic laws and policies in a wide range of areas have to be changed to bring them in line with these rules. According to several analyses, the Uruguay Round agreements will severely restrict or constrain the possible policy options in many areas. Non-compliance with the rules can result in complaints being brought against a country, and in the threat of trade penalties and retaliation through measures affecting trade and other activities. Due to the 'all or nothing' or 'single undertaking' nature of having to sign on to all the multilateral agreements of the Uruguay Round, and to the 'integrated dispute settlement system', countries also risk having 'cross-sectoral retaliation'. At the extreme, non-compliance can also lead to expulsion from the WTO, and thus, the loss of the automatic 'most-favoured nation' status granted to a WTO member by all other members. The WTO system therefore has a powerful system for ensuring compliance by member countries. It is the organization with the strongest 'bite' in getting its legally-binding rules enforced, and signing on to a WTO agreement is a very serious undertaking. In contrast, signing on to a UN Declaration, even a UN Declaration of over a hundred heads of government, has little enforcement possibility and only becomes a moral commitment.

It would be very difficult, if not impossible, for a developing country member to change the WTO rules, or to avoid compliance of obligations. The disciplines of the WTO are legally binding on present and future governments. Once the WTO agreements come into force, it would be difficult for a present government to have economic policies relating to foreign trade, investment, sectoral policies in services and agriculture, or technology policy (*vis-à-vis* intellectual property rights) that are in violation of WTO rules. Moreover, the rules are binding on future governments as well. Thus, should an opposition party have a different economic programme from the governing party, it would find it difficult or impossible to implement the programme should it come to power, if this were to contradict the WTO rules. In this way, policy options have been significantly narrowed, for a country's policies would have to be made (or changed) within the boundaries of what is permissible according to the WTO Agreements.

The Uruguay Round's unbalanced and inequitable outcome

The Uruguay Round negotiations that gave birth to the WTO resulted in a package of agreements that were, on the whole, unbalanced and inequitable in favour of developed *vis-à-vis* developing countries. Various aspects of the asymmetries and disadvantages to developing countries have been brought out in several studies (e.g. Raghavan 1991, 1996; Das 1997; South Centre 1995; Nayyar 1995b; Shahin 1996).

A comprehensive study by Das (1997) concludes that the Uruguay Round

> has been a unique negotiation in which most of the concessions have been made by developing countries without getting anything but meagre concessions in return. It is not because the negotiators or trade policy officials of developing countries ignored the interests of their countries. . . . The results are in fact characterized by the massive gap between the economic and political strengths of developed and developing countries.

A significant critique of the Uruguay Round outcome was also made in 1994 by Luis Fernando Jaramillo, then Chairman of the Group of 77 in New York and Colombia's permanent representative to the United Nations. In a speech after the Uruguay Round's conclusion, he stated:

> The Uruguay Round is proof again that the developing world continues to be sidelined and rejected when it comes to defining areas of vital importance for their survival. The Third World confined itself to a role of passive spectator of the decisions adopted. . . . The countries of the Third World have been put in a situation in which they already paid the price of accepting the new terms in different areas of interest for the industrialized countries, without obtaining in exchange satisfactory conditions of market access. . . . According to some estimates, the industrialized countries, which make up only 20 per cent of the GATT membership, will appropriate 70 per cent of the additional income that will be generated by the implementation of the Uruguay Round. It would seem that this does not allow one to conclude that the Uruguay Round will translate into a positive balance to developing countries. . . . Unquestionably, the developing countries are the losers both individually and collectively.

The Uruguay Round's combination of liberalization and protectionism

It is a mistaken notion that the Uruguay Round was set up to promote liberalization overall. As pointed out by Nayyar (1995b), the main asymmetry in the Uruguay Round's results was the liberalization of those areas which are of benefit of the major countries, whilst protectionism was given a major boost in the area of technology and IPRs, and liberalization of labour services (proposed by some developing countries) was unacceptable to the North.

When the Uruguay Round began in 1986, many Third World countries were strongly resisting the Northern countries' push to expand the GATT's powers into 'new areas' such as services, investments and IPRs. Until then, the GATT's jurisdiction was only in keeping the rules of trade in manufactured goods. The Southern countries were rightly concerned that the North was interested in liberalizing economic areas in which they had an advantage, where their corporations could penetrate and capture new markets which till then had been relatively protected by Southern governments. This was certainly the case in services, a fast expanding sector, with transnational enterprises ranging from banking and insurance to motion pictures eagerly awaiting the removal of barriers to their advance into Third World markets.

The negotiations over trade-related investment measures (TRIMs) were similarly initiated by the North to pressurize Third World governments to give up their powers to impose conditions on the entry and operations of foreign companies. The 'liberalization' of investments would clearly benefit the North, where most transnational companies are based. The South was concerned that with only weak restrictions permitted to be placed on these big corporations, the smaller-scale domestic businesses might not survive the onslaught of foreign investments. On the other hand, when it came to the subject of technology transfer, the North took an aggressively anti-liberalization stance and instead pushed for all GATT members compulsorily to introduce a standard set of national laws to protect trade related intellectual property rights (TRIPs). Since most patents are owned by transnational companies, this in effect meant the legal protection of technological monopoly by these Northern-owned firms, and a drastic curtailment of possibilities by the South to learn and use new technologies.

Although in the early and middle stages of the Uruguay Round, several Third World countries (including influential India and Brazil) put up a stiff resistance to the Northern push and interpretation of the 'new areas', by the final two years, the Southern fight had melted and, in the end, the Uruguay Round adopted texts to protect IPRs, liberalize services, and prohibit trade-related investment measures. All three issues have thus become integrated with trade in manufactured and agricultural goods, and all now fall under the jurisdiction of the WTO.

In effect, the Uruguay Round has most benefited the transnational corporations. The 'free trade' so much bandied around by the proponents of the Uruguay Round has come to mean, in reality, the vastly expanded freedom and powers of transnational corporations to trade and invest in most countries of the world, whilst correspondingly governments now have significantly reduced powers to restrict their operations; and at the same time, these corporations have 'freedom' from potential new competitors whose possibilities to develop technologically are now curbed by intellectual property provisions in TRIPs. The big companies, which were the powerful lobbies behind the Northern governments propelling the Uruguay Round from start to finish, have won many more rights without having to meet new obligations: indeed, previous obligations they may have had to observe have now been dropped.

Implications of WTO agreements for the South

On the whole, the Uruguay Round has benefited the rich industrial nations, and some developing countries (mainly the more advanced ones), while many countries (especially the less developed countries (LDCs) and weaker economies) have lost out. It is simply not true that 'we are all gainers, there are no losers', as some leading proponents of the Uruguay Round would have it. Some have gained more than others; and many (especially the poorest countries) have not gained at all, but may well suffer severe loss to their economic standing.

The Uruguay Round outcome is expected to bring some benefits to those developing countries able to take advantage of certain changes. A lowering of Northern countries' industrial tariffs will benefit those Southern countries with a manufacturing export capacity. The planned phasing out of the Multi-Fibre Arrangement (MFA) will have positive effects on textile-exporting Southern countries. (However, textile-exporting developing countries are disappointed and frustrated that due to end-loading of the implementation schedules of developed countries, the benefits accrue mainly at the end of the ten year phase-out period.) The reduction of agricultural subsidies would improve the market access of those Southern countries that export agricultural products.

These benefits will accrue mainly to the better-off developing countries that already have an export capacity. The weaker countries (and especially the least developed countries) would not be able to benefit, or to benefit much, from these. Several countries (especially in Africa, but also including Indonesia) are projected to suffer absolute losses as a result from the Uruguay Round agreements. The benefits (which fall significantly short of what had been requested by the developing countries) will also take a long time (10 to 20 years) to come on stream, while the problems of compliance are already being felt by developing countries, especially the poorer ones. The LDCs will be hit particularly badly.

At the United Nations Conference on Trade and Development's (UNCTAD) Trade and Development Board session in October 1996, the Secretary of the Bangladesh Commerce Ministry, Farouk, speaking on behalf of the LDC group, said the LDCs are not yet well placed to take advantage of the Uruguay Round's opportunities. He added: 'In fact, the opportunities for LDCs stemming from the Uruguay Round are expected to be indirect and would perhaps materialize in the long run. In contrast, the challenges arising out of it are more immediate.' This, he said, was due to four reasons: erosion of preferences; limited number of exportable items resulting in their inability to participate effectively in global trade; higher prices for import of food, pharmaceuticals and essential capital goods; and increased administrative cost of compliance with their Uruguay Round obligations.

In exchange for some uneven benefits in the Uruguay Round, the South as a whole has had to make major concessions, especially in agreeing to bring the new issues of services, investment measures and IPRs, into the GATT/WTO system. For particular groups of Southern countries, the Uruguay Round will also result in specific problems. For instance, the agriculture agreement could have severe negative effects on some Third World countries. Most of them (except the least developed countries) will also have to reduce domestic subsidies to farmers and remove non-tariff controls on agricultural products, converting these to tariffs and then progressively reducing these tariffs. This will impose competition on the domestic farm sector. Farmers unable to compete with cheaper imports may not survive. Agricultural liberalization will also raise world food prices, which may benefit food exporters, but about a hundred Third World food importers will face a higher food import bill and are likely to be among the biggest Uruguay Round losers.

The Uruguay Round also, for the first time, brought services into the GATT, and liberalization of services will be an important part of the WTO's agenda. Although the framework of the Services Agreement does not oblige countries to conduct blanket liberalization, as liberalization will be on the basis of a listing of positive offers, there will, of course, be far increased pressures for liberalization in reality. In many Third World countries, the services sector is relatively shielded and local enterprises in banking, insurance, trade, the media and professional services have been able to develop. It is feared that under the pressures of liberalization, the Northern transnational corporations involved in services will make further inroads, and in some countries, may come to dominate some of the services.

The South's collective loss is most acutely felt in the agreement on TRIPs through which countries are obliged to introduced IPR legislation similar to Northern standards. This will hinder Southern countries' indigenous technological development. It should be noted that the present industrial countries did not have patent or IPR laws, or laws as strict as those which will now be imposed through TRIPs, during their early industrializing period, which enabled them to incorporate technology design originating from abroad in their local systems. TRIPs will also give rise to increasing technical payments, such as royalties and licence fees, to transnational corporations owning most of the world's patents.

The new IPR regime will also have significant impact on raising the prices of many products. By restricting competition, the IPR rules will enable some companies to jack up prices of their products far beyond costs, and thus earn rents in terms of monopoly revenues and profits. This is clearly seen in the case of computer software. Also, most Third World countries have exempted agriculture, medicines, and other essential products and processes from their national patent laws, but with the passage of TRIPs, everything is subject to IPRs unless explicitly exempted. The prices of medicines are expected to shoot up in many countries, and foreign drug sales will increase rapidly at the expense of local products.

The TRIPs agreement also opens the door to the patenting of life-forms such as micro-organisms and modified genetic materials, thus providing the boost in incentives so much desired by the bio-technology industry. Many environmentalists are concerned that this will be detrimental to the global environment as the present lack of controls and accountability in bio-technology research and application will likely accelerate bio-diversity loss and could threaten natural ecosystems.

For plant varieties, TRIPs do permit countries the option to introduce either patents or an alternative 'effective' *sui generis* system of intellectual property protection for a trial period of four years, after which the agreement will be reviewed. Many farmers' groups (especially in India, where huge farmers' demonstrations and rallies have been held against the GATT) and environmentalists are concerned that in the end, Third World farmers will be disallowed the traditional practice of saving seed for the next season's planting (if the seed used is under the intellectual protection of a company), but will instead be forced to purchase new seeds. In the next few years, these farmers and their supporters may argue the case for a *sui generis* system to protect their rights as an alternative to corporate IPRs, and it will be interesting to see what Northern governments and the WTO consider to be 'effective' in protecting intellectual property rights.

In the area of TRIMs, the most important point is that national policies relating to foreign investments have also now begun to come under the ambit of the GATT/WTO system. Originally, the Northern countries proposed that foreign companies be given an automatic 'right to establishment' or 'commercial presence'. This would have given rights to foreign companies that were attained by the colonizers through war and bloodshed in the colonial era. Eventually, the objections of some developing countries prevailed. In the final TRIMs agreement, 'investment measures' such as local content (obliging foreign firms to use at least a specified minimal amount of local inputs) will be phased out.

This, of course, has serious enough implications in terms of prohibiting measures that promote local industry and greater linkages to the domestic economy, and that protect the balance of payments. Just as significant, once the area of 'investment' has been brought into the ambit of the WTO, even if only in relation to investment measures (which had already been part of the old GATT rules), it could be easily predicted that the Northern governments would soon resume the pressure to bring in the whole body of 'investment policy *per se*' into the WTO framework. This has now happened, with the current intense pressures by the North to establish a new Multilateral Investment Agreement (MIA) in the WTO.

Implications of the proliferation of 'trade-related issues'

In the post-Uruguay Round period, the developed countries have intensified the pressure to incorporate into the WTO more and more issues that are to their advantage. Developing countries, on the other hand, are unprepared, individually or as a group, for these new negotiations. It is likely that the WTO will be used for implementing more rules that could be detrimental to the interests of the South, unless officials and political leaders in developing countries prepare themselves much better and defend their interests more effectively in current and future WTO negotiations.

Northern government plans to link trade (and the possible use of trade measures and sanctions as enforcement mechanisms) to several economic and non-economic issues in ways that are to their advantage. Trade and environment is already being negotiated under the WTO's Committee on Trade and Environment. There have been strong attempts by some Northern governments (especially the US and France), under pressure from trade unions, to link trade with labour standards in the WTO. It is likely that in the future, a wide range of other issues, such as human rights, tax systems, and cultural behaviour, will also be linked to trade measures in the WTO.

The linking of issues to the possibility of sanctions – through the device of attaching a 'trade-related' prefix to the chosen topics – was successfully used in the Uruguay Round to inject IPRs (through a trade-related intellectual property rights agreement) and investment issues (through a trade-related investment measures agreement) into the GATT/WTO system. The justification for introducing these issues was that they were 'related to trade'. In fact, the real objective was to link the chosen issues to the threat of 'trade retaliation and penalties' for non-compliance of disciplines. The device of bringing in new topics by alleging that they are trade-related has continued to be used in ongoing WTO negotiations. In fact, the pretence of being directly trade-related is no longer even necessary and may unnecessarily restrict the scope of the issues being introduced. The prefix 'trade-related' has now been dropped in proposals for new issues to be brought into the trade arena; instead, this is now achieved through simply using the word 'and', as in 'trade and environment', 'trade and labour standards', and 'trade and investment'.

The device of linking trade with other issues (when the intention is really to link the dispute settlement system of the WTO to new policy areas) is being increasingly used for the purpose of further opening up Third World economies or to reduce their competitiveness in the scramble for world market shares. The WTO could also be used as an instrument to shift a great portion of the burden of future global economic adjustment (for instance, because of environmental imperatives) to the South, which presently has a very weak bargaining and negotiating position in the WTO forum. Indeed, it is precisely because the South is so weak in the WTO arena, coupled with the fact that the WTO carries the power of 'bite' in the form of trade retaliation mechanisms, that this institution has been chosen as a vehicle to institute reforms favourable to the North.

The Multilateral Investment Agreement initiative

By far the most important 'new issue' being promoted by Northern countries in the international arena is investment policy *per se*. What was dropped in the Uruguay Round TRIMs negotiations, as a result of strong opposition from the South, is now being pushed with tremendous energy and resources. The investment initiative was being promoted in two forums: the WTO and the Organization for Economic Cooperation and Development (OECD). The objective is to establish an international agreement that widens the rights of foreign investors far beyond the current position in most developing countries, and to severely curtail the right and powers of governments to regulate the entry, establishment, and operations of foreign companies and investors. This initiative is currently also the most important development in attempts to extend the scope of globalization and liberalization.

The agreement is termed the Multilateral Agreement on Investments (MAI) in the OECD and the Multilateral Investment Agreement (MIA) in the WTO context. For the proponents, the desired content of both is basically similar. The MAI was being negotiated by the 28 members of the OECD and was to be completed by mid-1997, whereupon non-OECD countries (who had not been invited to participate in the negotiations) would have been invited to sign up. However, owing to conflicts within the OECD, the MAI process was abandoned in 1998, shifting the focus on this front almost entirely to the MIA after the mixed fates of the TRIMs and MAI initiatives.

The MIA has been informally pushed, particularly by the European Union (EU), at the WTO. Due to opposition to such an MIA by many developing countries, the Northern countries instead proposed a 'study process' in the WTO to examine the links between trade and investment. They enlisted the support of some developing countries. This was endorsed by the Singapore WTO Ministerial Conference in December 1996, which established a new WTO working group to examine the relationship between trade and investment. In the working group, proponents are expected to advocate upgrading the study process to negotiations that would lead eventually to an MIA.

The acceptance of the MIA would have profound effects on the behaviour, operations, and effects of foreign investments world-wide, and on each country. Transnational companies would have freedom and rights to conduct business all over the world, free from the many government regulations they now face. On the reverse side, it would mean that governments would no longer have the right or the power to draw up their own basic policies or laws regulating the entry, behaviour, and operations of foreign enterprises in their economies. Existing national laws and policies that now place restrictions on foreigners would have to be cancelled or altered to fit the new multilateral investment treaty. This would, of course, have serious implications, since most developing countries now have policies that deliberately seek to promote domestic companies and to protect citizens from excessive control of the economy by foreign firms.

The MIA proposal attracted a negative response from international non-governmental organizations (NGOs). These NGOs stressed they are not against foreign investments as such, since they recognized that 'foreign investment may have a relevant and indeed significant role to contribute in the development process.' However, they believed that this role has to be placed in an appropriate policy context, which 'requires that governments continue to be given the right to regulate the terms and conditions for the entry and operation of foreign investment in the various sectors.'

The concerns of the NGOs have much merit. The experience of Southeast Asian countries with foreign investment is illuminating in this context. These countries have successfully attracted large volumes of foreign investments, but the companies have to operate within sophisticated regulatory frameworks. For instance, foreign investors may be welcome in some sectors (manufacturing, oil production) but local firms may be given preference in others (for example, plantation agriculture). Even in manufacturing, there are policies in many countries restricting full equity rights, requiring foreign investors to enter joint ventures with locals. In the sensitive services sector, many developing countries restrict the operations of foreign firms in banking, other financial institutions, media, and the professions.

There are compelling reasons why protection of locals in the area of investment, and the right of countries to regulate foreign investments, is necessary in developing countries:

a) Given the colonial legacy, local firms and farms are still too weak in many sectors to compete with large foreign firms. Giving total access to foreign investments would run many local enterprises out of business, leading to loss of jobs and livelihoods.

b) To retain a meaningful measure of sovereignty over national resources and economic activity (a principle affirmed by several United Nations' Charters and Declarations), developing countries require the right to limit the degree of foreign ownership overall and particularly in crucial resources (such as land) and sectors (such as finance).

c) To avoid a structural problem in the balance of payments, governments should have the ability to regulate foreign investments in such areas as equity share (so that some of the profits will be locally owned and retained), profit repatriation (so that there is sizeable reinvestment of profit) and import limitation (to prevent excessive imports of capital and intermediate goods).

d) To develop local enterprises (including small farmers), governments must have the right to promote their growth through subsidies or preferential policies, at least until such time when they can compete on more equal terms with the larger foreign firms. Removing the right to treat locals more favourably could well foreclose the possibility of domestic enterprise development, and perpetuate or worsen dependence on foreign firms.

e) The proposed treaty would also remove from governments the use of a key instrument of macroeconomic, financial and development management.

An additional reason to be wary of having the MIA in the WTO is that the WTO is an agency in which trade retaliation or sanctions can be applied against countries that do not live up to their obligations. The proposed MIA would also have serious implications for countries that have found it necessary to regulate foreign investments and to promote the growth of local firms. 'Trade and investment' is therefore not a 'technical trade issue' that can be left to trade officials on the negotiating field alone to handle. It is an issue with great economic, social, and political significance, as it will have an important bearing on economic sovereignty, ownership patterns, the survival of local enterprises, businesses and farms, employment prospects, as well as social and cultural life.

The MIA proponents argue that such rules are the best way to promote the entry of foreign investments into the South. Most developing countries are, indeed, trying their best to attract foreign investors. The issue, however, is not the desirability or otherwise of foreign investments. It is about the right of governments and peoples to choose the pattern and ownership of investments they want for their country and, in that context, the type of foreign investment they welcome, in which sector, and under what conditions. The power to regulate foreign investment, to obtain better terms and benefits from them, and the right to enact policies to aid the weaker local firms is essential to any country that wants to have a critical minimal degree of control over its economy and social life.

It should come as no surprise why the industrialized countries are expending great efforts to promote this issue. They would like their companies to be able to operate much more freely in developing countries, and thus are asking that current restrictions and regulations be removed. Gaining access to the resources and markets of the South, and to the right to invest and operate in the developing countries, has been a major strategic objective of the governments and companies of the North. It was this objective that largely prompted the take-over of the Third World's territories in the colonial era.

It was the need to recapture control over resources, and to have national policies in favour of domestic rather than foreign interests, that spurred the anti-colonial struggles that finally led most colonies to win independence. It would thus be a great irony if the ex-colonial master countries were to succeed yet again to obtain rights for their companies to establish themselves and to dominate the economies of the former colonies, this time not through military conquest, but through the device of a treaty to be agreed to by all parties. This would be the modern version of the 'unequal treaties', with possibly the same disastrous effect on many countries. It is likely that if governments are not allowed the powers to impose regulations on foreign companies, or to give a helping hand to domestic companies, then the bigger foreign firms will overcome the local ones and win an increasing share of the domestic as well as international markets. The irony would be all the greater should the developing countries agree to such rules without clearly understanding their full significance.

Seeing the growing resistance to initial negotiations on a MIA, in the latter part of 1996, the MIA proponents watered down their proposal to begin an 'educative process' in the WTO, with no commitment that there be negotiations for an agreement. At the WTO Ministerial Conference in December 1996, this was accepted, and a working group has been created to examine the trade–investment relationship, without any obligation that this would lead to negotiations for an investment agreement. Based on the recent record of negotiations on new issues in the Uruguay Round, there is a strong possibility that once an issue is accepted as within the competence of the WTO, even for an educative process, there will be strong pressure that this would proceed into negotiations and a treaty. The pressures within the WTO towards rule-making make the WTO an unsuitable forum for an 'educative process', since the process operates within an atmosphere of tension, fear, and suspicion.

As some developing countries at the WTO (and many NGOs) argued, a more suitable forum for discussion and an educative process would be the United Nations, where the issue can be seen in its many facets (especially the development dimension), and not only from the per-spective of rule-making and the trading system. At the UNCTAD-9 Conference of May 1996, UNCTAD was given the mandate to discuss the issue of trade and investment and the implications of a MIA at intergovernmental level. Thus, for the next few years, discussions and an educative process could take place at this forum. Arising from such a process, the role of the trading system can be better clarified. Never-theless, the case against a study process in the WTO did not succeed, and the working group on trade and investment will now be established. Developing countries have to prepare well for the forthcoming negotia-tions, or else, they may be overwhelmed by the intense pressures of the developed countries. An insight into the way issues are dealt with at the international arena can be gleaned from the workings of the recent WTO Ministerial Conference in Singapore.

The Singapore WTO Ministerial Conference

The preparatory process

The WTO's first Ministerial Conference was meant to be a 'review con-ference', in which members were supposed to review the Uruguay Round results three years after its conclusion, and (especially the devel-oping countries) bring up problems they faced in implementing their Uruguay Round obligations. However, it was clear during the prepara-tory process that review and implementation was low on the priority of developed countries. These member countries wanted to use the Con-ference to give the WTO a major push in widening further the scope of issues under its jurisdiction and to give another impetus to global liber-alization. They put forward new issues which they wanted the Ministers to endorse as the basis for new working groups and a work programme for the next few years. These new issues were trade and labour standards, trade and investment, trade and competition policy, and transparency in government procurement.

In the preparatory process, held mainly in Geneva, but also at several informal seminars and meetings around the world organized by individual countries, developing countries generally argued that they were against new issues being introduced at this stage in the WTO, as they were already finding it a great strain to adjust to the Uruguay Round agreements which require major changes to many domestic laws and policies. They had little resources left over to take on new issues on the trade agenda, especially since these could have significant implications for their economies. They argued that a discussion on yet more new issues would divert their resources and that of the Conference away from the tasks of review and implementation. Several developing countries also argued against the principle or timing of introducing new issues into the WTO. On labour standards, there was general agreement by developing countries that the issue did not belong to the trading system. They also viewed the attempt to link labour standards to the WTO as a move by the North to eventually increase labour costs in their countries, depriving them of their main comparative advantage.

On investment, many developing countries were strongly against the introduction of an MIA in the WTO. They argued that investment policy *per se* was not within the purview of the WTO, and that the relevant aspect of investment (trade-related investment measures) were already covered in the TRIMs Agreement. On competition policy and government procurement, several developing countries (similar to the those objecting to an investment study process) also voiced opposition to beginning a work programme on these issues as they had not yet had time to study the implications of bringing them into the WTO. There was also concern that the objective of the major countries was to use these issues to further open up developing countries' markets for the transnational companies.

Lack of transparency

Many Ministers and officials from developing countries were surprised and frustrated at the organization and decision-making process of the Singapore WTO Ministerial Conference, which reflected the lack of transparency in the functioning of the WTO system in Geneva. All Ministers were allocated time to make speeches at the open plenary meetings, but most developing countries were never even invited to the really important discussions, on issues where there were disputes and which took place in 'informal groups'. For most of the Conference, their Ministers and senior officials were kept in the dark as to what was going on. 'Lack of transparency' was the term most used by delegates,

NGO representatives, and journalists alike to describe the Conference's manner of operations.

The 'open' part of the Conference was the plenary session where the Trade Ministers of 120 countries made speeches. Those from developing countries were often articulate in pointing out their problems in having to liberalize their economies after the Uruguay Round agreements that came into force in January 1995. Many made the plea that no new issues (especially non-trade issues) be brought into the WTO since they were still unable to cope with the problems arising from their existing WTO obligations. But, embarrassingly enough, the Ministers were speaking to an increasingly emptier hall. There were no discussions at all on their speeches, and thus no opportunity to seek solutions to the problems raised.

Meanwhile, the negotiations of key issues had gone 'underground' in many informal meetings to which only 20 to 30 selected countries were invited by the Conference chairman, Singapore Trade Minister Yeo Cheow Tong, and WTO director-general Renato Ruggiero. The informal group negotiated whether and how the Northern proposals on labour standards and the new issues could be brought into the Conference's Ministerial Declaration. The lack of transparency in the decision-making process, in which the real negotiations took place within a closed-door informal meeting in contrast with the formal appearance of decision by consensus, enabled the minority of rich countries to have their way over the majority much more easily. Because the ratio of North-to-South countries in the informal group was more to the favour of the North than if the meeting were to involve all members, the Northern countries were much more able to pressure the developing countries present to give in. In contrast, discussions are normally held in an open forum in the United Nations and its Conferences.

The 'informal group' system of negotiations used at the Singapore Conference is an extension of the way the WTO operates as a matter of routine in Geneva. What the Conference did was to expose to the international press, to NGOs and to the Ministers themselves the lack of transparency and the disadvantage of developing countries in the WTO. Before the Singapore Conference, many developing countries had already registered their frustration at the lack of transparency in the Conference's preparatory process and, in particular, at the undemocratic manner in which the heads-of-delegation, led by the Director-General, had at informal sessions determined the new issues and the draft declaration. At Singapore itself, that dissatisfaction increased manifold and extended from the Geneva diplomats to Ministers, other members of the delegations, the NGOs and the media.

Despite the self-congratulatory satisfaction of the organization's top management and the major countries, which – in their own words – achieved all their objectives in Singapore, the WTO's credibility and legitimacy has suffered a major blow where public groups are concerned. At a briefing of the NGOs near the end of the Conference, Chakravarthi Raghavan, Chief Editor of the South–North Development Monitor, said that in his 18 years experience of following the GATT at Geneva, he had never found such an utter lack of transparency as he experienced in Singapore. 'The lack of transparency and democracy in decision-making had made the WTO and its agreements illegitimate,' he remarked. 'No institution or instrument lacking legitimacy can command or expect obedience or acceptance of civil society.'

For many developing countries, their faith in being able to really participate as members (and to avoid being manipulated by the major players or be used as rubber-stamps to produce 'consensus' against their own interests) has also been shaken. If it is only to regain some of that credibility, legitimacy and faith, the WTO has to tackle seriously the issue of transparency of information and process, and participation of all members, big or small, when it sits again to follow up on its decisions in Singapore. Will it be up to the challenge, or will it be 'business as usual', with the Quads (that is, the US, EU, Japan, and Germany) making the blueprints, drawing the policies, and through persuasion and pressure, with the help of the Secretariat, and via the secretive 'Green Room informal meetings', continuing to produce the 'consensus' to advance the cause of their global economic governance?

Unbalanced outcome, again

The Conference's neglect of the issues of importance to developing countries and its unbalanced results in favour of the North are reflections of the way the world trade rules in WTO are tilted against the poorer countries and how their concerns are marginalized. Although the developing countries form four-fifths of the WTO's membership, and the WTO is supposed to decide by consensus, the minority of Northern countries were able to place their priority issues on the Conference agenda, forcing the Southern countries in the frontline of the discussion to react in a bid at 'damage control'.

The imbalance at the Conference was reflected in the way liberalization of information technology products was put on a super-fast track via the Information Technology Agreement promoted by the US, while liberalization of products exported by developing countries (for example, textiles and clothing) were neglected. Concerns of the South over continuing protectionism by the North (for example, by the extension of the unilateral trade actions of the US and the protectionist use of anti-dumping measures against Third World products) were also brushed aside. The problems faced by developing countries in having to meet the Uruguay Round commitments, voiced by their Ministers in the open plenary sessions, were hardly discussed. Instead, most of the negotiating energy of the Conference was focused on the new issues put forward by the Northern countries. In the end, they succeeded in getting the Conference to extend the boundaries of the WTO to begin discussions and a work programme on new areas (investment, competition, and government procurement).

Damage control

Of all the new issues raised at the Singapore meeting, developing countries did best in protecting their interests in labour standards. The Director-General's draft declaration, carried over from Geneva, had not, in any case, placed labour standards as an item for a future work programme (unlike the other new issues), but in an early part of the declaration as a general statement. Thus, the negotiations in Singapore were not about a work programme on labour standards, but how to word the text and whether it should be included in the Declaration.

While a few developed countries (mainly the US and France) made a play for harder language for the WTO to have a larger say on the issue, developing countries in the end succeeded in establishing in the Declaration (para. 4) that the Ministers 'renew our commitment to the observance of internationally recognized core labour standards,' and that

a) the International Labour Organization (ILO) is the competent body to set and deal with labour standards;
b) growth and development promote these standards;
c) the comparative advantage of countries, particularly low-wage developing countries, must in no way be put into question; and
d) in this regard, the WTO and ILO secretariats will continue their existing collaboration.

The new issues

The developed countries succeeded in getting the Conference to form working groups and to agree to future work programmes in the new areas of investment, competition policy, and government procurement.

Developing countries were, however, able to build in some safeguards in the text of the Declaration, in an effort to protect their interests. There is no doubt, however, that these issues have now entered the ambit of the WTO and there will be intense pressures by the major countries on the working groups to have their interpretations and objectives adopted.

Some developing countries had come to Singapore with the intention of blocking the inclusion of any new issue in the Declaration, continuing the strenuous efforts taken by their diplomats in the gruelling preparatory talks in Geneva of the past year. These countries, including India, Malaysia, Indonesia, Egypt, Tanzania, Ghana, Uganda, and Haiti, had objected to the mention of investment in the Declaration. Several other countries also objected to competition policy and government procurement, whilst a vast majority of developing countries (supported by some developed countries) were against labour standards. They felt that integrating these areas in the WTO would allow the rich countries to gain unfair advantage over the South and open the door for them to link non-trade issues to the WTO and its dispute settlement system, including trade penalties for non-compliance. They feared that even a decision to 'study' or 'examine' these issues would already be accepting the principle and concept of the new issues being within the WTO's competence, and constitute a dangerous opening for full-scale negotiations and eventual binding agreements.

The expected resistance of the core group of developing countries opposing the acceptance of new issues softened considerably in the first days itself. First, one of the major resisting countries changed position from opposing the mention of issues on principle, to accepting the formation of the new working groups, but negotiating their terms of reference. Following this, more countries shifted their position and the negotiations changed from whether or not the new issues should be included, to how they should be worded. Damage control replaced damage prevention. From initially arguing against the principle of including new issues in the WTO (at least at this stage), developing countries shifted to an acceptance of starting discussions in the WTO on these issues and attempting to yield as little as possible and building in safeguards in the terms of reference for future discussions on the issues.

Trade and investment

Developing countries were able to put in some safeguards while agreeing to establish a working group on trade and investment, in an attempt to restrict the scope of the Work programme. Through the Declaration, the

WTO will 'establish a working group to examine the relationship between trade and investment.' The Declaration, however, has placed this examination within a complex set of terms of reference, including:

a) The simultaneous establishment of two working groups, one on trade and the other on competition policy;
b) The two groups will draw on each other's work;
c) The groups will link their discussions to existing WTO provisions including TRIMs;
d) The work undertaken shall not prejudge whether negotiations will be initiated in the future;
e) The groups will draw on the work of and cooperate with UNCTAD and other inter-governmental forums;
f) The development dimension will be fully taken into account;
g) The General Council will review the work of the two groups and determine after two years how their work should proceed;
h) Future negotiations, if any, on multilateral disciplines, will take place only after an explicit consensus among members;
i) In organizing the work, careful attention will be given to minimising the burden on delegations, especially those with more limited resources.

By the close of the Conference, sharply different interpretations of this text had already emerged. India's officials were clear that any reference to an MIA was rejected, that the investment study should be conducted as part of a TRIMs review, that there would not be a negotiation towards an MIA, and that 'investment does not belong to the WTO.' The EU had a clearly different view. The EU vice-president and trade commissioner Leon Brittan said:

> On investment, the most important theme of all for the future of the world economy, we have at last put WTO on the map. Investment indeed seems to me the top priority for WTO in the years ahead . . . . It is also an issue which is primarily for the WTO because it involves the development of an appropriate framework of binding rules...WTO rules will help provide the necessary underpinning.

The clear message from the EU is that the Declaration opens the road to a multilateral 'framework of binding rules' and that it will argue, once again, that this is necessary for foreign investments to flow to developing countries.

Unless developing countries organise themselves well, on both sub-stance and the tricky processes of the WTO system, the 'examination' of trade and investment in the working group could well prepare the ground for 'negotiations' for investment rules.

Trade and competition policy

One of the WTO Ministerial Conference's most important decisions was to establish a working group on 'trade and competition policy', a new issue that had figured quite prominently in the pre-Ministerial Confer-ence process. Concerns over the greater concentration of economic power in fewer giant corporations should, in any objective discussion, be the focus of a move to look at anti-competitive behaviour or curb monopolistic tendencies and practices around the world. 'Competition policy' in the WTO context has different meanings for different parties. The US and EU are aiming to get the South to establish 'effective' domestic anti-monopoly laws so their corporations can have better market access; Hong Kong wants to examine WTO rules in a 'globalizing economy'; developing countries back Japan and Korea in wanting to look at anti-competitive abuse of trade measures; and some South coun-tries want to bring in transnational companies and their restrictive business practices.

Many developing countries had opposed the introduction of this new issue into the WTO. It is likely that many, if not most, of the WTO members were not really aware of what they had agreed to, and this generated sharp controversy in the post-Conference press conferences. The Declaration agreed to: 'Establish a working group to study issues raised by members relating to the interaction between trade and com-petition policy, including anti-competitive practices, in order to identify any areas that may merit further consideration in the WTO framework.'

Most developing countries were unable to follow adequately the pre-Conference preparatory discussions in Geneva on competition. Some were, however, concerned that the EU proposal was aimed at ensuring greater market access for their transnational companies in the South. The EU was seen as using the WTO to commit developing countries to have domestic competition laws to break down local monopolies or practices that helped local companies maintain their market shares, so that the larger transnational monopolies could break into or enlarge their share of the domestic markets of developing countries. This suspi-cion was augmented by the lack of interest of the North in countering the international anti-competitive and restrictive business practices of transnational corporations (such as transfer pricing and other intra-firm practices) which harmed Third World economies (resulting for example in reduced taxes, higher prices or unfair commercial advantages). Proposals by some developing countries on this were received coolly. The EU proposal thus seemed aimed at ensuring that developing countries institute anti-monopoly laws at the national level, which their corporations and agents could invoke, but would not deal with the anti-competitive behaviour and restrictive practices of their transnational corporations at international level.

National businessmen of some developing countries were concerned that their business position might be adversely affected. In April, the ASEAN Chamber of Commerce and Industry Council, representing national chambers of ASEAN countries, issued a joint communiqué expressing concern about competition policy being advocated at the WTO, saying this issue 'must be dealt with care.' 'Competition laws existing in developed countries should not be limited to trade and should not be imposed on ASEAN,' it stated. 'The formulation of competition laws should be a domestic matter that is best left to each nation to decide.' Some businessmen worried, for example, that competition laws introduced via a WTO agreement would enable the transnational corporations to make use of local dealer networks built up by domestic enterprises – the kind of demand that the US made on behalf of its auto-giants in respect of the Japanese market and the Japanese auto manufacturers.

At an early stage of negotiations in the informal group at Singapore, a few countries that had previously opposed starting work on this issue, changed position by proposing changes to the text and thus implicitly agreeing to include work on competition policy in the declaration. On condition that the working group's mandate would also cover 'anti-competitive practices', many of the developing countries in the informal group agreed to the setting up of the working group. 'Anti-competitive practices' was a code for the abuse of trade measures (such as anti-dumping actions), and for some countries, the restrictive business practices of transnational companies.

When the inclusion of investment seemed inevitable, some of those who were opposed to the issue, saw much merit in simultaneous work on competition policy questions and the anti-competitive behaviour of transnational corporations. During the Uruguay Round negotiations, these countries had taken the view that investment measures were a justifiable response to the anti-competitive practices of transnational corporations. Thus, with the curbing of such measures through the TRIMs Agreement, they had proposed (in Article 9) that the review of

this Agreement after five years should include the question of investment and competition policy.

At the close of the Singapore meeting, developing countries felt that
they had built enough safeguards. But it remains to be seen if all parties
will abide by the 'bargain' struck at Singapore. In the post-Singapore
negotiations of the working group, it must be expected that the real
intent of the major countries, which the US has acknowledged, is getting greater 'market access' for their transnational companies in the
countries of the South. It remains to be seen whether the South can
defend its interests and promote its own issues.

Government procurement

The WTO Conference also agreed to establish a new working group to
study 'transparency in government procurement practices' and develop
elements for 'an appropriate agreement'. While the study, and the
agreement, only covers transparency (and not the practices themselves),
the major countries pushing this issue have made clear their ultimate
goal: to fully integrate the lucrative multi-billion dollar government
procurement market into the WTO rules and system. If they succeed,
governments in future will not be allowed to give preference to local
companies to supply goods and services or to carry out development
projects.

The system of government procurement has been taken for granted as
very much a matter of national prerogative. This situation is about to
change, through the working group. It will initially study only transparency in government procurement practices, and evolve an agreement
on this limited theme. But the prime mover of this initiative, the US, has
made it clear that in its scenario, this is only a first step towards a full-
scale opening up of the market for government procurement for foreign
companies. With the support of the EU, the US plans that an interim
agreement on transparency emerging from this working group will
eventually be upgraded into a full-blown agreement on government
procurement practices. This would give national treatment rights to
foreign companies (to have the same chance as locals to bid for and
win public-sector contracts), and most-favoured-nation treatment rights
to all WTO countries (to be treated in a non-discriminatory way in the
procurement awards).

The final Declaration states that the Ministers agree to 'establish a
working group to conduct a study on transparency in government
procurement practices, taking into account national policies, and
based on this study, to develop elements for inclusion in an appropriate

agreement.' In practical terms, this decision carries a heavier commitment than the decisions on the other new issues of investment and competition policy, which only mandated an 'examination' while the procurement group should develop elements for an 'appropriate agreement'. Developing countries appear to have accepted the decision because the working group, and the reference to an agreement, refers only to 'transparency' in procurement practices. However, the post-Conference statements by the US and the EU make it very clear that for them the working group is only an interim measure towards rules to ensure full access for their companies to the multi-billion dollar government procurement business in developing countries.

As far as the major countries are concerned, the transparency issue is only a first and tactical measure to draw developing countries, step by step, into the larger area of national treatment for foreign firms to obtain contracts for government procurement and projects. The developed countries have not attempted to hide this goal. In the heads-of-delegation process in Geneva over the past nine months, the American and EU papers made clear they considered government procurement to be a gigantic business which had hitherto remained outside the WTO's ambit and should be brought in through multilateral rules so that their companies could have full access to the developing country markets.

What the developed countries especially want to see eradicated in developing countries are the types of government procurement policies and practices that currently favour national enterprises and people – practices that the major industrialized countries had followed not too long ago within their countries and which had benefited some of their giant corporations. These policies are adopted in most developing countries in order to help build the domestic sector, strengthen domestic linkages and demand, and support local entrepreneurs. Since liberalization is proceeding so rapidly in other areas, government expenditure remains one of the few (and probably the most important) sectors of economic activity which can be used as an instrument to boost local business and domestic demand.

This crucial 'development dimension' is, however, lost in the 'market access paradigm' adopted by the Northern proponents of the idea of fully integrating government procurement in WTO rules and dispute settlement systems. At the working group, developing countries should thus be prepared with positions on the whole issue of government procurement, and not just the transparency aspect. For transparency is just a subset of the general issue of procurement policies and practices. And in the game-plan of the major countries, the negotiations for an 'interim arrangement' are only a means to a final agreement aimed at full integration of government procurement practices in the WTO multilateral discipline, single undertaking and dispute settlement system.

4
Replicating the Experience of the NIEs on a Large Scale

Robert Rowthorn

This chapter examines whether developing countries can follow the same pattern of export-led industrialization of the first-tier newly industrializing economies (NIEs), such as Hong Kong, Korea, and Taiwan, which was based on massive exports of labour-intensive manufactures to advanced countries. It also examines whether they can follow the more recent example of Malaysia, a second-tier NIE whose export-led growth has been driven by the direct investment of transnational corporations (TNCs).

Defining the issues

An individual small developing country can achieve a large percentage increase in its exports to the North without flooding the market and seriously reducing the price. However, this may not be true for developing countries as a whole; thus the fallacy of composition. Some studies have suggested that such a process is already under way; that is, manufactured exports from the South have been falling in price compared to those of Northern exports. However, this suggestion has been disputed and there is no consensus on the issue. After examining the arguments briefly, the discussion concludes that there is evidence of a modest decline in the manufacturing terms of trade of developing countries, most of which occurred in the mid-1980s.

Regardless of the past behaviour of the manufacturing terms-of-trade, the fallacy of composition could become a serious problem in the future for the manufactured exports of developing countries, as it has been for primary commodities, especially since there is now an increased emphasis on export-led growth. The ensuing discussion first illustrates this problem using the example of clothing, which is then followed by a more elaborate analysis of manufacturing exports, taking into account the impact of income levels and population on export performance. The main conclusions are as follows. There is considerable scope for growth in the exports of traditional manufactures, such as clothing, to the advanced countries, but the potential for growth is not remotely sufficient to allow the widespread imitation of NIEs like Hong Kong, Korea, and Taiwan, where economic development was based on such exports. Diversification into new types of manufactured exports would make it easier for developing countries to penetrate markets in the North, but even this might not allow them to export to the North on the scale achieved by the NIEs of East Asia. If a large number of developing countries seek to emulate these countries, the result could be either a wave of protectionism in the North or a collapse of prices.

Trade is not the only area in which there may be a fallacy of composition. Similar considerations arise in the sphere of foreign direct investment (FDI). A small, individual country may successfully replicate the experience of a country like Malaysia, whose export-led growth has relied heavily on inward FDI. But as we demonstrate below, this is not a viable path for the developing countries as a whole to follow, or even for a large subgroup of them. The scale of FDI required would far exceed what is likely to be available from the North. Exhortations to follow the example of Malaysia in either exports or FDI may at best lead to disappointment, and at worst may cause the developing countries to cut their own throats by forcing down the price of exports or the terms on which FDI is available.

These findings raise a number of policy issues which are discussed in the last part of the chapter. First, it is argued that large countries such as China or India do not need and never will achieve the same per capita exports or imports as the NIEs. Nor will trade achieve such a high share of gross domestic product (GDP). An outward-oriented strategy for such countries does not mean trying to emulate the per capita export performance of the NIEs.

Second, the developing countries can help to avoid flooding world markets with labour-intensive goods by diversifying their export mix. The more advanced countries or regions of the South can move up the value-added chain and supply more capital-intensive or skill-intensive exports to the North. Even less advanced countries may also be forced to move in this direction if the growth of Northern markets for labour-intensive goods remains sluggish.

Third, the main reason for the South to export to the North is to purchase capital and intermediate goods. The more consumer goods the South imports from the North, the more goods it must export in return, and the more danger there is of flooding the markets of the North; also, the more danger there is of a protectionist response in the North. Under these circumstances, balance of payments considerations, and also the need to stimulate domestic production, may make it desirable to restrict imports of consumer goods. It remains to be seen how far the required policies are compatible with the Uruguay Round commitments of developing countries.

Finally, there is scope for extensive trade within the South. This trade is likely to be hierarchical, with more advanced areas exporting capital-intensive and skill-intensive products to less advanced areas in return for products with a high resource or unskilled labour content. The outcome will be a 'flying geese' pattern, with the most advanced countries of the North at the apex and those of the South strung out behind at varying stages of development.

Difficult policy issues are raised by the likely shortage of FDI in relation to the number of countries now seeking it. Given that outside TNCs cannot in general be the motor of development as they have been in Malaysia, most developing countries will have to rely mainly on their own efforts to industrialize. This will require building up entrepreneurial capacities, acquiring technology in non-equity form from abroad and generating a high level of domestic savings. The measures needed to achieve these objectives may possibly clash with commitments already made under the Uruguay Round. A more serious problem is likely to be the proposal for an FDI Convention, which is currently being promoted by the European Commission as a sequel to the Uruguay Round. Such a convention may deny to developing countries many useful policy instruments for encouraging their own entrepreneurs, whilst failing to stimulate foreign investment on the scale needed for Malaysian-style growth.

Recent trends in the manufacturing terms of trade of developing countries

Since the celebrated work of Prebisch (1950) and Singer (1950), it has been frequently argued that the terms of trade between primary products and manufactures are on a downward trend. Developing countries wishing to boost their export earnings should, therefore, diversify away from primary products into labour-intensive manufactures for which income and price elasticities in the advanced economies are relatively high. The empirical basis of this last claim has been questioned by Sarkar and Singer (1991) in a paper analysing the manufacturing terms of trade of developing countries. They estimate that, over the period 1970–87, the price of manufactured exports from developing countries fell by an average of 1.0 per cent a year relative to the price of manufactured exports from developed countries. This finding suggests either that income and price elasticities for the type of manufactures which developing countries currently export are low, or else that demand for these exports is being artificially constrained by protection in the advanced economies.

Sarkar and Singer have been criticized by Athukorala (1993) because their definition of manufacturing does not accord with the normal practice of trade economists and is highly misleading. Trade economists normally define the term 'manufactures' to cover SITC categories 5 to 8, excluding non-ferrous metals (SITC 68). Non-ferrous metals are excluded because the manufacturing value-added component is small and variations in their price mainly reflect what is happening to the price of metallic ferrous ores. However, contrary to normal practice, the United Nations (UN) price series used by Sarkar and Singer include non-ferrous metals in manufacturing. This creates a potentially serious bias, since the price of non-ferrous metals fell sharply over the period in question. To correct for such a bias, Athukorala adjusts the UN series for developing country exports to exclude non-ferrous metals. He then uses regression analysis to demonstrate that the apparent deterioration in their manufacturing terms of trade virtually disappears when the adjusted series is used (Table 4.1).

Sarkar and Singer (1993) reply to this criticism by insisting that non-ferrous metals should be included in manufacturing, but their response is both very brief and unconvincing. However, there is a better response which they could have made. Chart 4.1 plots the manufacturing terms of trade of developing countries, showing both the original UN series, and an adjusted series which excludes non-ferrous metals from Southern exports. It is clear from this chart that the two series behave very differently prior to 1975, but are virtually identical thereafter. Thus, from 1975 onwards the bias arising from the inclusion of non-ferrous metals in the UN price index has been negligible. This is partly because the relative price of non-ferrous metals has varied less during the later period, and partly because of the declining weight of non-ferrous metals in the UN price series for developing country exports. Whilst in 1970 non-ferrous metals accounted for one quarter of developing country exports in SITC categories 5 to 8, their share had fallen to 12 per cent by 1975 and is now in the region of 4 per cent. What Athukorala's

Table 4.1 Trends in Net Barter Terms of Trade for Exports of Manufactures and Non-ferrous Metals of Developing Countries *vis-à-vis* Industrial Countries, 1970–87[a]

Commodity category[b]	Annual compound rate of exchange (%)	R^2	DW
Manufactures:			
SITC 5–8			
XUVDC/XUVIC	−1.00[c]	0.41	1.45
Non-ferrous metals:			
SITC 68			
NFUVDC/XUVIC	−3.60[c]	0.67	1.72
	(5.65)		
NFPDC/XUVIC	−4.43[d]	0.76	1.75
	(7.56)		
Manufactures:			
SITC 5–8 less SITC 68	−0.2		
XUVDC(a)/XUVIC	(1.06)	0.06	1.23
XUVDC(b)/XUVIC	−0.1	0.00	1.03
	(0.22)		

Notes: Estimate for manufactures in line 1 is from Sarker and Singer (1991). Others are Athukorala's estimates.

[a] Trend rates are obtained by fitting (using OLS) the equation: log $NBTT = a + rT$, where T is the time variable and the estimate of r is the trend rate. The t ratios are given in brackets.

[b] Variable notations: XUVDC = original (unadjusted) UN export unit value index for developed countries, XUVIC = UN export unit value index for industrial countries, NFUVDC = unit value index (specifically constructed by Athukorala) for non-ferrous metal exports from developing countries, NFPDC = UN price index for non-ferrous metal exports from developing countries, XUVDC(a) = XUVDC adjusted using NFUVDC, XUVDC(b) = XUVDC adjusted using NFPDC.

[c] Significant at 5% level.

[d] Significant at 1% level.

Source: Arthukorala (1993).

regression analysis picks up is the effect of an unusually large fall in the relative price of non-ferrous metals in the early 1970s, when these metals were of great importance in developing country exports. If we confine ourselves to the period from 1975 onwards, his adjustment makes little difference, and there is clear evidence of a decline in the manufacturing terms of trade of developing countries whichever series we use. Using the unadjusted UN series, regression analysis reveals that the relative price of developing country manufactured exports fell at the rate of 0.48 per cent a year over the period 1975–93. If an adjustment is made to remove non-ferrous metals, the rate of decline is 0.46 per cent a year.

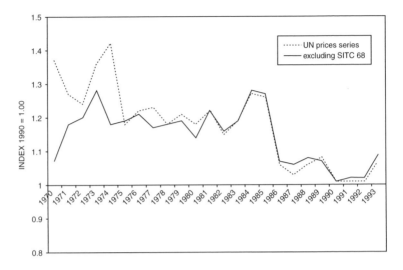

Chart 4.1   Manufacturing Terms of Trade: South *vis-à-vis* North
Source: UNCTAD, *Handbook of International Trade and Development Statistics, 1993.*

Minford *et al.* (1995) also argue that the relative price of manufactured exports from developing countries has been falling. To support their claim they use two different measures of the terms of trade. Following the same approach as Sarkar and Singer, they first compare the UN price series for manufactured exports from developing countries with the equivalent UN series for developed countries. Their second measure uses an alternative series for exports from developed countries based on the export prices of Machinery & Equipment and Services (Chart 4.2). This indicates a somewhat larger deterioration in the terms of trade of developing countries than the first measure.

Thus, there is evidence that the relative price of manufactured exports from developing countries has fallen since 1975. However, the overall decline is not very large and, as can be seen from the charts, has been mainly confined to a short period around 1985. The fact that developing countries have experienced only a modest shift in their manufacturing terms of trade tells us little about what might have happened if their exports had risen much faster than they actually did, or if they should rise dramatically in the future. The comparative stability of relative prices in the past may be merely a coincidence due to the fact that Northern markets were opened up just fast enough to absorb the actual growth in supply from the South. With a faster growth in supply, Southern export

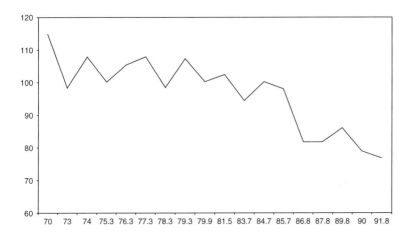

Chart 4.2 Ratio of Developing Countries' Export Prices (US$) to Developed Countries' Export Prices of Machinery and Transport Equipment and Services (US$)

Source: Minford *et al.* (1995).

prices might have collapsed in the past, and may do so in the future if the increase in supply is large enough.

The fallacy of composition: the example of clothing

It is sometimes argued that poorer countries should follow the development path pioneered by most of the first-tier NIEs. In the initial stages of development, they should direct their economies towards the large scale export of labour-intensive manufactures to advanced countries. To assess the feasibility of this strategy a number of points need to be taken into account. First, there is the question of markets. How large is the potential market in advanced countries for labour intensive products? And what fraction of this market can the poorer countries expect to capture? Secondly, there is the question of population. How large is the population which is likely to be involved in the development process in question? If the number is modest, then it may be feasible to emulate the little dragons. However, if the number is very large this may not be feasible.

To explore this issue, I shall initially focus on clothing which has been the major labour-intensive export from East Asia in modern times. Despite the rapid growth of clothing exports from developing countries, UN statistics on apparent consumption indicate that such goods still account for only a quarter of total expenditure on clothing by the advanced economies as a whole. Most expenditure goes to goods produced internally within these economies and a small proportion on goods from Eastern Europe.[1] Under the Multi-Fibre Arrangement, domestic clothing producers in most advanced economies enjoy protection against imports from developing countries. As a result, the output of clothing in many of them has remained roughly constant over the past 20 years (Chart 4.3), although employment has fallen everywhere because of rising labour productivity. Whilst protection has served to stabilize or contain the fall in domestic output in advanced economies, the demand for clothing has been rising and a widening gap has emerged between output and expenditure. This gap has been filled by imports from developing countries.

What would the situation be like in the absence of protection? Some indication is provided by the example of Sweden, which has virtually eliminated protection for the clothing industry. Over the past 30 years, the output of clothing has dropped by 80 per cent in Sweden and is still going down. This suggests that under free trade, the production of clothing and similar labour-intensive goods would fall dramatically in most advanced countries, although perhaps not as much as in Sweden, where the egalitarian wages policy has meant very high labour costs for the producers of such goods.

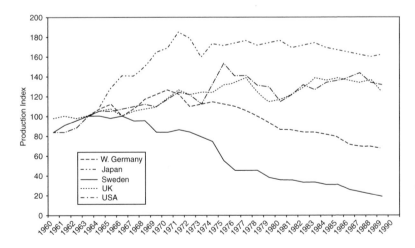

Chart 4.3   Clothing Production (Index 1960 = 100)

Source: UNCTAD, Handbook of International Trade and Development Statistics, 1993.

Following the Uruguay Round, it is envisaged that most of the restrictions on labour-intensive imports from developing countries will eventually be eliminated. Table 4.2 shows what this could mean in the case of clothing. In 1990–91, the apparent consumption of clothing by the major Organization for Economic Cooperation and Development (OECD) economies was US$258.1 billion, of which US$178.7 billion was spent on goods produced internally, US$57.9 billion on imports from the developing countries, and a further US$21.5 billion on imports from elsewhere. The table assumes that purchases of internally produced clothing in the North fall by 60 per cent as a result of free trade. It also assumes that expenditure in the North on clothing increases by 40 per cent by the time free trade takes full effect. Thus, developing country exporters enjoy the twin gains of access to expanding markets in the North and reduced output by their Northern rivals. The result is a 265 per cent increase in their exports to the North, from US$57.9 billion to US$265.2 billion. These figures are obviously very crude and their purpose is purely illustrative. Even so, they do indicate the orders of magnitude involved and the potential for developing countries to increase their exports of labour intensive manufactures provided the advanced economies abandon protectionism.

Steps towards free trade are likely in the wake of the Uruguay Round, but it remains to be seen just how far the advanced economies will actually go when the time comes. Moreover, protection is only one of the issues at stake here. If the advanced economies were to eliminate all trade barriers, this would give a major boost to exports from developing countries, but it would not be remotely sufficient to allow all of these

Table 4.2 Prospects for Clothing Exports to the North[a]

	Actual 1990–91 $ billions	*Hypothetical $ billions*	*Percentage change*
Apparent consumption in the North	258.1	361.4	40.0[b]
Production in the North	178.7	71.5	−60.0[b]
Imports from developing countries	57.9	211.3	265.2[b]
Other external imports	21.5	78.5	265.2

Notes: [a] North in this table refers to EEC, Canada, USA and Japan.
[b] Assumed.
Source: Data are from the UN *Handbook of International Trade and Development Statistics, 1993*.

countries to replicate the experience of the first-tier NIEs, whose growth
strategy was mostly predicated on huge per capita exports of labour
intensive goods to the advanced economies (Table 4.2). Such a strategy
has only been feasible because the first-tier NIEs are very small. Their
combined population is only 73 million (Table 4.3). This is not much
larger than the population of the Guangdong province of China (65
million) or the Philippines (64 million), and is well below the figures for
Indonesia (184 million) or the Chang Jian Delta around Shanghai (125
million). China alone has a population of 1,162 million, whilst
the developing countries as a whole contain around 4,000 million people. It is inconceivable that more than a small fraction of these huge
populations can simultaneously replicate the export strategy of the
first-tier NIEs. This does not mean that they cannot industrialize rapidly,
but it does mean that will have to pursue a different trade strategy.

Table 4.3   Population and GDP for Selected Countries in 1992

	Population (millions)	GDP (US$ billions)	GDP per capita (US$ thousands)
First-tier NIEs			
Singapore	3	46	16.44
Hong Kong	6	78	13.42
Taiwan[a]	20	249[b]	12.21[b]
South Korea	44	296	6.78
Total	73	669	9.20
Second-tier NIEs			
Malaysia	19	58	3.10
Thailand	58	110	1.90
Philippines	64	52	0.82
Indonesia	184	126	0.69
Total	325	347	1.07
Poor Large Asian			
China	1,162	506	0.44
Pakistan	119	42	0.35
India	884	215	0.24
Bangladesh	114	24	0.21
Total	2,280	786	0.34

Notes: [a] 1990.
[b] GNP.
Source: World Development Report, 1994 for all, except Taiwan; Taiwan figures are from the
Statistical Abstract of the United States, 1994.

Table 4.4 calculates what would happen if every developing country had the same per capita exports of clothing (and footwear) as the average first-tier NIE in 1992. Under this assumption, Chinese exports alone would be equal to US$403 billion. This is 16 times the present exports of clothing and footwear by the first-tier NIEs and six times the total exports of such items by all developing countries in the world put together. It was estimated above that in the absence of protection, clothing exports to the advanced countries would eventually rise by 265 per cent. Assuming a similar rise in footwear exports, we arrive at a combined figure of US$240 billion for potential clothing and footwear exports to the North. This is a very large increase over the present level, but it is not remotely sufficient to allow the developing countries as a whole to emulate the performance of the first-tier NIEs. For China alone to export on *half* the required scale, the advanced economies would have to abolish protection of clothing and footwear completely, increase their consumption by 40 per cent and purchase their entire imports of

Table 4.4 Exports of Clothing and Footwear to Developed Countries

Actual Situation in 1992	*Population (millions)*	*Export per capita (US$)*	*Exports (US$ billions)*
First-tier NIEs	73	346.6	25
Second-tier NIEs	352	26.3	9
China	1,162	7.6	9
Other developing countries[a]	2,962	7.7	23
Sum of above	4,549	14.5	66
Sum less first-tier NIEs	4,476	9.1	41

Hypothetical Situation with Export Performance of First-tier NIEs	*Population (millions)*	*Hypothetical exports per capita (US$)*	*Hypothetical exports (US$ billions)*
First-tier NIEs	73	346.6	25
Second-tier NIEs	352	346.6	122
China	1,162	346.6	403
Other developing countries[a]	2,962	346.6	1,027
Sum of above	4,549	346.6	1,577
Sum less first-tier NIEs	4,476	346.6	1,552

Note: [a] Includes Eastern Europe and former USSR.
Source: UNCTAD database.

such goods from China. If all developing countries were to emulate the experience of the first-tier NIEs, their total exports of clothing and footwear to the North would have to increase by a factor of more than 20. Even allowing for the effects of the Uruguay Round and future growth in Northern markets, such an increase is inconceivable.

These calculations illustrate the impracticality of generalizing the trade strategy of the first-tier NIEs. No large population area can expect to achieve per capita exports of traditional labour-intensive products on anything like the scale achieved by the first-tier NIEs, although a few small countries or regions might do so. Any widespread attempt to emulate the trade performance of the first-tier NIEs would merely flood the world market and lead to a collapse in the prices of such products. The danger of immizerization is widely recognized in the case of primary products, but the same considerations apply to labour-intensive manufactures. There is a limit to the amount which the advanced economies will spend on items like clothes, footwear or toys, no matter how low their prices.

Export dependence: effects of population and income levels

The preceding section has taken a simple-minded approach to the question of generalizing the export performance of the first-tier NIEs. This section follows a more sophisticated approach pioneered by Cline (1982). Cline was concerned not only with traditional labour-intensive goods, but with the entire spectrum of manufactured exports from developing countries. He also argued that crude per capita comparisons are misleading, since they do not take into account how variations in the size of countries or their income levels affect trade performance. Because of their huge populations, China and India will never be as dependent on trade as city states such as Hong Kong and Singapore, or smaller countries such as Korea and Taiwan. Moreover, the share of manufactured exports in GDP is an increasing function of per capita income, so that poor countries will have a low share, no matter what kind of trade strategy they follow. Such factors must be taken into account when defining what is meant by replicating the experience of the first-tier NIEs.

To handle this problem we shall follow Cline's approach. We begin by defining what he calls the 'cross-country norm' for manufactured exports. This is done as follows. Manufactured exports are expressed as a share of GDP, and this share is assumed to be a function of population and per capita income. The parameters of this function are then estimated for the year 1990, using a sample consisting of 54 developing countries, together with three East European countries.[2] The former account for around 90 per cent of all manufactured exports from South to North, so the coverage is fairly comprehensive. Using the estimated function, we can predict for each country what the share of manufactured exports should be, given its population and per capita income. The predicted shares of manufactured exports are shown in Column (2) of Table 4.5 under the heading 'cross-country norm', along with the actual shares which are shown in Column (1). The ratio of Column (2) to Column (1) indicates the extent to which a particular country deviates from the cross-country norm. Thus, manufactured exports from the average first-tier NIE to the North are 2.82 times as

Table 4.5 Manufactured Export Shares in GDP and Expansion Factors, 1990[a]

| Country | GDP share (%) | | Ratio (1)/(2) | Expansion factor to first-tier base[c] |
| | Actual | Cross-country norm[b] | | |
	(1)	(2)	(3)	(4)
Hong Kong	23.9	10.4	2.30	–
Korean Rep.	16.8	7.8	2.15	–
Singapore	58.6	11.4	5.16	–
Taiwan	26.8	7.8	3.44	–
First-tier NIEs	23.7	8.4	2.82	–
Indonesia	5.0	2.6	1.94	1.45
Malaysia	21.1	3.0	7.00	0.40
Philippines	5.5	1.7	3.23	0.87
Thailand	11.9	3.0	3.98	0.71
China	3.6	6.9	0.52	5.38
India	3.4	4.7	0.72	3.91
Other Asia	6.1	5.6	1.09	2.78
Argentina	1.1	5.6	0.19	14.48
Brazil	2.1	8.8	0.24	11.81
Chile	1.5	2.8	0.53	5.30
Mexico	4.1	5.9	0.69	4.11
Other Latin American	1.8	2.5	0.74	3.83
Africa	2.6	2.0	1.26	2.59

Notes: [a] This table refers to the manufactured exports of 54 developing countries (listed in the appendix). These countries include the first-tier NIEs and account for 90 per cent of exports from South to North.
[b] Estimated by OLS regression with dependent variable log (export ratio), and independent variables log (per capita GDP), log (population) and powers thereof.
[c] Equals 2.83 divided by Col. (3).
Source: UNCTAD database.

large as predicted from their population and per capita income. In contrast, manufactured exports from China, for example, are only 0.52 times their expected value. By comparing these two figures, we can estimate by how much exports from China would have to expand in order to replicate the performance of the first-tier NIEs, after adjusting for the effects of size and per capita income. The resulting 'expansion factor' is shown in Column (4), along with the corresponding factors for other developing countries.

Column (4) indicates that China would have to expand its manufactured exports to the North by a factor of 5.38 (= 2.82/0.52) in order to replicate the performance of the first-tier NIEs. For India and Indonesia, the expansion factors are 3.91 and 1.45 respectively. It is interesting to note that, with the exception of Indonesia, the second-tier NIEs lie even further above the cross-country norm than do those of the first-tier.

We can now estimate what would happen to manufactured exports from developing countries, were they to replicate the trade performance of the first-tier NIEs. Manufactured exports to the North would rise by a factor of 5.38 in the case of China, 3.91 in India, 1.45 in Indonesia and so on. In those countries where the expansion factor is below unity we assume no change in exports. The combined effect of these changes is to increase by 310 per cent the total manufactured exports to the North from the countries covered by Table 4.5. Assuming a similar increase for the developing countries excluded from the table, we estimate that manufactured exports from the South to the North in 1990 would rise from US$116.9 billion to US$479.6 billion. The share of such exports in Northern GDP would rise from 0.7 per cent to 2.9 per cent, and their share in the North's apparent consumption of manufactures from 1.3 per cent to 5.3 per cent (see Case A, Table 4.6).

The preceding estimates are static because they ignore the fact that GDP in the South is rising. In statistical terms, the rapid growth in manufactured exports from the first-tier NIEs to the North has been partly due to an increase in the share of manufactured exports in GDP and partly to the rapid growth in GDP itself. To get a full picture of what it would mean to replicate the experience of these countries, we must allow for the fact that GDP in the South is growing at the same time as these Southern countries are adopting a first-tier style trade orientation. This is done in Case B of Table 4.6. Case B assumes that: (1) countries of the South adopt the same external trade orientation as under Case A; and (2) GDP per capita in the South increases by 100 per cent. Since economic growth in the South would in practice be accompanied by

Table 4.6 Imitating the First-tier NIEs

Manufactured exports from South to North	Actual 1990	Hypothetical	
		A	B
US$ billions	116.9	479.6	1602.0
Per cent of Northern GDP	0.7	2.9	7.0
Per cent of apparent consumption of manufactures in the North	1.3	5.3	12.7

Note: 'South' refers to all developing countries excluding the first-tier NIEs. Hypothetical values assume that Southern countries are at least as export-oriented in manufactures as the first-tier NIEs (after adjusting for per capita income and population). Variant A assumes that per capita income in each country is unchanged; Variant B assumes the per capita income in the South increases by 100 per cent, whilst in the North GDP and consumption of manufactures increase by 40 per cent.

For Comparison: External Imports of Manufactures

	EEC	North America	Japan
US$ billions (1990)	268.2	325.0	92.0
Per cent of GDP (1990)	4.4	5.4	3.1
Per cent of apparent consumption (1990–91)	10.4	11.8	6.3

some growth in the North, Case B assumes that Northern GDP and apparent consumption of manufactures both increase by 40 per cent. Further details are given in the Appendix.

The effect of combining first-tier style trade orientation with economic growth in the South is dramatic. Compared with the actual situation in 1990, manufactured exports to the North are almost 14 times greater. Despite economic growth in the North, their share of Northern GDP rises from 0.7 per cent to 7.0 per cent, whilst their share of the North's apparent consumption of manufactures rises from 1.3 per cent to 12.7 per cent. Note that these figures refer to the South excluding the first-tier NIEs, which would continue to be major exporters to the North.

To achieve the average degree of penetration of Northern markets envisaged in Case B, the South would require to make massive inroads into many activities at present dominated by Northern producers, whilst simultaneously driving Northern producers out of areas, such as clothing and household electrical goods, where they still retain a significant presence. One can only speculate as to the identity of the former activities, but motor cars are an obvious example. Japanese and Korean car firms are currently investing, or planning to invest, on a large scale in Europe to serve the local market. A major factor behind this investment must be a fear of protection, which the Uruguay Round has not assuaged. If free trade were truly guaranteed, it would be more rational for these firms to locate their production in such countries as India or China, and then ship their output to the advanced countries. American car firms are already doing this in the case of Mexico, and the firms of other countries might follow their example under free trade.

The counterpart to massive exports from South to North would be the export of other types of manufactured goods, together with modern services, in the opposite direction. Such a development would have major implications for the economic structure of the North, hitting certain kinds of labour and certain regions badly, whilst benefiting others. In particular, it would exacerbate the difficulties faced by unskilled workers in the North, who have already suffered from the twin blows of technical change and imports from such countries as Korea and Taiwan. The scale of restructuring in the North would be much greater than what has already occurred due to competition from the South, and it could provoke widespread fear and resentment in the North. Amongst those affected would be not merely the obvious losers, such as the unskilled, but also many of the apparent beneficiaries, whose gain from cheap imports might be overshadowed by the insecurity arising from accelerated structural change.

The extent of these emotions and their political impact on the North would depend on macro-economic circumstances. In an expansionary environment, with high investment and rising output in the North, there would be new jobs available to replace those destroyed by Southern competition, and the structural changes involved could be absorbed fairly smoothly. Some people would still feel resentful and there would still be some fear, but these emotions would be less widespread and there would be fewer demands for protection against Southern imports. Conversely, with the kind of depressed demand conditions which have characterized the North over the past 20 years, the scale of import penetration envisaged here would cause profound social problems in the North. Demands for action against the South would multiply and the result would probably be a new wave of protectionism in the North. The North may have committed itself under the Uruguay Round to more open markets, but it is doubtful if this commitment would survive in the face of widespread economic distress.

Other evidence on the fallacy of composition

This section reviews briefly two empirical studies which have a bearing on the fallacy of composition argument. Faini *et al.* (1990) estimate price and income elasticities of demand for a sample of 23 developing countries. They find that the elasticity of developing country exports with respect to developed country income may be lower than previously estimated by other authors. They conclude that the export success of some Asian countries may be predicated on the failure of other developing countries to compete effectively in world markets. Estimated price elasticities for individual countries are quite high, but this is mainly because lower prices lead to more exports at the expense of other developing countries. Simulations suggest that most of the benefit from lower export prices disappears when other developing countries also reduce their prices.

In contrast to the work just reviewed, Martin (1993) is sceptical of the fallacy of composition argument because it is supposedly based on partial equilibrium reasoning, and ignores amongst other things the fact that successful increases in exports increase income levels which, in turn, increase the demand for imports. To correct this deficiency, he uses a simple global general equilibrium model with 13 trading regions and three commodities: manufactured exports, other goods and services, and non-traded goods. The composition of demand in each region is derived from a nested set of constant elasticity of substitution (CES) consumption functions. Commodities from different regions are assumed to be imperfect substitutes for each other, and the elasticity of substitution between them is assumed to be constant. Using this general equilibrium model, Martin conducts a number of simulations designed to explore the fallacy of composition argument. He finds that the static gains from trade liberalization are small, and sometimes negative when terms of trade losses outweigh the efficiency gains obtained from liberalization. However, if export growth is propelled by investment and technological advances, increases in exports from developing countries are mutually reinforcing rather than competitive. On the basis of this finding, he strongly rejects the fallacy of composition argument.

Martin's paper has several weaknesses. The first is his use of very broad aggregates and very high elasticities of substitution between the products of different regions. There is no distinction between manufactures of different types, and elasticities of substitution between the products from different regions are assumed to be 3.0 under all circumstances.

These are extremely misleading assumptions if the purpose is to examine the fallacy of composition argument with regard to manufactured exports from developing countries to the North. They ensure that no matter what type of manufactured goods the South exports, and no matter how much the South has already exported, the price elasticity of demand in the North for the exports of a single region, or for the developing countries as a whole, will remain high. Thus, no matter how much clothing the South exports to the North, only a modest reduction in prices is required to gain a further substantial increase in exports. Moreover, the price elasticity of demand in the North is just the same whether the South exports clothing or machinery.

Martin's analysis is also open to criticism for ignoring the costs involved in large scale restructuring in the North, and the difficulty of re-deploying the human and material resources displaced by competition from large scale Southern imports. It is these costs, the impact of which is unevenly spread, that account for the potential opposition to free trade in the North and underlie the warnings of such authors as Cline (1982) that large scale imports from the South might lead to protection. Martin responds to this warning by pointing out, correctly, that greater imports from the South would be matched by greater exports from the North. Moreover, taking efficiency gains into account, overall GDP in the North would rise. But, this does not really address the issue. As Wood (1994), Rowthorn (1995) and many others have pointed out, the restructuring associated with a new international division of labour could lead to unemployment, increased wage dispersion and poverty for many in the North, especially the unskilled. Martin is able to ignore these dangers completely because his simulations assume that full employment is maintained at all times and that the benefits of trade are uniformly spread throughout the population of each region.

Given his assumptions about employment, income distribution and elasticities of substitution, it is not surprising that Martin can reject the fallacy of composition argument in such a robust fashion. His model contains none of the features which might lead to market saturation in the North for the type of exports which poorer developing countries can most easily supply, nor those features which could stimulate protectionist sentiments in the North. On the other hand, his model does stress several important features which are underplayed by the export pessimists. The first is that trade liberalization would lead to an increase of trade in both directions between North and South, stimulating Northern exports and raising per capita income. The former would directly create employment in export industries, whilst the latter would increase the demand for labour in the non-traded sector, thereby helping to offset the loss of jobs in import-competing activities. These general equilibrium effects are simulated in Rowthorn (1995) which allows for unemployment and inequality, features that are ignored by Martin. Another strength of Martin's analysis is his stress on the importance of South–South trade, and the potential for increasing exports between developing countries. However, it is doubtful whether such trade would be sufficient to permit the degree of external orientation that certain Asian NIEs have displayed during their export-led growth.

FDI-led exports: the Malaysian example

The second-tier NIEs of South East Asia differ from those of the first tier in a number of ways. The latter are poor in natural resources and, with the exception of Singapore, their post-war economic growth was based initially on traditional labour-intensive manufactured exports, above all clothing. In contrast, the second-tier NIEs were rich in natural resources and were able to achieve relatively high per capita incomes on the basis of exports of primary commodities such as rubber, petroleum, and food. Their exports of traditional labour-intensive goods have been rising in recent years, but such exports will never be as important as they were in Hong Kong, Korea, or Taiwan, where fibres, textiles, and clothing still accounted for well over a third of manufactured exports and 30 to 45 per cent total exports in 1970 (Table 4.7).

If we exclude Singapore, which is a special case because of its role as an entrepôt and petroleum-refining centre, we can identify two paths of post-war development in East Asia. The first-tier NIEs started by exporting traditional labour-intensive manufactures, and then moved on to modern exports such as machinery and electronic goods. The second-tier NIEs began by exporting primary products and then moved directly to the export of modern goods without relying so heavily on traditional manufactured exports. The contrast is most extreme in the case of Malaysia, where exports of machinery and equipment have mushroomed and are now more than six times as large as those of fibres, textiles, and clothing (Table 4.7). Most of these modern exports are produced by TNCs, which have incorporated Malaysia into their production hierarchies, using the country as a location for low and medium-skill activities in the electronics industry. This is reflected in the high import content of Malaysia's manufactured exports.

Table 4.7 Composition of East Asian Visible Exports, 1970–92 (percentage shares)

	Total (millions)	Primary products[a]	Manufactures	Machinery & equipment	Textiles, clothes & fibres
Hong Kong					
1970	2 037	4.3	95.7	11.8	44.3
1980	19 704	8.9	91.1	19.5	28.2
1992	119 567	8.0	92.0	25.6	13.8
Korea					
1970	830	23.5	76.5	7.2	41.1
1980	17 451	10.5	89.5	20.3	29.9
1992	76 394	7.2	92.8	40.3	20.3
Singapore					
1970	1 554	72.5	27.5	11.0	5.6
1980	19 376	56.9	43.1	26.8	4.3
1992	63 386	23.3	76.7	52.1	4.7
Taiwan					
1970	1 429	24.2	75.8	16.7	29.0
1980	19 838	12.1	87.9	24.7	21.8
1992	81 337	7.1	92.9	48.0	15.1
Indonesia					
1970	1 055	98.8	1.2	0.3	0.2
1980	21 909	97.7	2.3	0.5	0 7
1992	33 816	52.5	47.5	3.8	18.1
Malaysia					
1970	1 687	93.5	6.5	1.6	0.7
1980	12 945	81.2	18.8	11.5	2.9
1991	34 375	39.4	60.6	38.0	6.0
Philippines					
1970	1 060	92.5	7.5	0.1	5.5
1980	5 751	78.9	21.1	1.8	9.3
1992	9 790	58.7	41.3	1.1	13.2
Thailand					
1970	685	95.3	4.7	0.1	7.5
1980	6 369	74.8	25.2	5.9	10.0
1991	28 324	34.5	65.5	21.8	17.4
China					
1970	6 328	58.2	41.8	1.5	
1980	18 270	52.2	47.5	2.9	
1992	84 940	21.3	78.7	14.8	30.8

Note: [a] Food and agricultural products, petroleum, minerals, etc.
Source: UNCTAD, *Handbook of International Trade and Development Statistics, 1993.*

Malaysia is often cited as an example of what FDI-led exports can achieve and as a model which other developing countries should emulate. The Malaysian experience has three aspects which are relevant in this context: (1) the export of primary products during the initial phase of economic growth, (2) a spectacular expansion of manufactured exports to the advanced countries of the North during the ensuing phase of growth, and (3) a heavy reliance on inward investment by TNCs throughout the entire process. To what extent can these aspects be replicated by poorer countries seeking to develop their economy?

Primary products

For a country to earn a substantial revenue from the export of primary products, it must be able both to produce these exports and to sell them at an adequate price. Many poor countries in Africa and Latin America have a large endowment of natural resources and could increase their primary product exports dramatically. This is not generally the case in Asia, where the population lives mainly in countries such as Bangladesh, China and India with small endowments of natural resources and no potential to supply primary exports on the per capita scale observed in Malaysia. In addition, there is the question of markets. A large increase of primary product exports from the developing countries could lead to a collapse in prices, nullifying most of the gains from greater production and realizing the fears expressed by economists such as Prebisch and Singer. Thus, both supply and demand considerations make it difficult to generalize the Malaysian example of financing the initial phase of economic growth through primary product exports, although this is certainly a possibility for some individual countries.

Manufactured exports to the North

In 1990, manufactured exports from Malaysia to the advanced countries of the North were equivalent to 21.1 per cent of GDP, which is one of the highest shares in the developing world. After adjusting for population and per capita income, Malaysian exports were seven times higher than the cross-country norm, which is an even greater divergence than that registered by Singapore and other first-tier NIEs (Table 4.5). We have already discussed how difficult it would be to generalize the export performance of the first-tier NIES. To replicate the Malaysian performance would be even more difficult.

Foreign Direct Investment

On both a per capita basis and relative to GDP, Malaysia had one of the largest stocks of inward FDI in the developing world in 1990. Since then, it has also been one of the largest recipients. UN statistics indicate that China has received more FDI than Malaysia in absolute terms, but spread over its huge population the inflow is small, averaging around US$13 per capita in recent years, as compared to US$240 for Malaysia (Table 4.8). The contrast is even more striking in the case of India, where the inflow of FDI averaged US$0.2 per capita in this period. These disparities highlight the difficulties which developing countries will face if they seek to base their economic growth primarily on inward investment as Malaysia has done. Malaysia has succeeded because it has managed to attract a grossly disproportionate share of the total FDI going to the developing world. For other developing

Table 4.8   Inward FDI into Selected Developing Countries, 1990–93

Country	FDI Stock 1990			FDI Inflow 1991–93 (annual average)		
	Dollars (millions)	US$ per head	% of GDP	Dollars (millions)	US$ per head	% of 1990 GDP
Hong Kong	13 413	2 351	17.9	1 419	248.9	1.9
Korean Rep.	7 874	184	3.1	1 112	25.9	0.4
Singapore	32 355	11 961	88.6	6 149	2 273.2	16.8
Taiwan	9 735	481	6.2	1 022	50.5	0.7
First-tier NIEs	63 377	886	12.1	9 702	135.7	1.9
Indonesia	38 883	218	36.6	1 754	9.9	1.7
Malaysia	14 117	799	33.0	4 273	241.8	10.0
Philippines	2 098	35	4.7	512	8.4	1.2
Thailand	7 980	145	9.3	1 948	35.3	2.3
China	14 135	12	4.0	14 346	12.6	4.0
India	1 667	2	0.7	201	0.2	0.1
Other Asia	30 977	177	12.7	1 557	8.9	0.6
Argentina	8 778	271	6.2	4 308	133.0	3.0
Brazil	37 143	250	7.8	1 076	7.2	0.2
Chile	6 175	469	20.3	688	52.3	2.3
Mexico	27 856	330	11.4	4 685	55.4	1.9
Other L. America	18 492	141	9.8	2 871	21.9	1.5
Africa	20 482	106	11.9	1 123	5.8	0.6

Note: The countries in this table are the same as in Table 4.3.
Source: UNCTAD, *World Investment Report, 1995*.

countries to attract investment on anything like the Malaysian scale, it would require a gigantic increase in the total flow of FDI into the South.

This can be illustrated by some simple calculations. Excluding the first-tier NIEs, the flow of foreign direct investment into the developing countries averaged US$16.5 per capita, or 1.4 per cent of GDP over the period 1991–93. For Malaysia, the figures were US$241.8 and 10.0 per cent respectively. Table 4.9 considers two hypothetical cases. In Case A, it is assumed that the average developing country receives the same per capita inflow of FDI as Malaysia. To achieve such an outcome would require a fifteen-fold increase in foreign direct investment going to developing countries and the total figure would be approximately US$2,000 billion annually. This is 3.5 times the total manufacturing investment of the entire OECD, excluding Mexico and Turkey (Table 4.10). In Case B, the objective is more modest, foreign direct investment into the average developing country is equal to the same share of GDP as in Malaysia. Even this outcome would require a seven-fold increase in FDI and the flow would be equal to 1.7 times the total manufacturing investment of the North.

These figures indicate clearly the huge amount of FDI needed for the average developing country to replicate the Malaysian experience. It seems inconceivable that the existing countries of the North, together with new capital exporters such as Korea or Taiwan, will provide FDI on anything like the required scale. Indeed, as more developing countries seek to attract foreign investment, the competition for such investment is likely to intensify, so that even Malaysia may be forced to rely less on outside firms and more on its own capacities.

Table 4.9 The Implications of Imitating Malaysia for FDI

	FDI inflow (1991–93 annual average)		
	Dollars billions	*US$ per head*	*% of 1990 GDP*
Malaysia	12.8	241.8	10.0
Developing countries (excluding first-tier NIEs)			
Actual	136.8	16.5	1.4
Hypothetical A	2007.8	241.8	20.9
Hypothetical B	957.7	115.3	10.0

Note: Hypothetical estimate A assumes that FDI per capita in the average developing country (excluding first-tier NIEs) is the same as in Malaysia; Hypothetical B assumes that the ratio of FDI to GDP is the same as in Malaysia.

Table 4.10 Gross Domestic Fixed Capital Formation in the North in 1992 (US$ billion at current prices and 1990 exchange rates)

	Whole economy (1)	Manufacturing (2)	Ratio (2)/(1)	Basis of estimated ratio
Canada	115.9	11.8	0.10	
US	932.5	122.3	0.13	
Japan	968.2	176.6	0.18[a]	as Germany
Australia	61.5	6.3	0.10[a]	as Canada
New Zealand	7.6	0.8	0.10[a]	as 1989
Austria	42.1	6.6	0.16[a]	as 1991
Belgium	38.5	9.4	0.24	
Denmark	19.7	3.1	0.16	
Finland	24.1	3.9	0.16	
France	247.8	36.6	0.15	
Germany	402.7	73.5	0.18	
Greece	17.6	2.6	0.15	
Iceland	1.1	0.1	0.10	
Ireland	7.5	1.2	0.17	
Italy	219.5	41.0	0.19	
Luxembourg	2.7	0.4	0.14[a]	as 1991
Netherlands	59.8	9.1	0.15[a]	as 1991
Norway	23.8	2.5	0.10[a]	as 1991
Portugal	19.8	4.8	0.24[a]	as 1989
Sweden	40.2	5.0	0.12	
Spain	117.1	28.7	0.24[a]	as Portugal
Switzerland	56.4	10.3	0.18[a]	as Germany
UK	170.4	22.6	0.13[a]	as 1991
Total	3596.2	579.1	0.16	

Notes: [a] Share of manufacturing estimated.
OECD *National Accounts* do not give manufacturing investment for Japan, Australia, Austria, Spain or Switzerland, the estimates in this table are based on the investment share of manufacturing in a similar country, as shown in the final column. In some cases, a detailed breakdown is not available for 1992; in such cases the 1992 share of manufacturing is estimated from published information for the year shown.
Source: OECD, *National Accounts, 1992.*

Policy implications for developing countries

The arguments presented in this chapter have implications for developing countries in the realms of both trade and FDI.

Trade

It has been argued that the developing countries cannot simultaneously grow by seeking to export traditional labour-intensive products on the scale observed in Hong Kong, Korea and Taiwan. What are the alternatives? There are several possibilities.

a) A few at a time

The first possibility is that economic development occurs in geographical sequence, with relatively small populations involved at a time. A few restricted geographical areas – small countries or regions – might grow rapidly on the basis of explosive exports of labour-intensive products to the advanced economies. As these areas mature, their exports of such goods would start to fall and production would move on to the next rank of developing areas, which in their turn would become dynamic exporters of labour-intensive products to the North, and so on until the whole world has industrialized. This is the sequence of events foreseen by some versions of the 'flying geese' theory. It is theoretically possible, but it ignores two things. The process would take several centuries, since only a small fraction of the developing world could be involved at a time in exporting labour-intensive products to the North on the per capita scale achieved by the first-tier NIEs. Furthermore, economic development is already occurring more rapidly than this scenario assumes. The second-tier NIEs, the coastal provinces of China, the dynamic parts of India and Latin America, have a combined population of around one billion. There is no way that even these areas can rely on labour-intensive exports to the degree that the first-tier NIEs did.

b) Diversify the export mix

A second possibility is for aspiring countries to export to the North on the same scale as the first-tier NIEs in their earlier development phase, but to rely on a wider product mix. In addition to traditional labour intensive products, such as clothing and toys, they could export products to the North which require a greater input of modern skills, but which are still within their capabilities. This is what the second-tier NIEs seem to be doing, but the obstacles to generalizing their performance are formidable since the required scale of exports to the North is massive.

c) South–South trade

Another possibility is to rely less on exports of any kind to the advanced economies. The larger developing countries could pursue a more inward-looking strategy than was followed by the first-tier NIEs, whilst the smaller countries could trade with each other. In this context, it is important to recognize that development is a very uneven process, and that some areas will grow much faster than others. As income levels between countries or between regions of the same country diverge, the conditions for specialization and trade will spontaneously develop. For example, Shanghai now has a per capita income more than seven times that of the poorest province of China, Guizhou. As Shanghai and the surrounding area continues to develop, labour-intensive production will migrate to cheaper parts of the country and the region will be forced to specialize in more advanced kinds of production.

d)   Import restrictions

The South exports to the North in order to purchase capital and intermediate goods. The more the South imports from the North, the more it must export in return, and the greater the likelihood of flooding Northern markets and of protectionist reactions in the North. In these circumstances, developing countries' balance of payments considerations may necessitate restricting imports of consumer goods, which will require the use of existing, or new, policy instruments that will both effectively restrict such consumption and are compatible with their WTO commitments.

The eventual outcome is likely to be a mixture of all of these possibilities. If protection declines in the North, there will be greater exports from the South of traditional labour-intensive products. The more developed countries or regions of the South will also increase their exports of more sophisticated products to the North. There will be a great deal of trade within the South, much of it internal to the large countries which have economies that will never be as open as those of their smaller counterparts. The less developed countries and regions will export resources or traditional labour-intensive products to the more developed countries in the South, which will sell their more advanced manufactures in return. Many of the latter goods will themselves contain a large input of sophisticated imports from the North. The result will be a hierarchical division of labour with the developed countries of the North at the apex, and the countries and regions of the South strung out behind them in 'wild-geese' formation. Such a division of labour is compatible with many different trade regimes, and many developing countries may continue to restrict imports for balance of payments reasons or to encourage domestic production. These restrictions will have to be compatible with Uruguay Round commitments, but in view of ambiguities in the relevant documents, the room for manoeuvring ability may be greater than it appears.

Foreign Direct Investment

Developing countries have become more receptive to foreign direct investment, and Malaysia is often cited as an example of what FDI-driven growth can achieve. The chapter has argued that Malaysia has succeeded because it has managed to attract a grossly disproportionate share of the total FDI going to the developing world. For the developing countries as a whole to attract investment on anything like the Malaysian scale would require an inconceivable increase in the total flow of FDI going to the South. Instead of seeking to replicate such an extreme example, a more realistic model for the average developing country to emulate might be Thailand, where FDI has played a strategic role in certain key sectors, but has been numerically small compared to the overall development effort.[3] For the major countries of Asia (Bangladesh, China, India, Indonesia, and Pakistan) to attract per capita investment on the scale of Thailand would require an annual inflow of FDI equal to approximately US$80 billion. This is an ambitious objective, but it is not beyond the bounds of possibility.

Notes

1 According to the UN *Handbook of International Trade and Development Statistics* (1993 edition, Table 7.1), the shares of apparent consumption of clothing in 1990–91 in the European Economic Community (EEC), United States of America (USA), Canada and Japan combined were as follows: imports from developing countries – 22.42 per cent, imports from Eastern Europe – 6.16 per cent, other external imports – 2.17 per cent.
2 The estimated function and the sample of countries are described in the Appendix.
3 Over the period 1991–93, FDI accounted for 5.0 per cent of gross domestic fixed capital formation in Thailand.

Appendix

This appendix describes some of the methods underlying Tables 4.5 and 4.6.

Table 4.5

The cross country-norm shown in Column (2) is derived by estimating the following equation for the year 1990:

$$\log(X_i/Y_i) \quad = \quad 13.405 + 0.791 * \log(y_i) - 2.959 * \log(N_i) + 0.0945 * \log(N_i))^2$$
$$\qquad\qquad\quad (1.25) \qquad\qquad (4.28) \qquad\qquad (-2.29) \qquad\qquad (2.40)$$

$$R^2 \qquad = \quad 0.310$$

where X_i/Y_i = manufactured exports from Country i to the North as a percentage of GDP, y_i = per capita income in US dollars, N_i = population; t-values are shown in parentheses. The above equation easily passes the Lagrange multiplier tests for functional form, normality and heteroscedasticity.

The developing countries in the sample used to estimate this equation are as follows: Hong Kong, Republic of Korea, Singapore, Taiwan Province, Indonesia, Malaysia, Philippines, Thailand, China, India, Cyprus, Fiji, Israel, Jordan, Malta, Mauritius, Oman, Pakistan, Papua New Guinea, Saudi Arabia, Sri Lanka, Syrian Arab Republic, Argentina, Brazil, Chile, Mexico, Barbados, Bolivia, Colombia, Costa Rica, Ecuador, El Salvador, Guatemala, Honduras, Jamaica, Nicaragua, Panama, Paraguay, Peru, Surinam, Trinidad and Tobago, Uruguay, Venezuela, Egypt, Algeria, Cameroon, Kenya, Madagascar, Malawi, Mali, Morocco, Senegal, Tunisia, and Zimbabwe. The remaining countries in the sample are: Hungary, Poland and Romania. The data were obtained from the UNCTAD database.

Table 4.6

For those developing countries included in Table 4.5 and for which Col(4) > 1, hypothetical exports in Case A are derived by multiplying actual exports by Col(4). For countries in the table with Col(4) < 1, hypothetical exports in Case A are the same as actual exports. For developing countries not covered by Table 4.5, hypothetical exports in Case A are derived by increasing actual exports by the same percentage as the average country included in Table 4.5 (except for the first-tier NIEs). Case B is derived from Case A by multiplying exports by a factor of $2^{(1+0.791)}$, where 0.791 is the elasticity of the export ratio X/Y with respect to per capita income y, as given by the above regression equation.

5
The Global Financial Casino

Hazel Henderson

Ever since the collapse of the Bretton Woods system in 1971, the global financial non-system has been characterized by increasing turbulence, mounting debt, widening poverty gaps within and between countries and a de-coupling of finance and currency flows from the real world economies of production, trade, and consumption that money is supposed to facilitate and measure. International financial operations escape national regulations and are centred in London, New York, Tokyo, Hong Kong, Singapore, and offshore tax havens: Switzerland, the Cayman Islands, the British Virgin Islands, Cyprus, Antigua, Liechtenstein, Panama, the Netherlands Antilles, the Bahamas, Luxembourg, and Jersey in the Channel Islands. More than 20 000 corporations are chartered in the Cayman Islands and deposits in its 575 chartered banks now total some $500 billion. Only 106 of these banks have a physical presence in Cayman and an estimated 1.5 million of such corporations now operate 'offshore' in secrecy – up from 200 000 in the late 1980s. Americans account for some 40 per cent of these assets (Morgenthau 1998).

The enormous lag between today's economic globalization and economics theories and textbooks with their assumptions of efficient markets, general economic equilibrium, rational actors in markets with perfect information all operating with negligible impacts on innocent bystanders and the environment have been detailed elsewhere (Henderson 1981/88; 1995; 1996/97). This theoretical lag has played a key role in justifying the existing system and entrapping millions in poverty, unemployment, under-employment, and in the loss of previously self-reliant livelihoods. Meanwhile, the promise of rising standards of living via Gross National Product (GNP)-measured economic growth was purveyed by similarly trained academic macroeconomists in both industrial and developing countries.

One thing has been learned in the past decade's tug-of-war between governments and market players: markets *need* rules. Democracies use two forms of feedback from individuals to decision-makers: *prices* in the market and *votes* to determine policies. But prices must be correct (including social and environmental costs) and votes must be uncorrupted by money. Even free market ideologues acknowledge that 'free' markets rely on government regulations of property rights, contracts, national and international law, accounting rules and disclosure, enforcement, police, courts, reliable tax collection (for infrastructure, health, education, and other public services) and civic values. Absent such social institutions, markets descend into anarchy, criminality, violence, and the mafia. Yet, *laissez faire* beliefs that markets are self-correcting die hard.

At the United Nations Earth Summit in Rio de Janeiro, 1992, I called for the retraining of consulting economists in more relevant disciplines: chaos and systems theory, game theory, ecology, biology, cultural anthropology, and social psychology. Unlike doctors, unlicensed economists can make whole countries sick and are quite unaccountable. Of course, economists are not alone in promoting the obsolete paradigm of the 'Washington Consensus': more free trade, liberalization, deregulation, opening up of domestic economies, privatization and exportled GNP growth. These failed remedies are still promoted by their employers: the World Bank, the International Monetary Fund (IMF), the Bank for International Settlements (BIS), the Organization for Economic Cooperation and Development (OECD), and most of the private market players, banks and global companies that benefit from these current institutional arrangements. The world's secretive private banking services (for clients with over $1 million) have risen from $4.3 trillion in 1986 to $10 trillion in 1997 and projecting $13.6 trillion by 2000. The largest players are Union Bank of Switzerland ($580 billion), Credit Suisse ($290 billion), and in the USA Citibank, Chase and Merrill Lynch (with $100 billion each).

At last, the social and environmental costs of fifty years of these 'Washington Consensus' policies are now visible. The horrendous price in human misery and environmental devastation became evident in 1997 as the Asian crisis spread from Thailand throughout the region. The world saw how the traditional money-denominated scorecards of wealth and progress, the Gross National Product (GNP) and its narrower version the Gross Domestic Product (GDP) together with less than full-cost prices have helped steer the world off course. New alternative indicators of quality of life and sustainable human development are bridging the theoretical gaps, such as the United Nations Human Development Index (HDI), the World Bank's Wealth Index, launched in 1995, as well as my own Country Futures Indicators (CFI) (Henderson 1996), the first version of which is the Calvert-Henderson Quality of Life Indicators for the USA, soon to be accessible on the web-site of the Calvert Group, Inc. family of socially-responsible mutual funds (see *www.calvertgroup.com*).

From GNP to Quality of Life Indicators

It is now imperative for the common good that national accounts in all countries and the United Nations System of National Accounts (UNSNA) include caring unpaid work to maintain family and community life. These changes have been recommended by me and an ethical minority of economists since the UNSNA was set up in the 1950s, after being designed originally to maximize war production in the United Kingdom during the Second World War. In 1995, the United Nations Development Program (UNDP) produced an estimate of $16 trillion of such unpaid caring volunteer work, simply missing from 1995 global GDP of $24 trillion (UNDP 1995), illustrating the enormity of this omission.

Such unpaid work (parenting, caring for old and sick family members, growing food for family and community needs, maintaining households, volunteering in community service, do-it-yourself home and community construction and repair projects) makes up some 50 per cent of all production in OECD countries and some 60–65 per cent in developing countries – depending on the size of their traditional village-based and indigenous economies (Henderson 1973; 1978). The environmentalists' critique of the UNSNA has been the most insistent and many 'green GDP' alternatives have been proposed such as Physical Quality of Life Index by David Morris (Henderson 1981) and the Index of Sustainable Economic Welfare of Herman Daly and John Cobb (Daly and Cobb 1989) now calculated in many versions in OECD countries including the UK and Sweden.

We measure according to our dominant cultural view of what is valuable. When GNP/GDP accounts were set up in the Second World War, bombs, bullets and war production were the goal, while the value of children, a healthy educated citizenry, infrastructure, social safety nets and the environment, were all set at zero. This statistical viewpoint is still perpetuated – not only by bureaucratic inertia but by the sectors, interest groups and politically powerful forces amplified by such a system of national accounts. Military budgets remain off-limits while social safety nets, health, education, environment and even repairs to infrastructure are pushed down national budget priority lists. A subtle disintermediation has occurred, slowly devaluing employment, caring work, parenting, social services and safety nets while over-valuing finance itself, i.e. paper asset-shuffling. The financial services sectors grew ninefold, out of all proportion to the real economies of Main Street they were designed to track and serve (Dembinski and Schoenberger 1998). This same sort of disintermediation has also devalued the commodities sector and natural resources, currently at a 12-year low. One could simply make more money by holding and trading financial assets.

Many critics have pointed out over the past 25 years that this over-blown finance sector was a 'bubble' and when it deflated, as on 19 October 1987, Main Street and the world's traditional resource and human-capital based economies of the world would actually benefit (*Utne Reader*, August 1997). Even though cyber-libertarians, internet entrepreneurs and electronic currency traders do not like earthbound constraints, the laws of thermodynamics still operate. One cannot fill a car's gas tank with a 'virtual gallon of petrol' or drive across the 'flow of services' of a bridge. All this was pointed out by Nicholas Georgescu-Roegen in his *The Entropy Law and the Economic Process* in 1971.[1] Although improvements in communications and materials sciences have since led to a profound de-materializing of OECD economies – today's debates involve the extent to which this process, which futurist Buckminster Fuller called 'ephemeralization', can continue substituting knowledge and communications for natural resources. Here is where social and human capital and investments in people and social infra-structure are key inputs. Societies cannot continue de-materializing their economies without investing in maintaining such social architec-ture and human capital for further advances in research (see, for ex-ample, Lamberton 1971). Knowledge, human capital, trust, cohesive values and sound management of the planet's bio-diversity and natural resources are now the key factors of production.

Today, globalizing electronic markets offer a 'fast-forward' view of what we can expect as they accelerate the dominance of the below full-cost price system over diverse traditional values, cultures, and insti-tutions, which form the 'cultural DNA codes' of different societies. Today's global economic crises exacerbated by the unfettered globaliza-tion of financial markets driven by deregulation policies, electronic trading and commerce have eroded the powers of all nation states.

Even the most democratically elected politicians' policies are 'disciplined' by computerized currency and bond traders in today's $1.5 trillion daily global casino (90 per cent of these flows are unrelated to trade or the real economy, i.e., they are speculative). Thus, maintaining adequate domestic macroeconomic policies, and investments in infrastructure, education, research, etc. to maintain social capital and safety nets to cushion unemployment and provide social services, have fallen victim to such volatile unregulated markets and the global financial 'bubble'.

Governments are still responsible

All this does not mean that governments are powerless (see, for example, Weiss 1998). Yet, we still see national governments and politicians ducking these responsibilities, which are often part of their electoral promises to voters. Even the most democratically elected politicians, once attaining office, too often renege on these promises and begin to cast their policies in line with the status quo and special interests. Money has become the curse of democratic political processes in many OECD and developing countries aspiring to become more democratic. Today in the USA, we see the spectacle of scandals and widespread corruption in campaign financing with the resulting catastrophic loss of trust in government. Only 30 per cent of US adults trust their elected representatives and public officials in Washington and the same survey found that US adults actually trusted the UN *more* than their government in Washington (*Americans Talk Issues* 1994).

In Europe, many other scandal-ridden governments put their taxpayers' funds on the global auction block, along with their workforces and natural and environmental resources, in the new global bidding war to lure (bribe) corporations, banks, and financial institutions to locate in their countries. These bidding wars broker taxpayers' funds to subsidize such new corporate facilities, often at absurd costs. For example, the London-based *The Economist* reported (1 February 1997, p. 25) that in 1991, Portugal paid Auto Europa, Ford, and Volkswagen $254 000 per job created, while the state of Alabama, USA, 'bribed' Mercedes-Benz with $167 000 per job created. These enormous corporate subsidies might have financed micro-businesses or provided guaranteed incomes for life to many of these prospective job holders as documented in the *Time* (November 1998; 'What Corporate Welfare Costs', www.time. com). Heads of state troop dutifully to the World Economic Forum in Davos to offer deregulation 'sweeteners,' subsidies, and tax breaks to corporate CEOs. They bargain away their citizens' taxes and sovereignty in the now-familiar global 'race-to-the-bottom.' Cronyism is endemic – not something recently discovered in Asia. This corporate–government collusion in OECD countries and developing countries is spreading world-wide. It is corrupting democracies, and betraying their citizens, voters, employees, and investors. Democracy is perverted world-wide to serve fictitious corporate 'humans': whose charters permit evading liabilities and public accountability.

Corporations' charters, granted by governments, limit their and their officials' liabilities. Worse, these charters allow them all the rights of 'natural persons.' These corporate and financial entities have grown over the years to wield enormous power over their nations' elected and governmental officials. Citizens in most OECD countries, organized for such government protection from corporate irresponsibility, and voters overwhelmingly have passed national laws and regulations. A joint statement was sent to the OECD by a coalition of 565 citizen groups in 68 countries opposed to the Multilateral Agreement of Investment (MAI) as 'a damaging agreement which should not proceed in its current form – if at all.' Many of the MAI's provisions favoured corporations over citizens and would counter already ratified UN protocols on bio-diversity, climate change, as well as the 50 years of UN treaties and standards on human and employee rights and environmental protection. Citizens must now be vigilant in preventing MAI being sneaked in under the IMF. Meanwhile, *The Economist*'s Clive Crook tells us that governments are not in retreat – but getting bigger – citing percentages of nations' GNPs spent by governments. These overall figures do not tell us how much of this government spending is steered by financial and corporate interests into the billions of annual subsidies they enjoy – along with their other legislative priorities, such as the MAI. Indeed, many governments have become corporate 'cash cows' while some have sunk into 'kleptocracies'.

Today, there is increasing alarm expressed by central bankers, finance ministers and market players themselves about the fragility of the global casino. Yet, few concrete steps have been taken to create the much-ballyhooed 'new international financial architecture'. After much huffing and puffing, the Group of 7 announced in Bonn, Germany on 20 February 1999, a new forum 'to assess the issues and vulnerabilities affecting the global financial system and to identify and oversee the actions needed to address them'. The forum of 35 top financial officials of the G-7 countries, the World Bank, the IMF, the BIS, and various regulatory bodies will meet only twice a year and its only authority will be 'peer pressure'. Developing countries will be excluded from the forum, while the new BIS-sponsored Financial Stability Institute will add its own ideas. Such insider-driven, top down approaches are unlikely to address any of the fundamental global issues of concern here.

Understanding the 'New Economy' debate

Today, many different hypotheses concerning the so-called 'New Economy' of information technology in the USA can be seen within today's global context of social system transition. Other hypotheses set local, ethnic, community, and nationalistic backlashes against the backdrop of globalization (see, for example, Møller 1995 and Huntington 1993). These 'New Economy' and other hypotheses stem from different paradigms and interpretations, which produce conflicting forecasts of: productivity, inflation, deflation, effects of the Asian meltdown, etc. Such statistical paradigms underlie GNP/GDP, Purchasing Power Parity (PPP) and Consumer Price Indexes (CPIs), and new approaches seek to include in national accounts, asset balance sheets, social and environmental capital, unpaid work, and externalities. Some of this statistical work is underway, but still under-funded – from retooling GNP/GDP to account for natural and human capital and subtracting social and environment costs to recalculating the CPIs. CPIs should reflect higher quality in some goods and the shift to services.

Macroeconomic policies should also account for the valuable public goods and services that add to quality of life but are unpriced (e.g. police and fire services, infrastructure, health and environmental protection agencies, etc.), without which complex technological economies cannot function. Thus, the US CPI may be overstated by as much 1.5 per cent, as the US Boskin Commission says, or by more than this if the value of unpriced public services are factored in. Energy and food prices continue to be excluded from the 'core' rate – along with depreciation of infrastructure and other national assets. *The Economist* now recommends adding financial and real estate asset inflation to Consumer Price Indexes (9 May 1998). All this statistical revisioning will end up recalibrating US Federal Reserve and other central bank policies and the NAIRU (Non-Accelerating Inflation Rate of Unemployment), as well as the budget, social security, and deficits.

Thus, futurists contend that most economic models in the public and private sector are still backing us into the future looking into the rearview mirror. Human agents *are* still seen as either the guinea pigs in the computer models of fashionable social simulators or as the golf balls or atoms of traditional Newtonian physics. This 'objective' view (which *does* make the mathematics easier!) assumes that all human actions in society are irrelevant, statistically damped out by the Law of Large Numbers. Even powerful producers in many computer models are assumed to have no impact on the structure of the economy. On the contrary, some economists and most futurists acknowledge that financial markets are influenced by large institutions – from governments to global corporations and institutional investors – in increasingly interwoven global real-time networks, where over-shoots and herd behaviour are amplified. Thus, game theory, chaos models and psychology become sharper tools for examining how markets are affected by the interactions of mutual expectations of players. Unfortunately, the 'Artificial Society' models of mathematical economists often program their simulated 'human agents' with the same competitive, self-maximizing, economic behaviour – and, unsurprisingly, recreate poverty gaps and trade wars (see, for example, Epstein and Axtell 1996). The now defrocked '*quants*' and 'rocket scientists' whose computer models calculate the prices of derivatives allowed a 20–40 per cent risk factor due to their own models, but this still led to huge losses. The red-faced Nobel Committee, which awarded the 1997 economic prize to two partners of the ill-fated Long Term Capital Management hedge fund, awarded the 1998 prize to Amartya Sen, who studies poverty and moral issues.

Of course, one or two innovative economists (borrowing models from systems and game theory and from chaos and complex adaptive systems studies) have moved beyond this Industrial Age, Cartesian–Newtonian worldview. For example, the Santa Fe Institute's W. Brian Arthur uses 50-year old cybernetic, feed-back driven systems models to illustrate that in network markets, there are increasing (not diminishing) returns to scale and path-dependency in innovation (i.e., initial conditions will amplify in non-linear systems).[2] This phenomenon underlies Microsoft's market domination. Buddhists call this 'laying down a path in walking'. Stanford University's Paul Romer reminds his fellow economists of what futurists have known for decades: that technology must be incorporated as a key variable in all macroeconomic models. Others include Michael Rothschild revisions economies as 'ecosystems', in terms long familiar to futurists and ecologists and echoing my *Creating Alternative Futures: The End of Economics* (Henderson 1978/96.) Clearly, interdisciplinary dialogues between all these worldviews would create sharper analytical tools.

All this underlies today's pop debate in the financial press about the nature of the 'New Economy' and the explosive US stock market rises and volatility, as well as whether US Federal Reserve Board Chairman Alan Greenspan's new view of the statistical lag in measuring productivity is correct. *Business Week* has frequently editorialized that globalization and the increasing competition it brings, *does* discipline even the biggest firm's pricing – just as it does wages – echoing calls for dumping the Phillips Curve. Even Phillips didn't believe in the Phillips Curve. All this *has* shifted the NAIRU into lower territory so that interest rates *can* be reduced and sustainable economic growth *can* proceed in a new virtuous cycle. All this sounds great as a market 'flow model' (i.e., the conventional monetarist 'bathtub' model of the national economy as a hydraulic system). In the UK, Roger Bootle makes a similar case in his *The Death of Inflation* (1996, 1997), but with a longer time scale interpretation beyond simple monetarism and a more radical conclusion: that OECD economies face a future of deflation. The deflationary effect of the Asian meltdown has not yet been fully felt in the world economy. The US and European stock market declines are still reverberating in the world economy. Indeed, the US and European stock markets have been pumped up with billions in flight capital seeking safer havens. A fast feedback loop is created by the 'herd behaviour' of asset managers who follow asset allocation theory and feel obliged to buy the big indexes: Dow Jones, Standard and Poor's, and London's FTSE100. This herd behaviour effect is reinforced in the USA by the 'prudent man rule,' which prevents asset managers from straying far beyond such blue chip stocks – thereby bidding up the big indexes. I call it 'the prudent lemming rule'.

Beyond these expanded economic models, the less examined other half of the story relates to assets (stocks of built, natural, and human capital) as well as liabilities, debt, and other aspects of restructuring outside much market data and models. Here, the gloomier view of the $1.5 trillion daily global casino emerges, with its $50 trillion in outstanding derivatives positions where individuals hedge their own risks by adding to systemic risks. Today's tidal waves of 'hot money' and speculation challenge central bankers charged with the now-impossible job of managing national economies and currencies. They still foolishly play at the same casino table with highly leveraged, profit-maximizing currency traders, who arbitrage interest rates and national government policies alike (Henderson and Kay 1996). The central bankers, under pressure from banks and financial interests, have stripped themselves of other macroeconomic tools: adjusting bank reserve ratios and stock brokers' margin requirements, as well as capital and currency controls. They now must rely on interest rates alone to cool inflation and financial bubbles. US and European central bankers are now *afraid to use* interest rates to cool their economies, not only because this throws the real economies of Main Street into recession and unemployment, but *also* because too drastic pricks in asset bubbles could cause further global deflation. Thus, central bankers today are left with 'jaw-boning' stock markets about 'irrational exuberance'. Even *The Economist* is re-visiting the issue of unregulated capital flows (23 May 1998, p. 72). A currency-exchange fee of 0.05 per cent is now back on the agenda of many governments. Russia has no option but to restore state control of some areas of its economy – an unfortunate, but understandable back-lash to the human misery of its economic meltdown.

Marginal reforms will not be enough. The G-7's $90 billion 'line of credit' pledged to the IMF on 30 October 1998 to help countries with 'sound economies' to 'ward off the global economic crisis' (i.e. currency speculators) was more orthodoxy and designed to please financial mar-kets. Stock markets rallied world-wide at the prospect of yet more public funds to buttress private markets. The world's taxpayers are aware of the moral hazard involved in bailing out reckless investors. So far, timid debates among G-7, G-10, G-22 leaders have not led to co-ordinated interest rate cuts or promised reform of the International Monetary Fund (IMF). Another global deflation is still imminent – and the dangers of political extremism grow, as they did during the Great Depression and led to the Second World War. In addition, the mountains of un-repay-able debt of the poorest countries must at last be written off. Currency exchange may need to be taxed (Henderson 1996/97; Summers and Summers 1989), unless the central banks implement proposals for a 'public utility' foreign exchange so that they can audit all trades and monitor fraud, money-laundering, tax evasion, speculation, etc. and impose fees and fines (Henderson and Kay 1996). Rhetoric from the G-7 of a 'new roadmap for a new century', increased global financial regulation and 'codes of conduct' for hedge funds and other market players must show results. Germany and France wanted tight controls on international capital flows (a key source of instability), but these were opposed by the USA and the UK (*Financial Times*, 30 October 1998).

More than ever, new multi-disciplinary metrics to measure quality of life must supplement current GNP/GDP systems of national accounts (UNSNAs), which must be corrected to account for social and human capital and ecological assets and unpaid work. Most urgent is the inclu-sion of an asset budget in such national accounts, so as to properly account for infrastructure and other public investments. Such huge investments have been 'expensed' in GNP/GDP – leading to massive budget 'deficits' and overstating of inflation. The USA followed the lead of New Zealand and Switzerland in 1996 in creating such an asset account for its public infrastructure – leading to its fiscal year 1999 budget 'surplus'. With even the London-based *Economist* calling for Japan to start 'printing money', i.e. monetizing its debt (10 October 1998, p. 18), it would surely make more sense to properly account for much of its 'debt' as public assets.

These public investments should be carried – and expensed – over their useful life, often 50–100 years. GNP/GDP are 'cash-flow' statements of money-denominated transactions, with such longer-term investments (infrastructure, education, infant health, etc.) treated as 'consumption' and written off each year. A corporation could not be run that way, that is, as a costly productive facility that could not be amortized over its useful life. This statistical correction reduced the US budget deficit by approximately $100 billion per year, by accounting for some infrastructure assets, but still not education or other investments in human or social capital (such as science, R&D etc.). The USA's budget surplus was also achieved by additional tax collected on Wall Street gains and some $100 billion reduction in still-bloated military expenditures. This budget 'surplus', claimed as the result of superior economic management (certainly improved accounting) attracted billions in flight capital from other jittery markets after Asia's meltdown went global, and to seek safe havens in the US stock and bond markets. Furthermore, if all other countries simply made the same re-calculations to their own GDPs, all would soon show similar budget 'surpluses'. The question is why don't they? Surely, such sensible corrections to all national accounts are preferable to the moral hazards of putting taxpayers at further risk, and become as proposed 'a global write-down of debt' (Editorial, *Business Week*, 7 September 1998).

European Union Member Countries (with an average of 11 per cent unemployment) have cut their domestic safety nets to attain the Maastricht criteria that included 3 per cent or less of budget-deficits. Some years ago, I urged that the Commission's policy staff might check their member nations' GDPs for asset accounts to see if infrastructure investments were missing. This might have saved painful budget cuts and the ensuing political unrest and strikes – particularly in France. The new euro, overseen by the independent European Central Bank (ECB) will constrain domestic economic policies further, exacerbated by the 'growth and stability pact'. Further straitjacketing of fiscal policies will force de-regulation and cuts in employment security and benefits for employees in the eleven euro countries and promote 'labour mobility' between them (i.e. more economic migration with its social costs unaccounted). Likewise, in the current global economic crisis, a great proportion of public debt in Japan, Korea, and other Asian countries, as well as in Europe and Latin America could be reduced along with unemployment by such accounting corrections.[3] It must be emphasized that such asset accounts in GDP should also include investments in long-term social capital (education, health, child development and R&D) to maintain a society's knowledge base and general quality of life. The World Bank's new Wealth Index, introduced in 1995, moves in the right direction – but still has little effect on operations.

Meanwhile, the UNSNA still over-values the goods and artifacts of the receding industrial era, while many OECD economies are approaching the USA's 70 per cent of services. Such services still do not include those of the Love Economy – eroding daily through neglect – in broken families, community breakdown, drugs, inner-city decay, and spreading epidemics such as tuberculosis, once thought contained. Statisticians in the USA are at work overhauling the categories of GNP/GDP, which still are dominated by widgets and goods, to include software, services, knowledge industries and intellectual capital. But the conceptual confusion continues as we proceed further into what I have called the *Age of Light*, based on deeper knowledge of nature and ourselves, and powered by renewable resources and solar energy (Henderson 1995, p. 261–72). Similarly, accounting firms are grappling with 'intellectual capital' and 'good will' in corporate balance sheets – all these overhauls represent the biggest advance in accounting since the invention of double-entry book-keeping. Before we can steer our economic policies back toward the common good, quality of life and sound environmental management, we must complete this accounting revolution. The current globalization of 'bubble finance' and the global economic crises it has exacerbated suggests the need for a crash program to correct all countries' GNP/GDP accounts – a prerequisite for all the other reforms of the global financial architecture now so urgently needed.

Furthermore, economists still bestride the policy process and offer concepts for managing global commons (e.g. ocean fish stocks and bio-diversity) based on extending property rights. They bring along their obsolete models of Pareto Optimality (which assumes away unequal distribution of wealth, power and information). Economists propose to enclose the last commons as 'property régimes' for economic efficiency while omitting the truth that all such schemes are essentially *political* allocations of resources. Futurists and systems theorists see them as closed systems requiring win–win rules. Today, economists are busy calculating the price of rainforests, bio-diversity, watersheds, etc. using opinion surveys of 'Willingness to Pay' (WTP) to preserve such commons. This forces ordinary citizens to bid for such resources (of no direct benefit to them) against commercial developers who would directly benefit. Such absurd WTP-derived 'contingency prices' are hopelessly inaccurate and drastically undervalue common resources. Only calculating replacement costs would suffice but these resources are often irreplaceable. So the task is beyond money equivalents and the skills of economists, and requires interdisciplinary teams and multiple metrics such as the Calvert-Henderson Quality of Life Indicators.

Policy makers fiddle while the crisis rages

Instead of making such needed corrections in national accounts, the G-7 called on governments to make their currency reserves, fiscal and monetary policies more transparent via an 'international code of conduct'. This will be a step forward only if their proposals that similar codes of conduct can be forced on central and private banks, transnational corporations (TNCs) and international speculators. What is needed is nothing short of a new 'Bretton Woods'. Times have changed since the international conference that, in 1944, created the first global economic architecture. The Bretton Woods gathering set up multilateral rules and agencies, including the World Bank and the IMF, which served the world economy until 1971, when Richard Nixon unilaterally pulled the plug by slamming shut the US gold window (removing the gold standard). Since then, the world has lurched from crisis to crisis – through a roller coaster of global recessions, currency gyration, and many ad hoc arrangements for floating currencies, capital movement controls and convertibility rules.

Back in 1995, at the UN Summit on Social Development at Copenhagen, a set of proposals emerged in the report of the Global Commission to Fund the United Nations (Henderson, Cleveland and Kaul 1995). It called for:

- A very small (0.05 per cent) tax on all currency trades, first discussed at Bretton Woods in 1944 and later versions proposed by US economists James Tobin and by Lawrence Summers. Such a tax would not hurt real, long-term investors, but would bite speculators who move money across borders often hundreds of times a day.
- A global version of the US Securities and Exchange Commission (SEC) to harmonize regulations of securities and currency markets. Such an

international supervisory body would curb today's unregulated global casino of insider trading, fraud, money laundering and capital flight. Today, speculators' 'bear raids' attack perceived weak currencies as for example in 1993 when such a raid drove the British pound down and out of the European Monetary Union (EMU).

- The proposal mentioned earlier that the world's major central banks get together and set up their own 'public utility' currency exchanges. Thus they could compete with today's money centre banks and speculators and properly oversee their currencies to protect their domestic purposes, just as they oversee their sovereign bonds.

The new Bretton Woods conference should be convened by the United Nations – to include all countries in designing cooperative new rules needed to tame the global casino. The world needs reformed financial institutions. But they will also need to be based on new accounting systems that can better monitor long-term investments, ecological assets, human and social capital and properly account for the loving services provided unpaid and voluntarily in the caring sectors of all economies. The paradigm error underlying the globalization of markets and market economics also involves its exclusive focus on competition. Such 'win–lose', zero-sum paradigms exist also in nation states, since the Treaty of Westphalia in 1648. Restoring the unaccounted-for role of cooperation at every level of society, and between now-interdependent nations is essential.

The extent to which the world's banks have mismanaged the global economy is only now becoming visible. Short-sighted, imprudent, secretive and badly supervised banking systems, as well as deregulated and virtually unregulated financial markets, changing technology and globalization have been at the heart of these problems (*The Economist*, 26 July 1997, p. 18). The BIS rule on 8 per cent reserve capital requirements, promulgated in 1988, has also proved inadequate.[4] All this costs the world's taxpayers, employees, small businesses and investors dearly. The world's poorest citizens remain the most tragic victims of mal-designed, mal-functioning financial systems and the debacles caused by the false promises of a generation of economists. One bright spot: technical and political challenges were met by the multibillion dollar costs of upgrading computer programs that handle the 'Year 2000 Problem'. Necessary, but not sufficient, is the cancellation of the debt of the most indebted countries, perhaps using US Chapter 9 Municipal Bankruptcy Law as proposed by the Vienna-based Kreisky Forum (Henderson 1996).

In the past few years since the publication of the Henderson and Kay (1996) paper advocating a transparent 'public utility' currency trading system for central banks, global currency markets have become more turbulent as predicted. Recently, we proposed in greater specificity than in our earlier paper, a Foreign Exchange Transaction Reporting System (FXTRS[sm]) for central banks whose specific technological features have been described briefly elsewhere (Henderson and Kay 1999; Henderson 1999). This screen-based 'ticker-tape' system can supplement the beneficial affects of non-technological methods to stabilize and improve these markets, while reducing their social and environmental costs. After the 1997 Asian meltdowns, debates over the need for currency boards, various kinds of capital controls, and taxation of currency trading increased markedly (Henderson 1998).

These debates continued after the Russian default of August 1998 and the near-bankruptcy and bailout of The Long Term Capital Management (LTCM) hedge fund a few weeks later. A consensus on charting proposals to change the world's 'financial architecture' among G-7 finance ministers and central bank governors was announced on 30 October 1998 by Britain's Chancellor of the Exchequer, Gordon Brown (*BBC Online Network*, 30 October 1998). US Federal Reserve Board Chairman Alan Greenspan's speeches to Congress and others explaining the Fed's assistance in the LTCM bailout used similar terminology. Greenspan and then US Treasury Secretary Robert Rubin[5] have referred to the destabilizing role of technology and inter-linked currency markets as requiring this 'new international financial architecture'. Calls for such concerted policy development also came from France, Germany and Britain, whose Prime Minister, Tony Blair proposed a new Bretton Woods conference, and from Canada, whose Finance Minister, Paul Martin urged a new global supervisor of financial supervisory bodies, an idea now widely endorsed. Since then, the introduction of the euro on 2 January 1999 has absorbed eleven formerly traded European currencies – taking them off traders' screens. Many in financial circles believe this has added to the pressure on other remaining important currencies, including those of Hong Kong, Canada, and Australia, the Czech *koruna* and those in Latin America, particularly the Brazilian *real*, which fell 30 per cent after its flotation on 15 Januray 1999. Argentina reacted by raising the possibility that it would abandon its *peso* (already under a currency board) and adopt the US dollar (*The Economist*, 23 January 1999, p. 69). Clearly, the existing international financial architecture – the Bretton Woods Institutions, and the IMF's financial assistance to the Asian economies and Russia, and even its $41 billion standby line of credit to Brazil – has proved inadequate to deal with all the recent volatility and financial contagion.

So far, few new policy initiatives have been offered beyond the standard set of prescriptions within 'the Washington Consensus' paradigm, i.e., exhorting countries to put their domestic economic houses in order, get their fundamentals right and get used to floating exchange rates, whatever their social costs. In this still 'pre-contagion' view, the remedies to prevent currency devaluations and speculative attacks are domestic matters for national policy makers. By now, it must be clear that the new global contagion and volatility can no longer be addressed by nations acting alone. They lie beyond the reach of domestic policy makers' unilateral efforts and long-term solutions are to be found at the global systemic level. Many global proposals were discussed at the Davos, Switzerland World Economic Forum in February 1999, but were vetoed by then US Treasury Secretary, Robert Rubin.

IMF traditional prescriptions and conditionalities imposed on Asia's domestic economies often produced counter-intuitive results. Orderly bankruptcy proceedings for distressed countries became a subject for debate (*The Economist*, 3 October 1998, p. 88). Malaysia took the risky route of closing its capital markets, essentially removing the *ringgit* from the interest of most currency traders. It nevertheless succeeded, in January 1999, in borrowing $1.35 billion from a consortium of 12 international banks at only three percentage points over LIBOR. Other familiar proposals were advanced or tried: trading bands, crawling bands, currency pegs, crawling pegs, fixed parity, raising interest rates, traditional currency intervention, early warning disclosures, currency boards, as well as versions of Chile's successful use of partial controls on short-term inflows. China has more options, with its huge internal market and the limited convertibility of its currency. Yet, most of these individual country-based policies will continue to fail, since they cannot address the now global, systemic nature of technologically interdependent financial markets.

These tightly-linked, real time globalized financial markets and the so-called contagion they create should have come as no surprise. These markets were deliberately deregulated during the 1980s and 1990s. Free markets, trade and privatization became the policy imperatives of many, if not most national governments, as the best path to accelerated GNP-growth. Few heeded the admonition encoded in the 1962 Fleming-Mundell model, still valid today: countries wishing to inter-link their economies in world trade cannot simultaneously achieve: 1) stable exchange rates; 2) autonomy of domestic economic policy; and 3) free global capital flows.[6] Since 1972, when the Bretton Woods system collapsed, national policy makers have been confronted with this axiom: they can achieve two of these goals, but not all three at once.

Other factors have also entered the global currency markets since the so far successful launch of the euro. The dollar had weakened against the *yen* and the euro's initial strength caused much discussion of the expected disintermediation out of dollars into euros. Today this new currency denominates some 30 per cent of world trade. A chorus of financial 'gurus' are urging the linkage of the dollar, the *yen* and the euro into a new de factor global currency regime in bid 'to end currency volatility' (*Business Week*, 25 January 1999, p. 126). Such proposals are unrealistic, due to the rigidity they would impose over vastly different countries, unless national currencies and regional currency unions are strengthened and local currencies are encouraged to co-exist to clear purely local markets (see, for example, Henderson 1996/97, Chapter 9).

Financial cyberspace: the newest global commons

As more citizens and businesses move their transactions into cyberspace, what are some key and broader implications? We address first electronic commerce. Most companies assume that money-based transactions will monopolize cyberspace through better security, encryption systems, credit card handling, and e-cash systems. However, electronic commerce does not *require* money-based transactions, and instead could lead to pure information-based transactions, i.e., high-tech barter. The implications of this are clear: money and information are now equivalent – we are already off the money and gold standard and on the information standard world-wide. Banks thrive on money-based scarcity and, understandably, are trying to control cyberspace transactions. Yet today, billions of dollars of services and goods are bartered each year in the USA by corporations and individuals on PC-based electronic trading networks. The implications for the world's central bankers are clear: if they don't improve their currency issuance and monetary management and control operations – through overhauling the Bretton Woods institutions and making credit widely available, not just to their cronies in governments and corporations – then they will be bypassed by pure information-based transactions. Today's state-of-the-art computer-based markets in cyberspace can make such information-based, high-tech bartering efficient with minimal transactions costs. Developing countries will no longer need to earn foreign exchange but can trade all their commodities among themselves – doing three, four, five and six-way trades with the computers keeping the audit-trails as to settlement agreements (which is what money is and does while also serving as a store of value).

There will be then a need for three different kinds of currency (Henderson 1996/97, Chapter 9): 1) a global reserve currency; 2) national currencies and monetary unions of them, where appropriate; and 3) local currencies to clear purely local markets. Nations will need to regain some of their lost sovereignty in order to maintain their political legitimacy and manage their domestic economies democratically for the benefit of the majority of their citizens. All this will now require international agreements to tax electronic commerce, and global mechanisms to protect human citizens, employees, and investors as opposed to paper financial institutions. There will likely be a shift to 'safe haven', high-tech barter transactions both locally and globally in order to create full employment and clear local markets. Local currencies and PC-based trading systems are flourishing in the USA, Canada, Europe, Australia, and New Zealand. Today, they are needed in Russia. Indeed, they can be used as leading indicators of the incompetence of central banks and macroeconomic management authorities in many countries.

We turn now to the issue of taxation. At the global level, tax-evaders are catered to by increasing numbers of small, island countries and regimes, deliberately offering anonymity, dummy corporations, money-laundering, and tax-havens. Internet-based commerce and internet-based trading make all of this easier (*The Economist*, 31 May 1997, p. 15). Conservative financial advisors are telling investors how to move offshore, obtain duplicate passports and dual citizenship, buy small islands, and suggesting other manoeuvres to evade taxation. Nation-states, now with chronic budget deficits due to tax losses from deregulation, are breaking up and some predict that there will be about 1,300 countries in a few years.

Local governments can resist pressures from global retailers, services chains, and mall developers to displace local merchants. These global TNCs still operate as free riders on taxsupported infrastructures at below-cost energy prices and at the exclusion of many social and environmental costs. This allows them to penetrate local markets with below true cost prices. Then after locals have been put out of business, they can raise prices without their competition. Development banks, local credit unions, and micro-credit groups should be favoured over branches of large national and global banks free riding on the unregulated information-structures of financial cyberspace. These banks, tied into the global casino, accept local deposits and pay-cheques but these funds tend to be 'vacuumed out' of the local branch bank each day onto the global electronic funds transfer systems (EFTS) to be lent out world-wide. At average global interest rates, local communities and businesses can no longer afford these interest rates to borrow back their own deposits for local development purposes. It is also important for local communities to engage in as much barter as necessary, including high-tech exchanges using personal computers, such as local exchange trading systems (LETS) and the many kinds of local scrip currencies now circulating in towns in the USA, Europe, and other OECD countries. These tools can complement scarce national currencies where monetary policy is ill conceived or too restrictive so as to help clear local markets, employ local people, and provide them with alternative local, purchasing power. Indeed, such local currencies in every state and most cities in the USA during the Great Depression helped local communities survive (Mitchell and Shafer 1984).

Perhaps the biggest paradigm shift involves these new information-based electronic markets, which are going from local to global, and were the underlying reason for the take-off of internet-based stocks and Initial Public Offerings (IPOs) of their shares. For example, the success of e-Bay.com, a San Francisco-based start-up, is based on LETS barter networks, offering second-hand auctions over the Internet, except that subscribers negotiate in money terms. The implications for both central banks and private banks are vast. If money-creation and management as well as money-based transactions and credit-availability are not overhauled drastically to serve the new needs of twenty-first century consumers (businesses, employees and investors), they will simply go around banks and money-based transacting to pure information-based transactions from high-tech barter, local scrip currencies, LETS systems to payments unions and counter trade. Banks are busy buying computer and information technology to reimpose scarcity and money-based transactions particularly on electronic commerce via e-cash, credit and debit cards, virtual banking, etc. The new competition from money-free, information-based, high-tech exchange will not go away. Banks and money-based exchange systems are very useful, but they now have competition for their basic functions of intermediation – for which the Internet is ideally suited. For example, a quarter of trading volume on Wall Street now is electronic and bypasses brokers, while floor-based 'open outcry' stock exchanges are being replaced daily. Seats on the New York stock exchange lost half their value in 1998.

I have argued (Henderson 1991, 1996/97) that the newest global commons is the Internet and the World Wide Web as well as financial cyberspace – all largely unregulated and with a host of issues around their use piling up. For example, the Internet's protocol and language codes are still informal and controlled by a handful of early technological innovators and programmers serving as volunteers on ad-hoc standards committees. Worse, while the Internet expands access to information, it is also rife with fraud, criminality and pornography. Little legal underpinning exists for the Internet, a common resource funded by tax dollars and currently overwhelmed by free riders. The next few years should see some kind of 'International Internet Standards and Oversight Agency' to deal with all of these free rider and commons issues, while interfacing with established agencies such as the World Intellectual Property Organization (WIPO) and the International Communications Union (ITU).

Money market players react

The Australian Prime Minister's (John Howard) Task Force on International Financial Reform, chaired by Federal Treasurer Peter Costello, with members including his Secretaries of Finance, Treasury, Foreign Affairs, the Governor of the Australian Central Bank and the CEOs of Australia's four largest banks, released its report of 31 December 1998 (Australian Treasurer, Official Press Release, 31 October 1998, *www. treasury.gov.au*). The Task Force acknowledged that a *global* response was required to address international markets' volatility and recent inappropriate risk assessments and investment decisions in the private sector. The Task Force's overall goal was 'soundly-based and more stable capital flows' with 'reforms needing to be progressed through international grouping, such as the G-22 – with active involvement of the private sector'. The report also stressed enhanced reporting and transparency. Since then, the G-22, convened by the USA in April 1998, was expanded into the G-26, to include smaller countries. Other approaches at the global, international and systemic level have also received attention. They include revived interest in currency exchange taxes. The debate concerning such a tax has been reviewed elsewhere (Henderson and Kay 1996), and since then these proposals have proliferated and received more intense scrutiny in many studies in Europe, the Americas and by the World Bank (ul Haq *et al.* 1996; Soete and Weel 1999).

Economist Jeffrey Sachs, then director of the Harvard Institute for International Development, proposed that the G-7 (now 8) should be expanded to G-16 to include eight democratically-governed developing countries including Brazil, India, South Korea, South Africa, Chile and Costa Rica. Sachs (1998) noted that:

> for a decade, we have had a phoney Washington Consensus – and almost no real discussions between rich and poor countries on the challenges facing a world of greater income inequity than ever before in history. The G-16 would establish parameters for renewed and honest dialogue.

Commenting on the Asian crisis, Sachs adds:

> The IMF worked mightily and wrong-headedly to make the world safe for short-term money-managers. The IMF encouraged central banks from Jakarta to Moscow to Brasilia to raise interest rates to stratospheric levels...investors do not (thus) gain confidence. The more these countries tried to defend their currencies the more they incited panic.

Henderson and Kay (1996) also pointed out this feedback loop regarding interest rate hikes. Many high-level financial officials are now calling for the IMF's role to be expanded to that of a global lender of last resort and also reversing their earlier views on the need for some small and emerging countries to use capital controls (*Business Week*, 8 February 1999, p. 64–77; *The Economist*, 30 January 1999, 'Global Finance'). Few refer to the G-15, a powerful group of developing countries that has met continuously since the late 1980s, and produced an influential report (South Commission 1990).

Other global proposals include investor/philanthropist George Soros' (1998b) concept of an International Credit Insurance Corporation to under-gird global markets. We agree with Soros' analysis, and support many of his initiatives toward the goal of a 'global open society' (where enhanced democratic political processes provide a social balance to market processes). However, such an International Credit Insurance Corporation, without additional restructuring of existing financial architecture, might well exacerbate current moral hazard problems. Indeed, Soros (1998b, p. 171) offers many other useful proposals to prevent what he sees as a 'disintegration of the global capitalist system and the evident inability of the international monetary authorities to hold it together'.

Soros also favours a special loan guarantee fund of at least $150 billion to enable developing countries with sound economic policies to regain access to international capital markets. This idea was floated by US Treasury Secretary Robert Rubin at the IMF annual meeting in October 1998, but received little support. Soros believes such a loan guarantee fund should be financed with a new issue of Special Drawing Rights (SDRs), which he points out over European bankers' objections, would not create additional money – but if they were ever issued, would merely fill a hole created by a default (Soros 1998b, p. 177). Soros also believes that IMF conditionalities should have included debt-to-equity conversions of non-performing loans and tighter policing of banks' capital adequach ratios by the BIS. These BIS rules exempted banks from such adequate reserves in the case of loans to Korea because it had joined OECD, whose 'rich country' membership enjoyed such 'low-risk' exemptions.

Soros targets several kinds of derivatives as needing regulation because they engender 'trend-following' or herd-behaviour, including delta-hedging and 'knock-out' options, and suggests that all derivatives should be licensed and registered with the SEC as 'new issues' of securities. Clearly the failure of many of these hedging strategies lies, as noted earlier, in their models' assumptions of efficient markets and perfect information. Other remedies widely discussed include imposing margin requirements and 'haircuts' on derivatives and other off-balance sheet transactions, as well as regulating hedge funds, proprietary trading operations of banks and investment banks' in-house hedge funds equally. Interestingly, Soros does not address the issue of speculative currency-trading directly – although he does not deny that he engaged in it and that it is widespread and a factor in current volatility and contagion. Alan Greenspan also reminds us that this increase in volatility is good news for traders, who thrive thereby. Yet, few blame traders who are playing by the rules of the current game and are not empowered to change it.

Thus, in systems' terms, the global economy, by virtue of its real time technological inter-linkages, has become the newest de facto 'global commons', i.e., a common resource of all its users. Such commons, as with others such as the world's oceans and atmosphere, require win – win agreements, rules and standards applicable to all users. If earlier competitive behaviour (win–lose) continues, the result is lose–lose as competition between players leads to sub-optimization and the system itself absorbs risks; this can eventually lead to a system break down.

The OECD countries are well into a new era of the 'Information Age', and are transiting to the 'Age of Knowledge', where scarce human time and attention as well as living eco-systems are recognized as more valuable than money. At the same time, we live in 'mediocracies' where a few media moguls now control the attention of billions of people – for better or worse – and which has changed politics forever. We are already living in the new Attention Economy (Henderson 1996/97, Chapter 5).[7] Indeed, we now live in Attention Deficit societies where each of us is bombarded with information overload from advertisers, media, politicians, teachers, health providers, not to mention junk e-mail. The good news is that this is forcing us to 'go inside ourselves' and ask some pretty basic questions: What do I *want* to pay attention to? Who am I and what do I want written on my tombstone? Such basic defensive reactions will define the growing sectors of our Attention Economies and their inexorable shift from material goods (as measured by traditional GNP/GDP per capita) to services and more intangible factors in living standards, measured by new scorecards such as the CFI. As economies dematerialize, it will be harder for governments to hype wasteful goods-based GDP-growth in the global economy without also measuring toxic wastes, resource-depletion, dirtier and shrinking water supplies, polluted air, unsafe streets, drugs, money-laundering, poverty and global epidemics.

In mature OECD countries, the limiting factor is now *time* rather than *money*. There are only 24 hours in each day, and already, in the USA, for example, the average citizen now spends $9\frac{1}{2}$ hours per day (up from $7\frac{1}{2}$ hours in the 1980s) watching TV, movies, etc., or online. If GDPs were re-categorized and re-calculated for the USA and similar OECD countries, we would find that these information/services sectors already are dominant. For example, mass media and entertainment are a growing percentage of global trade and tourism is the world's largest industry at 10 per cent of global GDP. In response, 28 per cent of US citizens are 'down-shifting' – a form of 'tuning out' this dominant culture of information overload and costly mass consumption oriented value system.[8] They are choosing more free time and less money income and moving to quieter, less expensive, rural towns where life is slower and communities are still intact. Consumers are seeking their own (not advertisers') definitions of 'quality of life.'

The new global standard-setting game

These Attention Economy characteristics include concern for more caring, attention-based health services geared to self-knowledge, prevention, and wellness, as well as cleaner, 'greener' products, eco-labelling (e.g. Germany's Blue Angel and US Green Seal) and the newer 'social' seals of approval (e.g. CEP SA8000 labour standards), as well as the rise of socially responsible investing. In addition, there are increasing demands for global corporations to reduce emissions, employ fair labour standards and promulgate Codes of Conduct (e.g., the Coalition for Environmentally Responsible Economies (CERES), CAUX and the Sullivan and McBride principles). The clash is escalating between individual value changes, concern with community and quality of life *vis-à-vis* market-driven globalization of finance and trade.

Institutional investors and corporations are responding by broadening their standard-setting activities in partnership with relevant government agencies, and civic and consumer groups. They build on the ISO 14000, 14001 and Environmental Management Systems (EMS) and eco-labelling and the prior 100 years of such voluntary standard-setting across a range of products from electrical goods to pharmaceuticals. Corporations continue publishing codes of conduct and fostering such global standards and best practices (see *Business Week*, Special Report, October 1995 and October 1996). The International Organization of Securities Commissions (IOSCO) has taken the leadership in bringing a greater transparency and order to global securities, currency, and futures markets. The big accounting firms and hundreds of new companies are increasing environmental and social auditing of corporate performance. Many institutional investors and portfolio managers have joined with these business leaders and those which have signed on to the CERES Principles, the Sullivan and McBride Principles, CAUX Principles, and those of the Minnesota Center for Corporate Responsibility. Much of this activity in assessing corporate performance owes its impetus to the pioneering work of New York's Council on Economic Priorities and its much-honoured founder, Alice Tepper Marlin, and that of other innovators such as Amy Domini and the Domini 400 Social Index, which regularly out-performs the Standard and Poor's 500. United Nations Secretary-General Kofi Annan's Global Compact urges corporate CEOs to raise these standards of good corporate citizenship voluntarily.[9]

Clear United Nations standards will also do much to dispel the growing suspicions among NGOs and smaller companies that the UN seems to favour the World Business Council on Sustainable Development (WBCSD) and other global corporate giants of the Industrial Era. Even as the giants strive for eco-efficiency, their power over governments still allows them to keep their huge, perverse subsidies, which still hamper the shift to sustainability. Meanwhile, the smaller, cleaner, greener businesses that have been pioneering uphill in the face of such subsidies feel shut out of the very game of sustainable development that they with NGOs have worked so hard for decades to create. It took decades of NGO pressure to get the World Bank to 'discover' micro-enterprises and micro-credit. The WTO is already in a firestorm of criticism for its high-handed and ignorant rule-making. The UN can do much better. By proactively embracing ethical and socially responsible small and medium-sized businesses (which are now recognized as the real engines of global job creation), the UN can demonstrate its commitment. Millions of such businesses world-wide can benefit from UN partnerships for sustainable development. The UN can, where necessary, assist those who need help in meeting its standards. Some agencies, including UNICEF and the ILO, have shown the lead, others, including UNDP, are following suit.

Only if we can *raise* the ethical floor under the global playing field can we hope to succeed in the long run. All of these global standards-setting mechanisms, from ISO 14001, SA 8000, and others, as well as eco-labels and the newer human rights labels, not to mention user fees, taxation and fines, are also important mechanisms for the shift to sustainability. Indeed, it will take an array of such policy mechanisms. Social and environmental auditing of corporations is vital. National governments need to shift tax codes around the world from incomes and payrolls onto resource depletion, waste, and pollution if we are to make the progress we seek on climate change and sustainability (Henderson 1990). Germany's new coalition government has already announced that it will begin shifting taxes from payrolls and incomes to natural resource use. Full-cost pricing, life cycle-costing, and internalizing social and environmental costs into capital asset pricing models as well, can reduce environmental destruction, irrational investments (particularly in the energy sector), and re-direct much of today's entropic world trade. When thermodynamic and economic models of efficiency are aligned, local and provincial efficiencies of scale are correct (Henderson *The Politics of the Solar Age*). But with all such policy tools, equity must be key if we are to address the needs of the 2 billion people still below the poverty line. Equity is especially important in emissions allowances, quotas, and all trading mechanisms.

Since the Asian crisis, more attention is now devoted to mitigating this systemic risk. The neo-classical assumption that markets are self-correcting is now severely strained. Many now admit that free markets, as well as trade and capital flows can indeed swamp many small emerging market economies with devastating effects rapidly felt world-wide. Even the London-based *Economist*, a bastion of free market orthodoxy, has changed its views. The magazine's editorials often call for interventions in markets, while respectfully covering such formerly taboo subjects as capital controls, tighter bank regulations, taxing currency exchange and even advocating that Japanese authorities to start printing money (*The Economist*, 10 October 1998, p. 18).

All these new systemic proposals, including those to deal with electronic commerce – which is now further loosening central banks' control over money aggregates – should be rigorously studied and debated. The technological infrastructure of today's global economy will not be dismantled; indeed it is becoming more complex, inter-linked and faster-operating every day. Economist Walter Russell Mead of the US-based Council on Foreign Relations and others address these new issues by proposing an international central bank (first proposed in 1930 by John Maynard Keynes) that might stabilize foreign exchange markets by maintaining its own currency as an international unit of account. Many others have made similar proposals as well as for reference baskets of currencies (former US Treasury Secretary James Baker); a 'board of overseers' of international financial markets (Henry Kauffman) and variations on all these proposals discussed herein,[10] including one to revive the Japanese proposal for an Asian Monetary Fund (G. Fred Bergsten).

Notes

1   I have regarded Georgescu-Roegen as the much sought-after 'new Keynes'. See Henderson (1971).
2   The United Nations University pioneered such work, for example, the Proceedings of its 1984 Symposium in Montpelier, France, *The Science and Praxis of Complexity* (Tokyo).
3   For information on the US Government's correction procedures, see 'New Methodology for Calculating Gross Domestic Product', Patrice Flynn, Flynn Research, Harper's Ferry, WV, USA.
4   See, for example, *Economic Reform*, published monthly by the Committee on Monetary and Economic Reform, 3284 Yonge Street, Suite 500, Toronto, Ontario M4N 3M7 Canada. e-mail: wkrehm@ibm.net
5   US Treasury Press Release 'Declaration of G-7 Finance Ministers and Central Bank Governors', 30 October 1998 and remarks by Alan Greenspan 'The Structure of the International Financial System' annual meeting of the Securities Industry, Boca Raton, FL, 5 November 1998.
6   The Robert Mundell and J. Marcus Fleming model (IMF Staff Papers, 1962) essentially showed that governments and central banks overseeing open economies cannot simultaneously maintain 1) the independence of their domestic monetary policies, 2) stable exchange rates, and 3) uncontrolled global capital flows.

7 This term has since been picked up by Arthur Andersen and *Wired* (April 1998).
8 Merck Foundation, Harwood Group, Silver Spring, Maryland, USA (1995).
9 Press Release, 'Secretary-General Proposes Global Compact on Human Rights, Labour, Environment', Speech in Davos, Switzerland, 31 January 1999. SG/SM/6881/Rev. United Nations, New York, NY.
10 Eichengreen (1999) is a useful overview of most current proposals. See also D'Arista and Slesinger (1998).

6
Financial Intermediation and Restraint

Chin Kok Fay with Jomo K. S.

The contribution of finance to economic development has long had the attention of economists since Adam Smith.[1] However, economists have not reached firm conclusions as to the link between financial development and economic growth. Views range from those who argue for the irrelevance of finance to those ascribing primary importance to the role of the financial system in economic development.[2] This controversy has made it difficult to identify financial policies for growth and industrialization in developing countries (Park 1994: 9). No consensus has been reached on what kind of financial policy to pursue. During the last decade, financial policies in both industrial and developing countries have increasingly stressed the role of market forces while the World Bank has been actively involved in fostering stock market development in Third World countries. But it has been pointed out that:

> In developing countries, the main impulse behind liberalization has been the belief based on the notion that interventionist financial policies were one of the main causes of the crisis of the 1980s, that liberalization would help to restore growth and stability by raising savings and improving overall economic efficiency.... However, these expectations have not generally been realized. In many developing countries, instead of lifting the level of domestic savings and investment, financial liberalisation has, rather, increased financial instability. Financial activity has increased and financial deepening occurred, but without benefiting industry and commerce.
>
> (Akyuz 1993a: 1)

The possible role of bank finance in promoting late industrialization is our main concern. This chapter considers different industrial financing

140

options, including the relevance of the Japanese, South Korean,[3] and German experiences. The financial system debate has focused on the ability of a country's financial system to promote long-term growth and financial stability. The remarkable economic successes of Japan, Korea, and Germany have generated much interest in banks as practical alternative for industrial financing. Recent theories of financial intermediation suggest that debt financing is more supportive of long-term productive investments than equity financing. The stock market may even adversely affect economic growth and structural change, especially at the early stages of economic development.

Financial systems are often classified into bank-based systems (sometimes referred to as the German–Japanese model) and market-based systems (often referred to as the Anglo-Saxon model). Following this classification, the United States and the United Kingdom are often characterized as having market-based systems, while Germany, Japan, and Korea are characterized as having bank-based systems. Recent academic research attributes the comparative failure of the stock-market-dominated financial systems of the United States and the United Kingdom – relative to the bank-based financial systems of Germany and Japan – to arms-length bank–industry relations and other features of the financial systems of these countries involving corporate control, industrial investment, and economic growth. Bank-based systems appear to be more efficient means of resolving corporate agency problems and providing long term resource commitments for industry. Earlier work has attempted to identify the theoretical considerations for considering different industrial financing options as well as the relevance of the Japanese, Korean, and German experiences (Chin 1996).

It has been argued that 'financial restraint' – that is, policy interventions creating rents that induce financial sector agents to undertake particular activities – is superior both to 'financial repression' and to *laissez faire*. The greater contribution of bank credit, compared to stock markets, to the economic development of post-war Japan, South Korea, and West Germany has been demonstrated. This has important implications for the relative advantages of different forms of financial intermediation for late industrialization.

Financial restraint[4]

Since the mid-1970s, the literature on financial development has been dominated by arguments for financial liberalization (see McKinnon 1973, Shaw 1973). This body of thought has attempted to relate capital market developments to long-term economic growth in developing countries (where capital markets are generally underdeveloped). They claim that 'financial deepening' – through growing financial intermediation and monetarization of the economy – aids economic development, and assert that 'financial repression' is detrimental to long-term economic growth. It is argued that fostering free competition and liberalizing the financial sector from interest rate ceilings and other restrictions facilitate economic development and growth. The theoretical and empirical foundations of the financial liberalization hypothesis have, however, received many criticisms.[5]

From a different perspective, Hellmann, Murdock, and Stiglitz (1994, 1995) propose a set of financial policies, constituting 'financial restraint', aimed at the creation of rents[6] in the financial and productive sectors in order to induce agents in the financial sector to engage in desirable or beneficial activities; financial restraint is argued to be more efficient than either financial repression on the one hand or *laissez-faire* policies on the other.

Unlike financial repression, where the government extracts rents from the private sector, financial restraint involves the government creating rent opportunities for the private sector. With financial restraint, the government can create rent opportunities, but allows profit maximizing firms to pursue and capture these rents, thus enabling private information to be utilized in making allocation decisions. As Hellmann, Murdock, and Stiglitz (1994: 1) put it:

> Rents in the financial and production sectors can play a positive role in reducing information-related problems that hamper competitive markets. In particular, these rents induce private sector agents to increase the supply of goods and services that might be underprovided in a purely competitive market, such as monitoring of investment or the provision of deposit collection.

Thus, this is a fundamentally different approach to conventional interventionist thinking, where the government undertakes the believed socially beneficial actions itself. By leaving the efficiency of execution to private agents, the numerous inefficiencies that can be expected from direct government action can be avoided. In addition, this approach differs significantly from the view of a government distributing rents through subsidies and other support programmes, which typically are not performance-based and may create greater dependency rather than self-sufficiency among subsidized firms.

In their analysis, Hellmann, Murdock, and Stiglitz agree with McKinnon in warning against the government depriving the private sector of a positive real return on financial assets, and with Shaw's view that improving the quality of financial intermediation is critical to increasing the efficiency of investment. Their analysis differs, however, from McKinnon's and Shaw's in arguing that selective intervention – financial restraint – may help rather than hinder financial deepening. They identify several ways in which financial restraint can foster financial deepening.

Using a simple demand–supply model of the market for loans, Hellmann, Murdock, and Stiglitz illustrate the effect of interest rate controls as a mechanism for the creation of rents within the financial sector. Figure 6.1a shows market equilibrium at an interest rate r_0 at the intersection of a household funds' supply curve and a corporate funds' demand curve.[7] If the government intervenes by regulating the deposit rate of interest r_d, rents are potentially captured by financial intermediaries. Given the equilibrium lending rate r_L, the difference between the equilibrium lending rate and the deposit rate $(r_L - r_d)$ defines the economic rents accruing to banks. In this case, the lending rate is greater than it would be in the absence of intervention, allowing banks to capture rents both from households $(r_0 - r_d)$ and from firms $(r_L - r_0)$.

There are two broad categories of rent effects in the Hellmann, Murdock, and Stiglitz analysis. First, it is argued that the rent effect on savings is large. Beyond interest rates, they claim that households are likely to be more responsive to deposit security and intermediation efficiency. This is because households are typically risk-averse, placing greater emphasis on the security of deposits. Besides, household savings

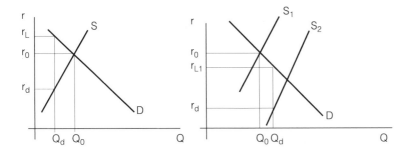

Figure 6.1   Effect of Interest Rate Controls on Rents

depend crucially on the available efficient facilities and infrastructure for deposit collection, in particular on the extent of the bank branching network and the efficiency of services provided to local communities (Hellmann, Murdock, and Stiglitz 1995: 5). Under financial restraint, the creation of rents in the financial sector can increase savings by inducing greater security and improving deposit infrastructure; this rent effect also dominates the interest rate effect. How rents can increase savings by affecting these two non-price factors will be discussed in the next few paragraphs.

A simple graphical way of illustrating this rent effect is a rightward shift in the supply curve from S_1 to S_2, as shown in Figure 6.1b. Given the controlled deposit rate, r_d, the excess for loans gives an equilibrium lending rate of r_{L_1} and banks capture rents of $r_{L_1} - r_d$. Despite the rent captured by banks, firms are better off with the rent effect. They obtain a greater volume of loans at a lower interest rate than they would under 'free market' equilibrium ($Q_d > Q_0$ and $r_{L_1} < r_0$). This is possible if the rent effect is large relative to the interest elasticity of savings.

Regarding the question of how rents can affect financial intermediation, Hellmann, Murdock, and Stiglitz (1995: 7–8) elaborate:

> We emphasise two important roles of the creation of economic rents for financial intermediaries under a regime of financial restraint. First, by creating an ongoing flow of profits from the continuing operation of the bank, these rents create incentives for banks to operate as a long-run agent (by creating a 'franchise value'[8] for the bank) so that they will work to monitor effectively firms and manage the risk of their portfolio of loans.... Second, by increasing the returns to intermediation, banks have strong incentives to increase their own deposit base. Banks will thus make investments to attract incremental deposits, for example, by opening new branches in previously unserved rural areas or by making other investments to bring new depositors to the formal financial system.

Here, rents do not so much involve the transfer of wealth as much as provide the opportunities to create wealth (Hellmann, Murdock, and Stiglitz 1995: 2). Unlike rent transfers, which alter the distribution of income without directly changing incentives for the parties competing for these transfers, rent opportunities are contingent on the agent's actions. With financial restraint, a bank may only capture rents through its own efforts by attracting new deposits for loans to rent-generating sectors and by rigorous monitoring of its portfolio of loans to ensure maximum return on its investments. As pointed out by Hellmann, Murdock, and Stiglitz (1995: 6), 'in the case of financial intermediaries, rent opportunities would include incentives to promote deposit mobilization – both in the wealth and intensity of financial services – and to encourage efficient portfolio allocation and loan monitoring on the part of banks.'

There are some further policies that are necessary to support financial rent creation. It is important to note the assumption, crucial to their argument, that the rents generated by the financial sector can persist even in the long run. Thus, the government needs to place restrictions on competition in the banking sector[9] as such competition could eliminate the rents. The government needs to control entry into the industry so that

> new entry does not erode the rents that are necessary to induce banks to value their franchise. Also, too much entry would prevent most competitors from achieving the efficient scale, thus lowering their ability and desire to invest in better information and monitoring capabilities, and worsening the overall quality of intermediation.
> (Hellmann, Murdock, and Stiglitz 1995: 17)

While there is no price competition under financial restraint, there can be non-price competition such as in the locality and quality of services. There is a possibility that rent will be competed away or at least reduced through non-price competition. In addition, there are other socially wasteful forms of competition, for example, 'a bank which opens a branch next to a competitor's branch does not mobilize any new funds; the new branch only competes for existing depositors' (Hellmann, Murdock, and Stiglitz 1995: 17). Thus, restriction on such competition is necessary to prevent socially wasteful duplication of activity.

Another set of policies is concerned with restricting households' ability to substitute out of financial sector deposits. An undesirable side effect of financial restraint is that deposit rate controls may lead to asset substitution, where depositors seek out alternative savings vehicles (Hellmann, Murdock, and Stiglitz 1994). Restrictions on competing asset markets are, therefore, necessary to limit inefficient reallocation of savings in response to deposit rate control.

There are four important asset alternatives that Hellmann, Murdock, and Stiglitz consider. First, in developed countries, bond and stock markets have become an attractive alternative for households to invest their savings. However, it is argued that the development of security markets may not be desirable as:

> ... security markets would compete with the banking sectors for household funds. Security markets can only be used by the largest and most reputed firms in the economy. If they were to go to the security markets, banks would lose some of their most profitable business and there is a loss of franchise value. It follows that security markets provide an alternative savings vehicle that undermines the rents in the banking sector, and may threaten the stability of the financial system.
>
> (Hellmann, Murdock, and Stiglitz 1995: 19)

Their argument suggests that security markets should not be emphasised during a stage of development when an effective banking system is being developed.

Foreign deposits are another alternative to deposit savings with domestic financial intermediaries. Serious attempts should be taken to control international capital movements. Alternative investment options can be provided to investors to make capital flight unattractive to them.[10]

A third threat to the formal banking sector is the informal sector, which invariably pays much higher rates to attract deposits. Hellmann, Murdock, and Stiglitz argue that the decision to deposit funds in the informal sector is not so much a function of the rate differential, but mainly a function of the efficiency and safety offered by the informal sector. If their argument is correct, then financial restraint may actually encourage and facilitate the flow of funds from the informal sector to the formal sector.

The fourth asset alternative is real assets such as gold. These assets are inflationary hedges as their value is not adversely affected by inflation. Real asset substitution poses a serious threat to financial sector deposits whenever real interest rates are negative. Consequently, the economy needs to have a stable macroeconomic environment, where inflation rates are low and predictable so that real interest rates will be positive. This is one of the pre-conditions that must be met in order for financial restraint to operate effectively.

Bank credit, economic growth and structural change

The traditional theory of intermediation is based on the concept of economies of scale. According to Gurley and Shaw (1960), financial intermediation can pool risk and diversify portfolios more cheaply than individual investors, given the fixed costs of acquiring investments. On the assets (lending) side, financial intermediaries can manage investments at lower costs than most individual lenders. Owing to the sheer size of the portfolio, financial intermediation can significantly reduce risks through diversification. It can also minimize the possibilities of liquidity crises by scheduling maturities appropriately. On the (borrowing) liabilities side, it can be seen as providing a form of insurance to risk-averse depositors against liquidity risk.

A disadvantage of intermediated finance is the increase in transaction costs due to the longer chain of transactions between the firm and the final investor. For the Gurley and Shaw argument to hold, the technology for issuing securities must be such that it is less costly for intermediation to do this repackaging (of the primary securities issued by firms into the indirect financial securities desired by final investors) than for investors to hold securities directly. However, transaction costs were not formally modelled by Gurley and Shaw who do not distinguish banks from other financial intermediaries such as mutual funds, which may also benefit from economies of scale (Davis 1992: 17). On the other hand, there are economists who argue that debt financing can be better performed through banks.

Recent theories of financial intermediation have focused on the role of banks in information production and transmission (see Leland and Pyle 1977, Campbell and Kracaw 1980, Diamond 1984). As noted, information asymmetries in the absence of complete contracts[11] give rise to a need for lenders to screen the quality of borrowers and to monitor their performance to avoid adverse selection and moral hazard.[12] The argument is that banks may have informational advantages over other outsiders in dealing with information asymmetries. The informational advantages arise from ongoing credit relationships, from access to a borrower's deposit history (Fama 1985), as well as from the use of transaction services (Lewis 1991).[13] Moreover, banks have a cost advantage because information production and provision of transaction and other intermediary services are complementary activities (James 1987: 217). The intangible nature of this information makes its transfer to markets or other lenders difficult. As a result, 'this will avoid the free rider problem typical of securities markets, where an individual investor in marketable securities can costlessly take advantage of information on borrowers produced by other investors, thus reducing the incentive to gather it' (Davis 1992: 18).

Diamond has developed a theory of financial intermediaries which explains why it may be efficient for investors to delegate monitoring to banks, given information asymmetries between borrowers and lenders.[14] The analysis focuses on financial intermediaries, particularly banks, that raise funds from many lenders (depositors) promising them a given pattern of returns, lend to entrepreneurs, and are delegated the task of monitoring and enforcing loan contracts with entrepreneurs that are less costly than those available without monitoring (Diamond 1984: 394). Diamond acknowledges that the tasks delegated to banks may give rise to incentive problems between banks and its depositors. A bank might cheat the depositors by claiming that all entrepreneurs had negligible profits so that it has insufficient loan proceeds to repay them. His solution to this problem is that the depositors sign incentive contracts with the bank, whereby the bank is obliged to pay a fixed debt claim to depositors. Banks which fail to fulfil this obligation are punished by bankruptcy. A bank must, therefore, choose contracts such that it has the incentive to monitor information in order to deter borrowers who may default,[15] and make sufficient payments to depositors to attract deposits. Providing such incentives is costly,[16] but Diamond shows that such costs can be reduced by portfolio diversification by banks.[17] This is due to the 'law of large numbers: as the number of loans to entrepreneurs with projects whose returns are independent (or independent conditional on observables) grows without bounds, we show that costs of delegation approach zero' (Diamond 1984: 395). As Diamond (1984: 402) puts it:

> The intermediary need not be monitored because it take full responsibility and bears all penalties for any shortfalls of payments to principals. The diversification of its portfolio makes the probability of incurring these penalties very small and allows the information collected by the intermediary to be observed only by the intermediary.

This allows depositors to costlessly observe whether or not the bank has undertaken the necessary amount of monitoring since if it has not, it would not be able to pay the promised rate of return.

Besides monitoring, it is also argued that banks can reduce the problems of moral hazard through control efforts. Managers are controlled directly and indirectly through both explicit and implicit contracts and by both lenders and shareholders. The lenders exert control through both the formal terms of a loan contract[18] as well as their refusal to renew a loan. Shareholders exert control through both the voting process as well as their refusal to provide additional capital. Stiglitz (1985: 140) argues that, to the extent that control is exercised, it is by banks and not by the owners of equity, despite the legal form that places responsibility for control in the hands of the owners of equity. Banks may exercise control more effectively because the nature of the loan contract enables them to do so without undertaking undue risk; they can focus their attention on information-gathering related to the probability of default and the net worth of the firm in case of low return. There is no tendency for a free rider problem as in the securities market, where if one shareholder takes action to increase his return, other shareholders who do not contribute will benefit equally, hence reducing the incentive for the active shareholder to acquire information to increase his return (Stiglitz 1985: 144). The consequence is that the shareholders, who have nominal control, cannot effectively exercise it. Thus, 'given that managers could not be effectively controlled, no one would turn over to them the capital required for the development of modern industry' (Stiglitz 1985: 143).

It is argued that banks are well placed to develop long-term relations and commitments to firms unlike the securities market (Mayer 1988, Sharpe 1990). Mayer's 'commitment in financing' hypothesis argues that banks will take the risk to commit themselves to rescue firms that are in financial difficulties, and resist the temptation to withdraw capital only if they anticipate being able to gain benefits from the expansion of business once the firm has been successfully revived. Competition in financial markets will only cause the future benefits from a successful rescue to be competed away. Thus, the more competitive the financial market, the less likely it is that firms will establish a long-term relationship with a lender. Long-term relationships will not develop in competitive financial markets as there is a problem of time inconsistency. That is, although a long-term relationship may be optimal *ex ante*, the bank or firm has the incentive to renege *ex post*. For instance:

A firm that is committed to a particular investment project that has not yet reached maturity is in a weak bargaining position when it comes to renegotiating further loans. The bank that takes a current loss in the hope of a future return is reliant on a more advantageous arrangement not being presented to the firm. *Ex ante* the bank would like to commit itself to a loan that specifies the terms of future finance, thereby encouraging the firm to undertake the investment. *Ex post* there will be incentive for the firm to renege on this arrangement. The firm will therefore seek protection in the form of long-term finance. Conversely, the company that is currently seeking rescue finance will *ex ante* be willing to commit itself to one bank but *ex post* be tempted by more competitive offers.

(Mayer 1988: 1179)

Thus, competition in financial markets prevents a firm and investors to commit to each other. The time-inconsistency problem results in a conflict between commitment and competition. The absence of commitment and long-term relationships, Mayer argues, forces firms to rely on internal financing for investment projects.

Banks are said to be able to mitigate the time inconsistency problem because they have more information about clients as discussed earlier. Superior information on the part of banks allows them to enjoy an information monopoly over firms as the information generated in prior relationships with their customers cannot be verified by potential new lenders (Sharpe 1990: 1069). Since other lenders are not able to distinguish between good risks and bad risks due to information asymmetries, they may charge the good risks higher rates, compared to what their old banks would charge them. Adverse selection makes it difficult for a bank to attract another bank's good customers without attracting the less desirable ones as well (Sharpe 1990: 1070). Thus, close debtor–creditor ties can reduce the lender's expected cost of providing capital, which may in turn reduce loan rates. While close debtor–creditor ties reduce the lender's expected costs, they also increase its information monopoly and, as a result, cost reductions are not passed on to the firms in the form of lower loan rates. Despite some monopoly power which the banks acquire over borrowers in the course of lending,[19] they may not, in fact, choose to exploit it, as Sharpe postulates that competition for new business encourages banks to maintain a reputation for non-exploitative behaviour:

> In the context of our loan market, if a bank exploits its 'optimal' customers, it is likely to lose market share as potential new customers learn of such practices. Broken agreements in the past would be punished by the loss of future credibility'.
>
> (Sharpe 1990: 1080)

Thus, reputation of banks is vital as firms will only be willing to commit themselves to creditors if they believe that their creditors will not exploit their position.

In conclusion, these studies, which apply the economics of information, imply that the more pronounced the information asymmetries, the more preferable banking arrangements will be to direct securities markets. Bank intermediation can reduce information and incentive problems by monitoring borrowers (Diamond 1984). Besides, banks are better equipped than securities markets to exercise control over managers more effectively (Stiglitz 1985), as well as develop long-term relations with and commitments to firms. This led Park to conclude that the role of banks is more important in developing countries, where information problems are severe, because accounting and auditing systems are typically less reliable than in advanced countries (Park 1994: 13).

The stock market, economic growth and structural change[20]

In theory, the stock market has a number of distinct functions: it allocates scarce capital among competing users and uses, and provides signals to firms making investment decisions (see Baumol 1965: 3). How well are these supposed functions actually performed by real stock markets? Economists have long assumed that stock markets fulfil these roles through two kinds of market mechanisms: the pricing process and take-over mechanisms (Singh 1992b: 24).

Tobin (1984) distinguishes between two concepts of share price efficiency: 'fundamental valuation' efficiency and 'information arbitrage' efficiency. The former refers to how well relative share prices of firms reflect their expected profitability. An efficient pricing process will reward well-managed firms by valuing their shares more highly than those of unprofitable firms. 'Information arbitrage' refers to how quickly all available information is disseminated throughout the market and incorporated into share prices. According to the efficient market hypothesis, a stock's price reflects the current market value of its expected future income stream, that is, its fundamental value. If a stock's price is less than the value of its expected income stream, investors will buy the stock, and the buying pressure will push up its price. It follows that highly profitable firms will have higher stock prices than unprofitable firms.

Steinherr and Huveneers (1990) cite a large number of studies on stock market efficiency; these studies show that the market efficiently reflects publicly available information, does not directly capitalize current earnings, and does reflect gains from investments and cost reductions (Benston 1994: 128). Nevertheless, not many studies suggest that share price movements are systematically related to current, past, or future underlying performance variables of companies or to long-run equilibrium considerations rather than to short-run trends (Singh 1990: 165). If stock prices do not reflect fundamentals, then the stock market will not necessarily perform its allocative function well: an inefficient stock market does not direct investment funds to their best possible uses.

Many empirical studies have shown the domination of stock market prices by short-term considerations.[21] It has been alleged that investment institutions' provision of finance for industry has generally failed to finance the economy's new areas (Coakley and Harris 1983: 102).[22] Equity financing may therefore be damaging, especially since fund managers are primarily concerned with short-term financial gains as signalled by the vicissitudes of the stock market. Although some fund managers invest for the longer term, most turn over their stockholdings to try to maximize the current value of their investment portfolios, since this is the main criterion against which their own performance is judged. It is alleged that this short-termism results in a reluctance to lend except when returns are more or less assured (Barberis and May 1993: 47). Keynes expressed his scepticism about the virtues of the stock market in relation to a country's investment needs:

> Speculations may do no harm as bubbles on a steady stream of enterprise. But the position is serious when enterprise becomes the bubble on a whirlpool of speculation. When the capital development of a country becomes a by-product of the activities of a casino, the job is likely to be ill-done.
>
> (Keynes 1936: 159)

Besides, not many small companies at the forefront of new industries would issue shares on the stock market. The reason is that to be able to raise funds by selling new shares on the market, a company has to meet various conditions. In addition, share prices of small companies are highly susceptible to wild fluctuations (Coakley and Harris 1983: 104). Small companies only issue a small proportion of their shares for sale on the market and, as a result, only a small amount is left over after investment institutions have taken their stakes. If many private investors try to obtain shares, their prices will rise dramatically: Apart from that, the small volume traded also means that when a few investors become pessimistic and sell their shares, their prices may fall dramatically. Indeed, there are many in need of finance who might have no credit access at all if not for the banking system.

'Efficient' prices, in the sense suggested above, are not sufficient for the stock market to perform essential tasks. In addition, sufficiency requires that the 'take-over mechanism' be efficient so that all those companies, whose profitability under their existing managements may be lower than under some other management, can be acquired by the latter (Singh 1992b: 27). However, empirical studies of actual take-overs on stock markets do not show that only unprofitable companies are taken over, or conversely, that the greater the profitability or the stock-market valuation of a company, the lower the likelihood of it being acquired. Evidence from a wide range of studies for the United Kingdom, the United States, and other industrial countries indicates that take-over selection is based on profitability only to a very limited degree; much more relevant is the size of a company. A large, relatively unprofitable company has a much greater chance of being immune to take-over than a small, but much more profitable company. In fact, in actual stock markets, making an acquisition to increase size might be a tactic to avoid take-over (Singh 1990: 164).

Allegedly, take-overs provide a mechanism by which capital markets ensure that non-owner managers perform their duties in the interest of shareholders and firms.[23] However, there are several reasons why this has not been, and is not likely to be, an effective control mechanism (see Stiglitz 1985: 137–9).[24] Even in advanced capitalist economies with highly organized capital markets, the stock market is a poor disciplinarian of large management-controlled corporations (Singh 1990: 173).

As far as the savings function is concerned, it turns out that the stock market makes a very limited contribution to social savings, at best. In fact, Mayer (1988) used flow-of-funds accounts to show that between 1970 and 1985, new issues in the United Kingdom and the United States made negative contributions to financing capital formation (see Mayer 1988: 1170–2). As he documents: 'The reason for this is cash expenditure on acquisitions. Repurchases of shares have not until recently been permitted, but the corporate sector as a whole has in effect been buying back shares in the process of making cash financed acquisitions' (Mayer 1988: 1172). Furthermore, there are several factors which explain management's reluctance to turn to securities markets to source funds (Baumol 1965: 74–6). In such circumstances, the securities market does not allocate much capital in an economy. Very often, large corporations in capitalist countries finance their investments through retained profits or by borrowing from banks (Singh 1990: 163).

Besides all the problems faced by well-organized stock markets in advanced countries, research suggests that most Third World stock markets too have certain negative features. First, stock markets in developing countries exhibit much greater volatility than those in advanced economies. Table 6.1 shows that during the period 1985–89, the standard deviation of monthly percentage changes in share prices in

Table 6.1   Standard Deviations of Developing- and Developed-country Monthly Share Price Indices for 1985–89

Market	Number of months	Standard deviation	Mean of % changes
Latin America			
Argentina	60	37.05	7.14
Brazil	60	21.07	2.51
Chile	60	8.26	3.41
Colombia	60	6.10	1.59
Mexico	60	16.09	4.47
Venezuela	60	11.59	0.29
East Asia			
Korea, Republic of	60	8.16	2.93
Philippines	60	11.15	5.62
Taiwan, Province of China	60	15.15	5.46
South Asia			
India	60	8.76	1.56
Malaysia	60	8.23	1.05
Pakistan	60	2.92	0.33
Thailand	60	7.90	2.69
Europe/Mid East/Africa			
Greece	60	12.39	2.45
Jordan	60	5.41	0.00
Nigeria	60	11.24	−1.00
Portugal[a]	47	18.17	5.53
Turkey[b]	36	23.67	4.90
Zimbabwe	60	8.71	3.39
IFC Regional Indices			
Composite	60	7.06	2.14
Latin America	60	13.91	2.14
Asia	60	7.98	2.82
Developed Markets			
USA (S&P 500)	60	5.16	1.39
UK (FT-100)	60	5.88	1.31
Japan (Nikkei)	60	4.08	2.17
EAFE	60	5.25	2.61

Notes: [a] Since January 1986.
[b] Since December 1986.
Source: Singh (1992: 35).

developing countries stock markets tended to be considerably higher than in developed markets.[25] A market characterized by a high degree of volatility is inherently more risky. The high degree of volatility not only makes share prices much less useful as a guide to resource allocation, but also discourages risk-averse savers and investors.

In retrospect, the equity market was a much more important source of corporate finance in advanced countries at an earlier stage of development than subsequently. This is reflected in Table 6.2, which shows the sharp decline in the use of stock issues as a financing source: they remain very low by pre-war standards. One might, therefore, conclude that equity finance is more important for firm growth in the initial stages of development and hence, developing countries should follow the footsteps of the advanced countries, a view shared by the World Institute of Development Economic Research (WIDER 1990: 6). However, it has been pointed out that:

> ... research suggests that the greater degree of equity financing in the US at the turn of the century does not much indicate the significance of new share issues for financing corporate growth, but rather reflected the gigantic merger movement which swept American industry during that period. The stock market was used by J.P. Morgan and others to float shares to carry out the huge amalgamations of the era. Moreover, in Italy, France, Germany and Japan, even at an earlier stage in the development of these economies, the stock market played a small role in the financing of firm growth: the banks were much more important in this respect.
>
> (Singh 1992b: 20)

Kumar (1994: 341–3) is sceptical about the supposedly well-functioning equity markets as claimed by Cho (1986). Kumar provides the following reasons why equity markets are not free from allocative distortions. First, asymmetric information may give rise to principal–agent problems.[26] Because of asymmetric and incomplete information, each economic agent is tempted to use his informational advantage to pursue his own interest, which may differ from the objectives of those (principals) who are influenced by his action. Incentive problems may worsen when a firm is equity-financed as managers are less restricted in diverting profits for their private use. With debt financing, managers have less flexibility in diverting profits for their private use as lenders have the power to discipline managers by withdrawing their funds. This acts as a sanction that may be more effective than

Table 6.2   Flow of Funds Data: Proportions of Total Financing Accounted for by Particular Sources of Funds

Period	Total Debt	Long-term Debt	Short-Term Liabilities	Internal Funds	New Stock Issues
	Total Sources (1)	Total Sources (2)	Total Sources (3)	Total Sources (4)	Total Sources (5)
1901–12	.31	.23	.08	.55	.14
1913–22	.29	.12	.17	.60	.11
1923–29	.26	.22	.04	.55	.19
1930–39	negative	negative	negative	1.14	.19
1940–45	.15	negative	.20	.80	.05
1946–59	.30	.16	.14	.64	.05
1960–69	.36	.18	.18	.62	.02
1970–79	.45	.21	.24	.52	.03

Sources: Taggart, cited by Singh (1992: 39).

shareholder control via share voting in which majority rule applies, or via take-overs, which are not likely to be an effective control mechanism.

Information imperfections limit the ability of a firm to raise equity capital due to 'signalling effects' (Greenwald, Stiglitz, and Weiss 1984: 195). Signalling effects may arise because attempts to sell equity may convey a strong negative signal about a firm's quality. It is believed that 'good' firms tend to be more willing to rely on debt capital, as both the absolute level of bankruptcy risk, as well as any incremental increase in risk due to added debt, will be smaller for 'good' than for 'inferior' firms. That is to say, equity will be predominantly sold by 'inferior' firms rather than by 'good' firms. The effective marginal cost of capital comprises the monetary cost of interest plus the marginal increase in expected bankruptcy costs associated with additional debt. Thus, adverse signals associated with issuing equity may restrict a firm's access to equity markets as the cost of equity is prohibitive for many firms. It may reduce a firm's value, as indicated by some empirical studies.[27]

In addition, the limited liability of the modern corporation restricts the aggregate claims of various claimants on the corporation to the market value of the firm. Thus, a corporation's limited liability induces corporate insiders to make investment decisions that are sub-optimal from the perspective of the welfare of all stakeholders. This, in turn, results in a conflict of interest between equity stockholders and other stakeholders (suppliers, customers, and workers).

With asymmetric information, managers may prefer to rely on internal financing and may prefer debt to equity if new capital is needed. Managers may be reluctant to issue new shares, even at the cost of passing up good investment opportunities. Thus, real capital investment is misallocated. The distortions in investments in developing countries may be even worse, since ownership and management of many small and medium-sized firms are usually in the hands of families.

Conclusion

This chapter has attempted to identify some analytical considerations in considering different industrial financing options as well as the relevance of the Japanese, German, and Korean experience for late industrializing economies. It does not intend to suggest that the Japanese, German, or Korean models are perfect, or that they are suitable for total emulation and can be replicated in Malaysia. Given the different historical and institutional settings, lessons must be drawn and institutions adapted accordingly to serve similar policy priorities in different contexts. We have argued that 'financial restraint' – understood as a set of policies creating rents to induce financial sector agents to undertake particular activities – is more desirable for late industrialization than either financial repression or *laissez faire* policies. By distinguishing between bank-and market-based financial systems, we considered the relative contribution of bank credit and stock markets to economic growth and structural change, both in terms of economic theory and empirical evidence; by referring to finance–industry relations in Japan, Korea, and Germany, we suggested how different financial institutions and arrangements better served industrial financing than would otherwise have been the case under a more liberal financial regime. Another important lesson drawn from these experiences is that the nature and quality of state intervention does matter.

A broad conclusion from this study is that financial restraint, based on stylized analysis of the policies of some high performing East Asian economies, may be a desirable policy for late industrialization. A securities market-based system and a banking-based system can develop simultaneously while being of different significance at different times for different players (Patrick 1994: 370). The analytical rationale for financial restraint suggests that the securities market should not be emphasized while an effective banking system is being developed. Given the imperfect and asymmetric information in the credit market, the experiences of Japan, Korea, and Germany show that their bank-based systems were able to develop close long-term relations with industrial firms as well as monitor them effectively, and hence, had the incentive to rescue or resuscitate potentially viable manufacturing firms in financial distress. Consequently, these countries have relied heavily on their banking systems, rather than on stock markets, for corporate finance and governance. Evidence seems to suggest that their banking systems play a vital role, not only in the expansion, but also in the survival of existing firms. Although there may be an increasing role for the securities market, the Malaysian financial system should not hastily embrace the 'arms-length' market-based system without considering the implications of the alternatives for growth and structural change.

Notes

1   Adam Smith, as cited by Drake (1980: 31), observed that: 'I have heard it asserted that the trade of the City of Glasgow doubled in about 15 years after the first erection of the banks there, and that the trade of Scotland has more than quadrupled since the first erection of the two public banks in Edinburgh ... that the banks have contributed a good deal to this increase cannot be doubted.'

2   For a survey of these views, see Kitchen (1986: Chapter 3) and Drake (1980: Chapter 3).

3   South Korea will hereafter be referred to simply as Korea.

4   The discussion in this section is inspired by Hellmann, Murdock, and Stiglitz (1994, 1995).

5   See Akyuz (1991: 2), Akyuz and Kotte (1991: 7) and the literature cited therein, and Cho and Khatkhate (1989).

6   By rents, they mean returns in excess of those which would be generated in a competitive market, and not income that accrues to an inelastically supplied factor of production.

7   This simple demand–supply model assumes no transaction costs in intermediation.

8   An important aspect of franchise value is that it creates long-run equity that cannot be appropriated in the short run since banks have an ongoing interest to stay in business. Thus, franchise value creates commitment for the bank to act as a long-run agent.

9   Hellmann, Murdock, and Stiglitz distinguish between two potential sources of competition. First, there may be excessive entry into the banking sector. Second, there can be excessive competition among existing banks.

10 See, for example, Hellmann, Murdock, and Stiglitz 1995: fn. 33.

11 Debt is a highly complex contract because it entails a promise the fulfilment of which by repaying principal and interest on a loan is, by its nature,

uncertain and will differ among borrowers. Complete contracts would have to specify the behaviour of the borrower in every possible contingency.

12 With asymmetric information and incomplete contracts, there is an incentive for a borrower to change his behaviour after the contract has been agreed, so as to maximize his wealth at the expense of the lender. For example, the borrower might use the funds to engage in high-risk activities that entail a lower possibility that the loan will be repaid. Thus, the lender must monitor the borrower after the loan is granted to ensure that the borrower is not acting contrary to his interest during the contractual period.

13 The borrower's deposit history provides the information that banks require to sort out good from bad risks.

14 Schumpeter assigned such a role to banks as he points out that ' ... the banker must not only know what the transaction is which he is asked to finance and how it is likely to turn out but he must also know the customer, his business and even his private habits, and get, by frequently "talking things over with him", a clear picture of the situation' (Schumpeter 1939: 116).

15 In case of such a default, that is, failure of the borrower to comply with the terms of the debt (contract), the bank monitors the situation and uses the information to renegotiate the contract at a new interest rate and contingent promises (Diamond 1984: 395).

16 Diamond termed these 'delegation costs'.

17 In his model, diversification occurs when the intermediary invests in a large number of firms with independent payoff risks.

18 A loan contract allows managers (borrowers) to retain control as long as they do not default. But in the case of default, control transfers to lenders as they have certain rights of intervention defined by the loan contract.

19 For example, banks often retain much discretion in altering the premiums they charge on loans.

20 The analysis in this section draws on Singh (1992b).

21 See, for example, Poterba and Summers (1988). They examined monthly data on the New York Stock Exchange returns from 1926 to 1985 and annual returns from 1871 to 1985. They also analysed monthly data for 17 other equity markets over various periods. In each case, the results suggested that the presence of important transitory components in stock prices resulted in deviation 'from the stocks' fundamental values. For a non-technical analysis, see Dertouzos, Lester, and Solow (1990: Chapter 4).

22 While banks and insurance companies provide long-term finance for Japanese industrial firms, they do not do so in the United States due to short-termism. For details, see Dertouzos, Lester and Solow (1990: Chapter 4).

23 If the managers were not maximizing the market value of the firms, this would render the firms attractive to take-over raiders.

24 The argument is based on recent developments in the economics of information. For instance, outsiders face difficulty in determining whether a firm is or is not efficiently managed. Moreover, the take-over mechanisms are ineffective since current managers are often in a position to take strategic actions that deter take-overs.

25 The distributional form of stock price changes reflects the riskiness of an investor's investment and its standard deviation is used as a measurement of this risk.

26 The information problems are sometimes referred to as 'principal–agent' problems as each agent's action affects the welfare of the principal and the principal tries to ensure that each agent will behave according to the principal's interest.
27 See, for example, Asquith and Mullins (1983).

7
Financial Liberalization and Globalization: Implications for Industrial and Industrializing Economies[1]

Ajit Singh

Contrary to the widespread enthusiasm in international economic cir-cles for the liberalization and globalization processes currently sweeping the world economy, this chapter expresses deep scepticism about the virtues of these developments. It questions particularly the benefits of financial liberalization and the integration of the global capital and currency markets, (a) for the world economy as a whole, and (b) for developing countries. The chapter argues that on the basis of the experi-ence of advanced economies, where these processes have progressed the furthest, liberalization and globalization have not delivered over the last 15 years. Further, there are reasons to believe that they are unlikely to do so in the foreseeable future.

In 1995, Sachs and Warner were very impressed by the benefits of 'openness' for developing economies. They were therefore also con-cerned with the question, why did these countries take so long (not until well into the 1980s, or the 1990s in many cases) to abandon their *dirigiste* and illiberal economic policies? The present author, who is not so impressed with the economic record of the liberalized global regime, asks the opposite question, that is, how does one explain the unwar-ranted euphoria for these developments on Wall Street, the City of London, in the multilateral international organizations as well as among many orthodox academic economists?

The next four sections concentrate on leading advanced economies and show how their uninspiring performance in the recent period is causally linked with financial liberalization and the increasing integra-tion of the capital markets which has occurred in these countries since the late 1970s. The remainder of the chapter considers the case of developing countries. Here, special attention is given to the very fast expansion of stock markets, which has been a salient part of the financial liberalization process in these countries in the recent period. The chapter argues that, on balance, further financial liberalization will hinder rather than help industrialization and long-term economic growth in these economies.

Liberalization and globalization in advanced economies

The terms liberalization and globalization are used here in their narrow economic sense. The former connotes the free movement of goods and services as well as investment and capital flows between countries. The latter encompasses both the integration and unification of the product and capital markets as well as the cross-national production activities of the multinational corporations.[2]

Liberalization and globalization have occurred at varying speeds and to different degrees in countries and regions throughout the post-war period. However, the important point is that these are invariably cumulative processes that have advanced furthest in leading industrial countries. For all practical purposes, these countries have been operating under a regime of more or less free trade in manufactures and free capital movements since about 1980 (for a fuller justification of this statement, see Singh 1996).

The experiences of advanced economies during the last 10 to 15 years therefore provide important evidence for assessing the effects of liberalization and globalization. However, as outlined below, the economic record of advanced countries in the relevant period has, unfortunately, been far from comforting. In short, it would appear that the liberal economy has so far failed to deliver in important dimensions.

Tables 7.1 and 7.2 give information on the growth of output and productivity in leading industrial countries as well as for the European Union (EU) and the OECD as a whole, for various periods between 1960 and 1993. Four sub-periods are identified. The first, 1960–73, is a segment of the post-Second World War Golden Age economic boom, which lasted for nearly a quarter of a century until the first oil price rise in 1973. The significant point here is that during this period, the economies of industrial countries, compared with today, were extensively regulated, both externally and internally. Not only were they subject to international capital controls under the Bretton Woods regime, they also had a plethora of controls, regulations and other restrictive practices in the domestic product, capital and labour markets.

Table 7.1   Real Gross Domestic Product (GDP) in Industrial Countries, 1960–93 (Average Annual Percentage Changes)

	1960–73	*1973–79*	*1979–89*	*1989–93*
United States	3.9	2.5	2.5	1.7
Japan	9.6	3.6	4.0	2.5
Germany	4.3	2.4	1.8	2.9
United Kingdom	3.1	1.5	2.4	0.0
Total of G7 Countries	4.8	2.7	2.7	1.6
Total EU15	4.7	2.5	2.2	1.2
Total OECD	4.9	2.8	2.6	1.7

Source: OECD, *Historical Statistics*, Paris, 1995.

Table 7.2   Real GDP per Capita in Industrial Countries, 1960–93 (Average Annual Percentage Changes)

	1960–73	*1973–79*	*1979–89*	*1989–93*
United States	2.6	1.4	1.5	0.8
Japan	8.3	2.5	3.4	2.2
Germany	3.7	2.5	1.7	2.1
United Kingdom	2.6	1.5	2.2	−0.3
Total of G7 Countries	3.7	2.0	2.0	1.0
Total EU15	4.0	2.2	2.0	0.8
Total OECD	3.7	1.8	1.8	0.9

Source: OECD, *Historical Statistics*, Paris, 1995.

The second period in Tables 7.1 and 7.2, 1974–79, is the time span between the two oil shocks, sometimes called the 'inter-shock' period. In retrospect, these five years are best viewed as an interregnum during which industrial countries attempted to deal with the post-1973 economic crisis, basically by following the broadly Keynesian policies of the Golden Age. These policies were finally abandoned in 1979, and the industrial countries, at greater or lesser speed, have been implementing the present liberal economic regime, both externally and internally. Apart from external liberalization in terms of trade and capital movements, this regime is characterized domestically by privatization, deregulation and the supremacy of market forces (Singh 1995a, 1995b).

The two tables show that the long-term trend rate of growth of output and productivity in industrial countries since 1980 has been approximately half that achieved by these countries during the illiberal and regulated 1960s. It is significant that the deterioration in long-term economic growth has been across the board rather than just confined to a few countries. Of the 22 OECD countries, 21 of them have recorded lower growth rates both in the 1980s and in the 1990s, compared with 1960–73. Further, most analysts agree that the long-term growth performance of industrial countries is unlikely to be better in the 1990s than in the 1980s; indeed, all present indications are that it is likely to be worse (see Economic Commission for Europe 1996).

The 1980s and 1990s were only marked by slower economic growth, but were also much more unstable. Apart from Gross Domestic Product (GDP), other important economic variables – nominal as we as real exchange rates, short-as well as long-term nominal and real interest rates – have also been subject to far greater fluctuations in the recent period than in the 1960s (see further, Felix 1995).

The most conspicuous failure of the liberalized global economy in the last decade or so has been with respect to employment. After enjoying more or less full employment during the 1950s and 1960s, leading European countries were faced with the spectre of mass unemployment in the 1980s and 1990s. As Table 7.3 indicates, the average rate of unemployment in the European Union countries increased from a little over 3 per cent in the 1960s to over 10 per cent in 1993. In the OECD as a whole, there were eight million people unemployed in 1970; in 1994, there were 35 million. If unemployment in the form of involuntary part-time work, short-time working and discouragement of job seekers in looking for new employment are included, another 40 to 50 per cent could be added to these unemployment figures (OECD 1994).

Table 7.3 Standardized Unemployment Rate, 1964–93 (Average Annual Percentage Changes)

	1964–73	*1974–79*	*1980–89*	*1990–93*
United States	4.5	6.7	7.2	6.5
Japan	1.2	1.9	2.5	2.2
Germany	1.1	3.2	5.9	4.9
United Kingdom	3.0	5.0	10.0	9.1
Total of G7 Countries	3.1	5.0	6.8	6.4
Total EU15	2.7	4.7	9.3	9.2
Total OECD	3.0	4.9	7.3	7.0

Source: OECD, *Historical Statistics*, Paris, 1995.

The record for the US with respect to employment is apparently better than that of the European Union countries. However, these relatively low US unemployment figures must be seen in the context of the fact that real wages in the US have not increased over the last two decades and, indeed, real wages have fallen over this period for unskilled workers. One reason for the lower unemployment in the US is that compared with Western Europe, it has relatively little public provision to assist the unemployed. The result is that the latter are obliged to work, however unremunerative the job may be. In other words, in the absence of an adequately developed welfare state, a number of US workers are employed in low-productivity jobs of the kind which Joan Robinson described in the 1930s as 'disguised unemployment' (see further Singh and Zammit 1995, Eatwell 1995).

There is, however, a silver lining to the economic record of the recent period. The rate of inflation in industrial countries is now as low as it was in the 1950s and 1960s. Inflation had accelerated in many countries in the 1970s in the wake of the economic crisis triggered[3] by the first oil shock. The economic policies of the 1980s and 1990s can be credited with containing price increases and bringing inflation down to its Golden Age levels (see Table 7.4).

Alternative hypotheses concerning industrial countries' performance

The generally poor economic record of industrial countries under liberalization and globalization over the last 10 to 15 years,[4] especially when compared with their performance in the illiberal Golden Age, raises two important analytical questions:

Table 7.4 Gross Domestic Product: Implicit Price Index, 1963–93 (Average Annual Percentage Changes)

	1963–73	*1973–79*	*1979–89*	*1989–93*
United States	3.6	8.0	5.0	3.0
Japan	6.0	8.1	1.9	1.6
Germany	4.4	4.7	3.0	4.1
United Kingdom	5.1	16.0	7.4	5.1
Total of G7 Countries	4.4	8.5	4.9	3.2
Total EU15	4.7	9.4	6.5	4.7
Total OECD	4.4	8.5	5.5	5.4

Source: OECD, *Historical Statistics*, Paris, 1995.

1) Could the observed deterioration be due to exogenous factors rather than any intrinsic features of the liberal and global regime itself?
2) If the poor economic performance is not due to exogenous factors, then why has the liberal economy failed to deliver (contrary to the predictions of the orthodox economic models)?

These questions have been examined in detail in Singh (1997a, 1997b). The main points of this analysis are summarized below.

On the question of exogeneity, one major argument concerns the role of technology. It is argued that the poor employment record of industrial countries in the recent period is not due to the economic regime, but rather, brought about by exogenous changes in technology. The pace of technological progress, it is suggested, has been so fast that it has resulted in 'jobless growth'. However, evidence for industrial countries provides no support for this contention. Although the average rate of economic growth was halved in the recent period compared with the Golden Age, productivity growth in this period has fallen even more sharply. As a consequence, the employment elasticity of growth has risen, not fallen (Boltho and Glyn 1995). Thus, the reason for much higher unemployment in the post-1980 period is not 'jobless growth', but rather, a much slower rate of economic growth than before.

There is, however, another more subtle argument of exogeneity in defence of the economic record of the post-1980 liberal economy. Here, the contention is that although the post-1980 period does not compare favourably with the Golden Age, it is very much in line with the long-term historical record of industrial countries in the pre-Golden Age period. Thus, it is suggested that it is not the recent period which has unusually poor performance, but rather, it is the Golden Age that had an extraordinary record. The latter, it is argued, was made possible by exogenous factors, specifically the exceptional circumstances of that period, for example, the post-war reconstruction boom and the 'catch-up' effort by European countries to reach the US levels of productivity.

It is indeed true that in statistical terms, the Golden Age is an aberration and the post-1980 period is not. During the Golden Age, the economies of industrial countries expanded at a rate of approximately 5 per cent per annum which is twice their trend rate of long-term economic growth in previous phases of economic development since 1820 (Maddison 1982). Thus, after 1980, these countries appear to have reverted to their normal long run growth trajectory.

However, a close analysis of the period shows that the Golden Age was not simply a chance product of a favourable combination of circumstances, or that industrial countries were not just plain lucky. This dynamic period was the outcome of a fundamental change in economic strategy, indeed, a new model of economic development which leading West European countries adopted in the quarter century following the end of the Second World War. This model differed radically from that followed by these nations during the inter-war period or that which has been implemented since 1980. The Golden Age model of social market economy emphasized cooperation, both at the international level between nation states, and at the national level between workers, employers and governments.[5]

The cooperative social and economic environment of the Golden Age, in a regulated national and international economy, provided the necessary long-term stability and certainty required for high rates of private investment, which in turn made possible high rates of productivity growth (Eichengreen 1996). Real wages rose in step with productivity, and the share of profits in national income remained more or less stable during this period. As long as the system was working, it had a strong positive feedback mechanism, generating high rates of growth of production, consumption and employment (Kindleberger 1992).

Thus, the high growth path of the Golden Age was based on a unique model of economic development. Post-Second World War reconstruction as well as the 'catch-up' of the European countries with the US were important stimuli for economic growth. However, without the social market economy and the social consensus that it embodied, such stimuli may not have translated into greater rates of investment and faster overall economic growth. As Matthews and Bowen (1988) point out, the European levels of productivity relative to those of the US were as low in 1913 as they were in 1950. Yet, there was no 'catch-up' in the inter-war period. Similarly, post-war reconstruction at the end of the First World War did not lead to 25 years of sustained economic growth and full employment, as happened in the Golden Age.[6]

Turning to the post-1980 period itself, it is not a valid argument to suggest that because economic growth during these years has broadly been in line with the long-term historical record of industrial countries bar the Golden Age, it is therefore satisfactory. The important point here is that the level and the growth of economic activity achieved in the 1980s and the 1990s was not sufficient to meet the needs of the people. Mass unemployment and stagnant or slow growing real wages (despite the supply-side *potentialities* of the new information technology revolution) constitute eloquent evidence of economic failure.

Why has the liberal economy not delivered?

Orthodox analysis ascribes many virtues to a liberal trading order and free capital movements. As Chakravarty and Singh (1988) note, the case for trade openness is, in principle, very robust. Apart from the usual comparative static advantages of trade emphasized in text books, openness can also be a source of great advantage for an economy for any of the following reasons: it may enable a country to concentrate its relatively specialized resources in areas of production where world demand is highly income- and price-elastic; it may lead to diffusion of knowledge, which may considerably raise the quality of local factors of production; through increased competitive pressure, trade may reduce or eliminate x-inefficiency; trade may lead to changes in the distribution of income, which can result in a greater share of accumulation in national output; trade may accelerate a Schumpeterian process of creative destruction and thereby yield faster economic growth.

However, some of these potential dynamic positive advantages of free trade can also easily go in the opposite direction. Thus, instead of leading to a higher rate of investment, a redistribution of income towards profits may simply increase capitalist consumption or lead to capital flight. With incomplete and imperfect markets in developing countries, the role of the government in monitoring and coordinating activities of entrepreneurs becomes critical in order to avoid negative outcomes and to increase the likelihood of positive benefits. This is especially so in relation to the question of 'learning' from trade.[7]

However, even if there were appropriate government policies at the national level, the benefits of trade liberalization may not materialize because of coordination failures at the international level leading to a low level equilibrium for world demand, output, and employment. Based on the experience of the 1930s, Keynes was particularly worried about this problem in relation to the post-World War II period. He noted that:

> the problem of maintaining equilibrium in the balance of payments between countries has never been solved...the failure to solve the problem has been a major cause of impoverishment and social discontent and even of wars and revolutions...to suppose that there exists some smoothly functioning automatic mechanism of adjustment which preserves equilibrium if only we trust to matters of *laissez faire* is a doctrinaire delusion which disregards the lessons of

historical experience without having behind it the support of sound theory.

(Moggridge 1980)

During the Golden Age, the problem of the balance-of-payments surpluses and deficits between nation states was indeed resolved at high rates of growth of world demand, output and employment. This was made possible by international coordination, achieved through the post-war Bretton Woods system, and also, importantly, through the activities of the US government as the hegemon in that system. The US provided adequate liquidity to the international economy to permit high rates of growth of world demand and output. This was done in the early post-war years through the Marshall Plan, and subsequently, through US military expenditures and foreign investment abroad. The latter policies, however, contributed to the persistent US balance-of-payments deficits in the 1960s, which ultimately led to the demise of the Bretton Woods system in 1971 with the ending of gold convertibility by the US government (Panic 1995, Glyn *et al.* 1990).

In the post-1980 period, with financial liberalization, the problem of international coordination failures, in the sense outlined above, has become very serious. There is much less economic cooperation between leading industrial countries today than was the case when the US was the single hegemonic power, and was thereby able to foist its own design on everyone else. In the absence of adequate international cooperation, the financial markets have come to dominate. This is not to suggest that there is no inter-governmental cooperation at all in the field of money and finance. There is still the International Monetary Fund (IMF), but its role has long been restricted to monitoring and disciplining the Third World. Leading industrial countries, which have effectively been outside the IMF disciplines, only occasionally and episodically cooperate on an *ad hoc* basis as, for example, with the Plaza Agreement in September 1985. In general, however, as Panic (1995) notes, the degree of international cooperation during the last 10 to 15 years has been limited to the minimum level necessary to stop the repetition of the mutually destructive acts of the 1930s, such as the competitive currency devaluations.

The increasingly globalized financial markets have, in general, worked in a 'deflationary' way, penalizing governments that follow expansionary policies.[8] In the formation of average market opinion, far more weight is given to the perceived dangers of inflation rather than to the need to obtain full utilization of resources. Eatwell (1995) outlines the process by which such market psychology becomes pre-dominant.[9]

Apart from these international coordination failures arising from the operation of liberalized global financial markets, which may lead to deflation, low rates of growth of demand and/or instability, there are also other channels through which such markets may produce negative outcomes. Specifically, unfettered capital movements provide enormous scope for destabilizing speculation, which in turn leads to high volatility of both monetary and real variables.

The sheer size of transactions on the global foreign exchange markets today is gigantic. The average daily volume of trade in the global foreign exchange market has risen from a mere US$15 billion in 1973, to US$60 billion in 1983, to US$1,300 billion in 1995 (*Economist* 1995). These enormous foreign exchange dealings are largely driven by short term differences in interest and exchange rates, rather than by fundamentals (Felix 1995, Eatwell 1995). Such market behaviour has, in part, been responsible for the prolonged over-valuation or under-valuation of key currencies (for example, the US dollar in the 1980s), which in turn contributes to the volatility of other financial variables. Fluctuations of financial variables can affect real variables such as investment, both directly and indirectly. Investment is discouraged directly by the rising cost of capital, which is in part caused by volatility in financial variables. In addition, overall uncertainty, which now increasingly characterizes the economic environment, as well as greater fluctuations in the components of final demand[10] also have a negative effect on the corporate inducement to invest. Despite the rise in profits in the 1980s and booming stock markets, the trend rate of growth of investment in industrial countries since 1980 has been about half of what it was in the Golden Age. The fluctuations in interest and foreign exchange rates are by themselves likely to have been significant in this outcome.

To sum up, financial liberalization can, in principle, increase economic welfare by a more efficient allocation of scarce capital resources. Further, in addition to its potential merits noted earlier, trade openness, under certain conditions, can also promote convergence in the sense of factor price equalization. Financial openness can reinforce that process and lead to quicker convergence. However, economic analysis and experience indicate that such benefits of openness can only be realized, provided there are no coordination failures in the domestic as well as international markets. As Stiglitz (1994) has noted, unregulated financial markets are particularly prone to problems of coordination failure.

These have played a significant part in contributing to the poor economic performance of industrial countries in the post-1980 period.

Poor economic performance and the sustainability of liberalization and globalization

The poor economic performance of industrial countries with respect to the growth of output, employment and productivity under a liberalized global regime and the causal links between these failings and financial openness lead to the question posed in the introduction to this chapter: why is there such uncritical enthusiasm for liberalization and globalization in international circles? The most likely answer to this puzzle is that provided by Krugman (1995) in a related, but somewhat narrower context.[11] He suggests that such irrational behaviour by the institutions of economic establishment is perhaps best explained in terms of the sociology of the formation of conventional wisdom. In the analogous case of the mistaken euphoria concerning the benefits of the 'Washington Consensus', Krugman observed as follows:

> ...the endless round of meetings, speeches..., occupy much of the time of the economic opinion leaders. Such interlocking social groupings tend at any given time to converge on a conventional wisdom, about economics among many other things. People believe certain stories because everybody important tells them, and people tell these stories because everyone important believes them. Indeed, when a conventional wisdom is at its fullest strength, one's agreement with that conventional wisdom becomes almost a litmus test of one's suitability to be taken seriously.
>
> (Krugman 1995)

Unfortunately, this euphoria concerning liberalization and globalization is not only unwarranted, but also misleading and potentially dangerous. This is because the future of the present liberal international economic regime itself depends on its ability to meet people's legitimate needs for remunerative jobs and productive work. As Hicks observed with respect to the 1930s:

> The main thing which caused so much liberal opinion in England to lose faith in Free Trade was the helplessness of the older liberalism in the face of massive unemployment, and the possibility of using import restrictions as an element in an active programme fighting

unemployment. One is, of course, obliged to associate this line of thought with the name of Keynes. It was this, almost alone, which lead Keynes to abandon his early belief in Free Trade.
(Hicks 1959, quoted in Bhagwati 1994: 233. On this point, also see Fischer 1995)

Although the view that liberalization and globalization will lead to faster economic growth in industrial countries is not justified by available evidence,[12] what is indeed true is that faster long-term growth of output and employment is *necessary* to sustain the liberal and global economic regime. Not only the history of the 1930s, but also that of the post-Second World War period, suggest that if the problem of mass unemployment and/or low real wages in industrial countries is not solved, it is likely to lead to a negative sum *ad hoc* protectionism in these countries, particularly against Third World products (for a fuller discussion, see Singh 1994b). That would be a negation of the globalized liberal economy.

The following discussion turns now to an analysis of the effects of financial liberalization on developing countries.

Financial openness, stock market development and industrializing economies

Although financial liberalization in developing countries has not proceeded anywhere as far as it has in advanced economies, nevertheless, during the last decade or so, many developing countries have been engaged in far-reaching reforms of their financial systems, liberalizing them and making them more market-oriented. An outstanding feature of this process has been the establishment and very fast expansion of stock markets in these countries. Between 1983 and 1994, the total combined capitalization of companies quoted on the 38 emerging markets included in *The Economist*'s list rose from less than a hundred billion to nearly two trillion US dollars (the sources of these statistics are Feldman and Kumar 1994 for 1983, and El-Erian and Kumar 1995). The corresponding growth in the combined capitalization of industrial countries markets was a little more than threefold – from three trillion to ten trillion US dollars. A number of leading individual emerging markets (e.g. Mexico, Korea, and Thailand) recorded more than a twentyfold increase in total market capitalization over this period of companies quoted on the stock exchanges. By the early 1990s, the latter figure for many of these markets was greater than that for the average medium-sized advanced country market in Europe (e.g. Sweden, Denmark, and Finland) (Singh 1997b).

If market capitalization is considered as a proportion of GDP, the degree of stock market expansion in a number of leading industrializing economies during the 1980s was particularly impressive. On the basis of the historical data Mullin (1993) notes, for example, that it may have taken as many as 85 years (1810–95) for the US capitalization ratio to rise from 7 per cent to 71 per cent. In contrast, the Taiwanese capitalization ratio rose from 11 per cent to 74 per cent in the ten years between 1981 and 1991. Feldman and Kumar (1994) report that the corresponding ratio for Chile increased from 13.2 per cent in 1983 to 78 per cent in 1993. The striking growth of market capitalization relative to GDP was also recorded by a number of other emerging markets during this period – for example, in Jamaica, the ratio rose from 2.8 per cent to 107 per cent; in Mexico, from 2 per cent to 43 per cent; in Korea, from 5.4 per cent to 36.2 per cent; in Thailand, from 3.8 per cent to 55.8 per cent.

Other indicators of stock market development (for example, the volume of shares traded) also rose very sharply during this period. The total value of shares traded on developing country markets included in the International Finance Corporation (IFC) composite index increased from nearly US$25 billion in 1983 to almost US$600 billion in 1992. In Turkey alone, the traded value rose from a mere US$7 million in 1984 to US$23 billion in 1993. Trading volume, either as a proportion of GDP or as a proportion of total market capitalization, for a number of developing country stock markets is now similar to that of the average stock market of advanced countries (Demiriguc-Kunt and Levine 1995).

The breadth and depth of stock market development in industrializing countries in the recent period may be illustrated by considering the specific case of India. Compared with many other semi-industrial countries, India has been rather conservative in initiating financial liberalization. The Indian stock market cannot literally be regarded as an emerging market since the first stock market was established in the country as long ago as 1875. However, up to 1980, stock market development had ebbed and flowed, but in general had been quite slow. In 1980–81, total market capitalization in the Indian stock market as a proportion of GDP was only 5 per cent. As a result of the liberalization measures initiated in the 1980s, by 1990, the ratio had risen to 13 per cent. With the major change in government policy and acceleration of the pace of liberalization in 1991, stock market growth has been explosive. By 1992–93, total market capitalisation had reached 40 per cent of GDP. The number of shareholders and investors in mutual funds rose from 2 million in 1981 to 30 million in 1992–93 (Mayya 1993). In terms of the number of companies listed on the stock markets, the Indian stock market today is the second largest in the world, only slightly behind the United States. In 1992, there were 6,700 companies quoted on Indian stock markets, compared with 7,014 companies in the US, 1,874 in the UK and only 665 in Germany. The average daily trading volume on the Bombay stock market has been about the same as that in London – about 45 000 trades a day. At the peak of stock market activity, trading has occurred at double that rate. Any large Indian city worth its name can now boast a stock exchange. There are functioning stock exchanges in 22 cities, the latest being Coimbatore.

Although there was rapid expansion of emerging markets during the 1980s and 1990s, it should be emphasized that even the most advanced among them are far from being fully mature. On many dimensions (for example, the thickness of the market), developing country stock markets have still got a long way to go. Typically, most of the trading takes place in a small number of stocks. For example, in Argentina in 1993, the share of total market capitalization accounted for by the ten largest stocks was 65.7 per cent. The share of value traded by the ten most active stocks was 68.4 per cent. The corresponding figures for Colombia in that year were 69.6 per cent and 58.6 per cent respectively (El-Erian and Kumar 1995: Table 7). Leaving aside the small number of blue chip and actively traded shares, even in the most developed of the emerging markets, there are serious deficiencies in available information and disclosure requirements regarding the performance and prospects of the shares of other corporations. There are similar weaknesses in the transparency of transactions on these markets. The less developed emerging markets suffer from a far wider range of informational and other deficits.[13] Nevertheless, during the last decade, with financial liberalization as well as other pro-active government measures to encourage stock market development, emerging markets have made considerable progress.

Apart from their role in domestic financial liberalization, in recent years, the stock markets have also been very important for the external financial liberalization of developing countries. In the 1990s, these markets emerged as a major channel for the flows of foreign capital to developing countries. International equity flows to 38 emerging markets increased from US$3.3 billion in 1986 to US$61.2 billion in 1993.[14] Indeed, as the IMF economists El-Erian and Kumar (1995) note, 'when compared to other episodes of large private capital flows to developing countries in the last 20 years, the [present] phenomenon differs in one basic respect: the dominant role of foreign portfolio flows as opposed to bank financing.' These portfolio flows have taken place through a number of distinct channels as external liberalization has progressed. Initially, advanced country investors purchased emerging market equities through country or regional funds; subsequently, there was direct buying of developing country corporate shares by individuals and institutions in industrial countries. In addition, during the last four years, a growing and significant amount of capital has been raised by the direct placement of developing country equities on industrial country markets.

It is generally agreed that both 'pull' and 'push' factors have been at work in attracting these huge amounts of foreign portfolio capital flows to developing countries (also see Eduardo and Montiel 1996, Smith and Walter 1996). The 'pull' factors have included external liberalization measures making it possible for foreigners to hold developing country shares, as well as a general shift in developing country strategies from *dirigisme* to privatization and market orientation. Some of the main 'push' factors have been the lower US interest rates in the early 1990s and the desire of institutional investors in industrial countries to diversify their portfolios.

Stock markets and economic development: alternative schools of thought

A central question is, will the financial liberalization and the associated development of stock markets in the developing countries in the 1980s and the 1990s help or hinder their industrialization and long-term economic growth? The traditional literature on financial liberalization – associated with McKinnon (1973) and Shaw (1973) – has paid relatively little attention to stock markets (also see Singh (forthcoming)). However, the recent development of endogenous growth models by Roemer (1989), Lucas (1988) and others has led to a large and growing amount of theoretical and empirical work on the role of financial markets and financial intermediation in economic growth.

Essentially, this literature[15] argues that financial intermediation, as well as the stock market, helps economic growth by (a) increasing the rate of investment, and (b) improving the productivity of investments. In addition, the stock market, through the take-over mechanism, can ensure that past investments are also most profitably utilized. The markets and the intermediaries carry out the functions of screening and monitoring investment projects, which individual investors on their own will find too uneconomical to undertake. These intermediary and market functions help diversify systemic risk and enable individuals to participate in investment projects, which they may otherwise not have been willing to do. Thus, the economy experiences a higher rate of investment than would otherwise have been the case. Further, to the extent that the financial intermediaries (such as banks) and the stock markets are actually successful in carrying out these monitoring and screening tasks, this should lead to an increase in the efficiency of investment. In this paradigm, the effect of the growth of financial intermediaries and financial markets on private household savings is ambiguous. This is because, as Pagano (1993a) notes, one effect of financial intermediation is more efficient risk sharing, which, depending on the individual's utility function, can have a negative effect on his or her savings.

In the recent endogenous models of finance and development, King and Levine (1993) emphasize the merits of financial intermediation with respect to the promotion of technical progress and entrepreneurship. Others have stressed the risk-sharing, monitoring and screening functions which the stock market may perform with respect to new investment projects (Allen 1993). Levine and Zervos (1995) suggest that the two main channels of financial intermediation – banks and the stock market – complement each other. However, Atje and Jovanovic (1993) conclude that while stock markets positively effect growth, raising it by a huge 2.5 per cent per annum, banks have little influence. This leads them to enquire why 'more countries are not developing their stock markets as quickly as they can as a means of speeding up their economic development.'

The empirical work in the above studies is invariably based on Barro-type inter-country cross-sectional analysis. Quah (1993), Lee, Pesaran and Smith (1996), and Arestis and Demetriades (1997) have emphasized the limitations of this kind of cross-sectional methodology in drawing causal inferences. Equally significantly, Singh (1997b) has pointed out that these empirical exercises represent reduced form analyses which abstract from the precise channels through which the stock market performs its tasks. The relevant channels are the pricing process and the take-over mechanism.

The stock market critics contend that, contrary to theory, in practice, these two mechanisms operate imperfectly, so that even well-functioning stock markets (such as those in the US and UK) do not perform the monitoring, screening and disciplinary functions at all well. For example, both analytical work and evidence suggest that actual stock market prices – although reasonably efficient in Tobin's (1984) 'information arbitrage sense' – are subject to whims and fads, often dominated by 'noise traders' and, therefore, not necessarily efficient in the critical sense of reflecting fundamental values.[16] Similarly, on the take-over mechanism, empirical evidence suggests that competitive selection in the market for corporate control takes place much more on the basis of size than performance. Due to various capital market imperfections, a large unprofitable firm has a greater survival probability than a small efficient firm. Indeed, the former may increase its chances of survival by further increasing its size through the take-over process itself (for a recent review of corporate take-overs, see Singh 1992a).

The critical school further contends that the actual operation of the pricing and take-over mechanisms in the well-functioning US and UK stock markets, leads to short-termism and lower rates of long-term investment, particularly in firm-specific human capital.[17] It also generates perverse incentives, rewarding managers for their success in financial engineering, rather than creating new wealth through organic growth. These deficiencies put the Anglo-Saxon economies at a competitive disadvantage with respect to Japan and Germany, which operate without hostile take-overs and where stock markets have historically been unimportant in industrial development (Porter 1992, Dore 1985). Thus, Porter (1992: 65) observes that:

> ... the change in nature of competition and the increasing pressure of globalization make investment the most critical determinant of competitive advantage ... yet the US system of allocating investment both within and across companies is failing. This puts American companies at a serious disadvantage in global competition and ultimately threatens the long-term growth of the US economy.

Stock markets and developing countries

There are important implications of the above analysis for developing countries that require examination. If even well-organized stock markets do not perform their disciplinary, allocative and other tasks satisfactorily and may impair international competitiveness, developing country markets are likely to do worse in these respects. This is because even leading emerging markets (such as Taiwan or India) do not possess the regulatory infrastructure for well-functioning markets[18] or adequate information-gathering and disseminating private firms. Moreover, the young firms on these markets will not have long enough records for their reputations to be accurately assessed. All this will lead to a noisy stock market environment, with arbitrary pricing and considerable volatility (Tirole 1991). In such circumstances, the monitoring, screening and disciplining functions of the stock markets may be more efficiently performed by financial intermediaries such as banks (Mayer 1989).

A central weakness of a stock market system with respect to finance–industry relationships is that it provides investors with almost instant liquidity. Although seen as a virtue by orthodox economists, this liquidity also means that the investors need not have a long-term commitment to the firm (Bhide 1993).[19] The bank-dominated financial systems, by contrast, can ensure such commitment. Further, because of close bank–corporation relationships, German–Japanese type banks can cope far better with asymmetric information, agency costs and transaction costs than the Anglo-Saxon stock market system (Hoshi *et al.* 1991, Allen and Gale 1995).

Stock market volatility and financing of corporate growth in developing countries

For the reasons outlined above, share prices in emerging markets may be expected to fluctuate more than those in well-developed markets. However, a high degree of volatility is a negative feature of a stock market for several reasons: (a) it can undermine the financial system as a whole; (b) it makes share prices much less useful as a guide to resource allocation; (c) to the extent that it discourages risk-averse savers and investors, it raises the cost of capital to corporations; (d) it may also stop risk-averse firms from raising funds on the stock market, or even (e) from seeking a listing on the stock market (Pagano 1993b).

Evidence supports the prediction of much higher share price volatility in developing countries compared with industrial countries (Davis 1995). In extreme cases, El-Erian and Kumar (1995) report that between 1983 and 1993, stock market volatility in Mexico was nearly 15 times, and Turkey more than 20 times as large as that in the US or Japan. There is also evidence of information-arbitrage inefficiency in developing country share prices (Feldman and Kumar 1994). More significantly, share prices in many emerging markets would appear to have deviated considerably from fundamentals in the share price booms of the last decade (see below).

However, some of the other implications of stock market volatility are not supported by the experience in developing countries during the last 15 years. During this period, not only has there been a big increase in emerging market activity and listings, but firms in developing countries have been raising considerable capital on stock markets.

In the first large-scale empirical studies of corporate finance for developing countries, Singh and Hamid (1992) and Singh (1995a) examined the financing of corporate growth of net assets (that is, the long-term capital employed in the firm) in the 1980s in several countries – India, Turkey, Brazil, Malaysia, Thailand, Zimbabwe, Korea, Jordan, Pakistan, and Mexico. Singh's (1995a) sample consisted of the top 100 listed corporations in each country. This research showed that, in general, large corporations in developing countries rely heavily on (a) external funds, and (b) new share issues to finance their net assets growth. In five of the ten sample countries, over 70 per cent of corporate growth during the past decade was financed from external funds. In another two, the external financing proportion was more than half. Similarly, the importance of equity finance for corporations in developing countries is indicated by the fact that in five of the nine sample countries with the relevant data, over 40 per cent of the growth of net assets in the 1980s was financed by new share issues. In another two countries, equity finance accounted for over 25 per cent of corporate growth during the relevant period.

These results are surprising for several reasons. The financing pattern in developing countries is not only different from that observed in advanced countries, it is also counter-intuitive and contrary to the predictions of most economic models. Advanced country corporations normally follow the 'pecking order' and issue very little equity, being funded largely by retained profits (Mayer 1990; see, however, Meeks and Whittington 1975, and Singh 1995a). In view of serious capital market imperfections and high volatility, corporations in developing countries may be expected to rely much more on internal, rather than external funds, and resort far less to equity finance than industrial country firms. Further, since the former are more likely to be family-controlled than the latter, this should also discourage corporate equity issuance for fear of losing control.

How then are these anomalous phenomena of the fast expansion of stock market listings and heavy reliance on equity finance by the big corporations in developing countries in the recent period to be explained? Singh (1995a) provides a set of inter-linked hypotheses to account for these observations. Briefly, the stage of development theory of equity financing is rejected. It is argued that unlike the US and the UK in the nineteenth century, stock market development in developing countries today is not simply an evolutionary response to market forces.

Rather, for various reasons (such as privatization programmes), many governments in developing countries have played a major proactive role in the expansion of these markets.

Further, Singh (1995a) suggests that an essential reason why corporations in developing countries resorted so much to equity financing in the 1980s was that the relative cost of equity capital fell significantly during these years. This was due to a large rise in share prices, which was, in turn, brought about by both internal and external financial liberalization.[20] At the same time, the relative cost of debt financing increased because of the steep rise in international interest rates as well as financial de-repression measures, which several countries embarked on during this period. Thus, the cost of equity capital relative to that of debt became much more favourable to equities during the course of the 1980s. To illustrate, Amsden and Euh (1990) note that in 1980, the average price/earnings ratio on the Korean stock market was about 3, and therefore, roughly, the cost of capital through share issues was 33 per cent. By 1989, the average price/earnings ratio had risen to 14 reducing the cost of equity capital to 7.1 per cent. Euh and Barker (1990) estimate that in terms of cash flow, taking into account the tax element, the latter cost to the Korean corporations in 1989 was only 3 per cent. This compares with a figure of 12.5 per cent for preferential commercial bank loans.

Thus, contrary to most economists' expectations, stock markets in developing countries have contributed significantly to corporate growth in the 1980s and 1990s. However, important questions from the perspective of long-term economic growth are: has this led to increased aggregate savings and investments, or raised the productivity of investments. These issues have not been systematically investigated for most developing countries (Claessens 1995). Some useful evidence for India (Nagaraj 1994) shows that financial liberalization and capital market growth in the 1980s simply led to portfolio substitution from bank deposits to tradable securities, rather than greater aggregate national or *financial* savings.[21] Nagaraj notes that despite the stock market boom of that decade and the substantial resources raised there by Indian corporations, corporate investment in fixed assets declined. Nor does he find evidence of increased output growth in the private corporate sector. The sector apparently used the new stock market funds to alter the corporate capital structure by increasing the proportions of equity capital and substituting securitized debt for bank loans. Both Singh (1995a) and Nagaraj report a secular fall in corporate profitability in India during the 1980s, which could, in principle, be due to product market liberalization. However, it then becomes difficult to explain the stock market boom except in terms of market psychology and speculation (see also below).

External liberalization, the stock market and the real economy

Foreign portfolio investment, following external financial liberalization in developing countries, has been particularly important for the foreign exchange-constrained Latin American economies in the recent period. The enormous portfolio flows to these countries in the 1990s helped to alleviate the constraint and enabled a modest economic growth (about 3.5 per cent per annum during 1990–94) after the 'lost decade' of the 1980s. At the microeconomic level, the portfolio inflows helped generate the stock market boom, lowering the cost of capital to Latin American corporations. In Mexico, much of the inflow went into the stock market and leaving aside the question of fluctuations, the share price index rose from 250 in 1989 to around 2,500 in 1994.

However, as Rodrik (1994) and Krugman (1995) point out, these portfolio flows to Latin America were not responding to fundamentals, but represented a misplaced euphoria and a 'herd' instinct.[22] The market was not rewarding virtue, frugality and restraint but, in many countries, subsidizing consumption instead at the expense of investment. Despite evidence that countries like Mexico were running huge current account deficits and using inflows largely for current consumption, such flows continued. The Mexican trade balance shifted from a small surplus in 1988 to a deficit of US$20 billion in 1993; the current account deficit was about 6 per cent of GDP in 1993 and 9 per cent in 1994. Financial and trade liberalization policies led to a fall in private savings from roughly 15 per cent to 5 per cent of GDP despite high interest rates (Taylor 1996). Notwithstanding huge capital inflows in the l990s, Mexico's rate of economic growth during 1990–94 was only 2.5 per cent per annum – barely equal to the rate of population growth.

The speculative bubble burst in December 1994, when portfolio flows to Mexico suddenly stopped. Share prices fell sharply, not only in Mexico, but also, through the 'contagion' effect, in most emerging markets.[23] The impact on the real economy was devastating – real GDP fell by 7 per cent in 1995 in Mexico and by 5 per cent in Argentina. Thus, even when financial markets have been expansionary,[24] their bandwagon and herd characteristics generate considerable instability for the real economy.

Portfolio capital was recommended to developing countries for being less vulnerable to external interest rate shocks than debt (WIDER 1990). However, in practice, these inflows have proved to be just as destabilizing. As Akyuz (1993b) points out, external liberalization through opening stock markets to non-residents leads to close links between two inherently unstable markets – the stock and currency markets – even when the capital account is not fully open. Faced with an economic shock, the two markets may interact with each other in a negative feedback loop to produce even greater instability for the markets and the whole financial system. Moreover, the gyrations in these markets may discourage aggregate investment through various channels, for example by depressing business expectations because of greater uncertainty, thereby causing greater instability in aggregate consumption because of wealth effects caused by large fluctuations in stock market prices. These factors contribute to the instability of the real economy and may also reduce long-term economic growth.

Such negative feedback effects will be particularly pronounced if external financial liberalization is carried out in 'disequilibrium' conditions of high and unpredictable inflation and fluctuating exchange rates. However, because of the structural characteristics of developing countries, which make them more subject to external and internal shocks than advanced economies, many of these unfavourable outcomes are likely to prevail even under 'normal' conditions, and even if there were a correct 'sequencing' of financial reforms.

Summary and conclusion

There exists today a palpable euphoria in international economic circles and among multilateral institutions concerning the benefits of liberalization and globalization. This chapter has argued that the euphoria is unwarranted by evidence and, at a policy level, it is dangerously misleading.

The first part of this chapter considered the case of leading industrial countries. It was noted that these economies have effectively operated under a regime of more or less free trade in manufactures and free capital movements for the last 10 to 15 years. The experience of these countries therefore provides a useful test case for assessing the benefits of liberalization and globalization.

The chapter shows that the economic record of industrial countries in the post-1980 period is far from inspiring. It is argued here that this poor performance has not been caused by exogenous factors, but is directly linked to the intrinsic features of the new market-supremacist liberal economic order. Specifically, it was argued above that these countries have been harmed by liberalized global financial markets (that is, financial openness) in a number of interrelated ways. First, in the absence of adequate international cooperation between governments, the balance-of-payments equilibrium between countries has only been maintained at low rates of growth of world demand. Secondly, individual industrial countries have been obliged by financial markets to follow generally restrictive policies which, by themselves, would discourage investment. Thirdly, the much greater volatility of key financial and economic variables under liberalized global markets would reinforce that trend. This would result in lower rates of growth of output and employment. The net result has been the observed low rates of growth of output and employment.

Moreover, the chapter suggests that there is little likelihood that under the current market-supremacist, liberalized, global economic regime, industrial countries will be able to achieve the trend increase in economic growth required to create sufficient numbers of good jobs to meet the needs of the people. This will jeopardize the sustainability of the liberal regime. The paradox is that faster growth may not follow from liberalization and globalization, but is nevertheless required to sustain the liberal trading order. This chapter indicates that in order to achieve the latter purpose, the freedom of the unruly financial markets may need to be curbed.

The second part of the chapter has concentrated on the role of the stock markets in both the internal and the external financial liberalization in developing countries in the 1980s and the 1990s. This process is continuing with the encouragement of the Bretton Woods Institutions: several more stock markets are being established in Africa and in transition economies.

The main conclusion here is that these developments are unlikely to help in achieving quicker industrialization and faster long-term economic growth in most developing countries for several reasons. First, the inherent volatility and arbitrariness of the stock market pricing process under developing country conditions make it a poor guide to efficient investment allocation. Secondly, the interactions between the stock and currency markets, in the wake of unfavourable economic shocks, may exacerbate macroeconomic instability and reduce long-term growth. Thirdly, stock market development will undermine the existing bank–industry relationships in developing countries, which despite their many difficulties, are not without merit in several countries, at least in the highly successful East Asian economies.[25]

This is not to overlook the problems with these relationships in many other developing countries (such as crony capitalism, monopolistic abuses, inadequate government regulations) (Singh 1993). However, even these countries would have been better off reforming and expanding their extant banking systems rather than establishing stock markets (see further Akyuz 1993b). Reforming the existing banking system would not only have absorbed less resources directly, it would also have been an easier option, in terms of institutional capacity, for most developing countries,[26] compared with the infrastructure required for well-functioning stock markets.

Stock markets are potent symbols of capitalism but, paradoxically, capitalism flourishes better without their hegemony. Contrary to a view expressed by the World Bank (1989), stock market expansion is not a necessary natural progression of a country's financial development. Historically, such progression has not occurred in leading continental European economies. Similarly, in the more recent post-World War II period, countries like Germany and Italy have been able to achieve their economic miracles with little assistance from the stock market (de Cecco 1993, Pagano 1993a). Stock markets have also not been significant in the post-war industrialization of Japan, Korea, and Taiwan (World Bank 1993). There is evidence that Japan deliberately encouraged the development of the banking system, rather than the stock market, after the War (Somel 1992). Developing countries simply cannot afford the luxury of stock markets. As Keynes (1936: 159) noted, 'when the capital development of a country becomes the by-product of the activities of a casino, the job is likely to be ill-done.'

However, notwithstanding Keynes, in the post-Cold War international economic order, realistically, whatever their merits, stock markets in developing countries are now here to stay. Singh (1993, 1994a) has suggested two areas of immediate policy concern with respect to these markets. The first involves the control of portfolio capital flows. Many countries, notably including Chile and South Korea, restrict such flows to their economic advantage (Akyuz and Cornford 1994). In the wake of the Mexican crisis, the case for controls is, if anything, strengthened. The important analytical point here is to throw sand into the interactions between the foreign exchange and the stock markets, even if it may be infeasible and/or undesirable to sever the connection altogether.

The second area concerns the market for corporate control, which can compound the negative effects of stock markets. So far, take-overs have not been significant in corporate growth in developing countries. However, as there exist, in many emerging markets, potentially predatory large domestic conglomerates (see further Amsden and Hikino 1994), and there is growing institutional investment, a market for corporate control will soon emerge. This would hinder the growth of small firms, reduce product market competition and lead to dynamic inefficiencies (Singh 1995a). Governments in developing countries must take timely steps to restrict the emergence and operation of such a market. The cross of the stock market is heavy enough for the developing countries to bear without also being landed with an Anglo-Saxon-type market for corporate control.

Notes

1   This chapter draws heavily on Singh (1997a) and Singh (1997b) and was originally written in July 1996, well before the present financial crises in Southeast and East Asia. The author is grateful to Blackwells and Oxford University Press, the respective publishers of the two papers, for permission to reproduce material from them for this chapter.

2   The reader will note that free movement of labour across national boundaries has not been included in the definition of liberalization and globalization above. This is not because it is wrong or illogical to also consider labour markets under this rubric; on the contrary, it may be regarded as illogical to include some factor markets (e.g. capital) and not others, such as labour. However, the reason for adopting the more restricted definition in this chapter is to sharpen the debate with the World Bank by using the same definition as theirs. Nevertheless, as Singh (1996) observes, although there is relatively little free international movement of labour, there has been considerable deregulation of domestic labour markets in many industrial countries in the 1980s and the 1990s.

3   There is no suggestion here that the oil shock 'caused' the crisis. Also see Singh (1995b, 1997a).

4   It may be argued that the market supremacist liberal economy was not properly operational until the mid-1980s and, therefore, the relevant period for assessing performance of such a regime should be 1985–95. However, economic performance in industrial countries over the last 10 years has been no better than over the last 15 years.

5   For an analysis of how this new cooperative model arose out of the harsh experience of the Great Depression and the political conditions of post-war Europe, see Glyn *et al.* 1990; Singh (1995b).

6   For an analysis of the fall of the Golden Age, see Glyn *et al.* (1990), Kindleberger (1992).

7   See Singh (1995c) on the East Asian experience in this respect; also see Free-
    man (1989).
8   The markets have sometimes also been expansionary, as in the case of Latin
    America in the 1990s. This is discussed further below.
9   This is, of course, the Keynesian view of price formation in foreign exchange
    markets. For a discussion of the rational expectations perspective, see Dam
    (1982). For a critical analysis of the rational expectations view, see Felix
    (1995).
10 UNCTAD (1995) notes that financial deregulation has made aggregate
    demand more unstable by increasing the volatility of consumption expend-
    itures, exports and imports. Easier access to credit has enabled consumers to
    spend more freely, but their accumulated debt has made their current expend-
    iture more vulnerable to changes in interest rates. The increase in the
    coefficient of variation in the volume growth of private consumption in
    five major OECD countries from 1961–73 to 1982–94 ranged from 78 per
    cent to 167 per cent. Export and import volatilities have also increased due to
    sharp changes in competitiveness brought about by exchange rate fluctua-
    tions and by swings in economic activity.
11 Other plausible hypotheses for this phenomena are discussed in Singh
    (1997a)
12 Sachs and Warner (1995) suggest that developing countries which are more
    'open', grow faster. However, openness here refers only to trade, not finance.
    Moreover, the main indicator of the lack of trade openness is essentially the
    black market premium. However, the latter variable is problematic since it is
    not just a function of lack of 'openness', in the sense of restrictive trade
    practices, but is much more a reflection of the macroeconomic disequilibria
    of the economy. See the interchange between Warner, Srinivasan, and Dorn-
    bush in the General Discussion on Sachs and Warner (1995: 106).
13 Feldman and Kumar (1994) divide emerging markets into four groups accord-
    ing to their stage of development. However, also see Demiriguc-Kunt and
    Levine (1995).
14 The source of these data is *Baring Securities: Cross Border Analysis*, as reported
    in Table 3 of El-Erian and Kumar (1995).
15 For a recent overview of these contributions, see Pagano (1993a).
16 For a review of the issues and evidence, see the papers in *Journal of Economic
    Policy* (1990).
17 For a review of the issues see Singh (1995b), Porter (1992). For an opposite
    perspective, see Marsh (1990).
18 With respect to Taipei, *The Economist* (9 September 1989, p. 20) noted,
    'Taiwan's stock market is a rigged casino with a phenomenal turnover....
    Its family-controlled firms equate accountancy with tax-evading creativity.
    Its courts react... to the nudges of the influential.... it is as free-wheeling
    and corrupt as the Philippines, but then we admit it is a free-wheel that
    works.'
19 Levine and Zervos (1995) and Atje and Jovanovic (1993) find, in their econo-
    metric work, a positive relationship between stock market liquidity (proxied
    by turnover) and economic development. However, as noted earlier, the
    question of causality here is problematical. For example, in some high-
    growth countries such as Taiwan, it may be perverse to ascribe causality to

stock market liquidity, even if there is perfect co-movement between the two variables. This is because *The Economist*'s description of the Taiwanese stock market as a 'rigged casino with a phenomenal turnover' – in the earlier note – is an apt one. In 1989, the average value of shares traded for each three-hour trading day on the Taipei stock market was nearly three billion US dollars. That was one billion US dollars a day more than in London, and more than half of New York's trading. On 28 August 1989, Taipei recorded a trading volume of 7.6 billion US dollars. The world's biggest stock market, Tokyo, traded just 4.2 billion US dollars worth of shares on the same day. Share prices on the Taiwanese market in the relevant period were subject to huge medium-term swings, which were not justified by changes in economic prospects (Singh 1993). This kind of high turnover of shares is generated by a public taste for speculation and gambling. It is likely to diminish, rather than promote economic growth as it undermines the capitalistic ethic by destroying the link between effort and reward.

20   Prior to liberalization, most developing country savers had limited avenues for savings due to financial repression. With internal liberalization and easier access to the stock market, share ownership and stock market participation greatly increased in many countries in the 1980s. Furthermore, a significant additional source of demand for corporate equities in developing countries came from advanced country institutional investors seeking to achieve portfolio diversification (Singh 1995a).

21   For scattered evidence on these issues for other countries, see Singh (1993, 1995a).

22   Krugman (1995), in effect, ascribes this euphoria to the mistaken belief that once a developing country follows the path set out in the Washington Consensus, it will achieve fast economic growth. However, 'conventional wisdom' was so wedded to this view that it ignored all evidence and analysis to the contrary. As noted earlier, Krugman outlines the sociological process through which such mistaken beliefs are termed and tenaciously held by the economic establishment.

23   'The Mexican financial crisis...resulted in a linked collapse of stock market values in almost all developing countries, *regardless of economic policies and performance*. The "contagion" effect was clear...' (Smith and Walter 1996, emphasis added).

24   As noted earlier, in advanced countries, financial markets have generally worked in a 'deflationary' way, penalizing governments that follow expansionary policies (Singh 1996).

25   On the relationships between banks and industry in East Asian economies, see, for example, Cho (1989), Amsden (1989), Wade (1990), Kojima (1995), Singh (1996).

26   If a developing country is not capable of running an above-board banking system, the establishment of a stock market is unlikely to help and may compound the problem. The recent history of both developing countries and advanced countries is rife with stock market scandals such as the huge 1992 stock market scam in India and regular scandals in Taiwan and Japan.

8
International Financial Liberalization and the Crisis of East Asian Development

Jomo K. S.[*]

After months of international speculative attacks on the Thai baht, the Bank of Thailand let its currency float from 2 July 1997. By mid-July 1997, the currencies of all three second-tier Southeast Asian newly industrializing countries (NICs) – i.e. also Indonesia and Malaysia – had fallen precipitously, with their stock markets following suit. The Philippines was also similarly affected, although not as badly. Before the end of 1997, despite its rather different economic structure, South Korea too collapsed. Most other economies in East Asia have also been under considerable pressure, either directly (e.g. the attack on the Hong Kong dollar) or indirectly (e.g. due to the desire to maintain comparative cost advantage against the now greatly devalued currencies of Southeast Asian exporters).

Contrary to the impression conveyed by many economic journalists and commentators as well as by the International Monetary Fund (IMF), there is still little agreement on how to understand and characterize the crisis. One manifestation of this has been the debate between the IMF and its critics over the appropriateness of its negotiated programmes in Thailand, Indonesia, and South Korea. While policy debates have understandably captured the most attention, especially with the public at large, the East Asian crises have also challenged international economists.

Some still see the crisis as essentially a currency crisis, although perhaps of a new type, different from those previously identified with either fiscal profligacy or macroeconomic indiscipline. Approaching it slightly differently, other economists see it as a balance of payments crisis, emphasizing the current account deficits sustained by some of the economies affected. However, a growing number now seem to agree that the crisis started off as a currency crisis and quickly became a more generalized financial crisis, before impacting on the real economy due to reduced liquidity in the financial system and the consequences of official policy and other responses.

There is also considerable debate about the implications of this crisis for economic development, particularly for the debate over whether the East Asian experience of the last three decades offered different lessons and prescriptions for development from those advocated by the 'counter-revolution' against development economics. As is now well known, this neo-liberal reaction has maintained that development economics and its prescriptions constituted bad economics, based on distortions of neo-classical welfare economics, which exaggerated the extent and implications of 'market failure' and underestimated the likelihood of 'state failure' and its consequences.

Influential economists at the World Bank and elsewhere have cited the East Asian financial crisis to criticize the Bank's 1993 *East Asian Miracle* volume as flawed. In particular, the critics denounce the study's acknowledgement of the success of 'directed credit' and what has come to be known as 'financial restraint' – said to have been authored by the Bank's recent Senior Vice-President and Chief Economist, Joseph Stiglitz, who has also dissented on the appropriateness of IMF prescriptions for the current financial crisis.

With the mid-1997 crisis starting not long after Paul Krugman's (1994) claims that East Asian growth is not sustainable because it is based primarily on factor accumulation – eventually subject to diminishing returns – rather than productivity growth ('perspiration rather than inspiration'), many critics – from across the political spectrum – have seen the East Asian financial crisis as evidence of Krugman's argument, or of some variation thereof. Often, there is more than a touch of neo-liberal triumphalism in hasty pronouncements of the end of the Asian miracle, or in word plays of 'miracle or debacle', 'tigers or fat cats' and the like.

Meanwhile, in recent years, there has been growing recognition of major structural and systemic differences among the eight high performing Asian economies (HPAEs) studied by the World Bank (1993), namely Japan, South Korea, Taiwan, Hong Kong, Singapore, Malaysia, Thailand, and Indonesia. The last three have been increasingly grouped as second-tier or second-generation Southeast Asian newly industrializing countries (NICs), with characteristics quite different from the others, and of course, even among themselves. It has been argued that industrial policy or selective state intervention has been of much poorer quality and less effective in these economies for various reasons. Instead, there has been much other state intervention motivated by other, less developmentalist considerations, especially in Malaysia and Indonesia (Jomo *et al.* 1997). It appears that such interventions bear some of the responsibility for the vulnerability of the second-tier Southeast Asian NICs to the factors which have precipitated the mid-1997 financial crisis in the region.

Macroeconomic problems

Rapid economic growth and structural change, mainly associated with industrialization in the region, is generally traced back to the mid-1980s, when devaluations in all three countries as well as selective deregulation of onerous rules helped create attractive conditions for the relocation of production facilities in these countries and elsewhere in Southeast Asia and China, especially from Japan and the first-tier or first-generation newly industrializing economies of South Korea, Taiwan, Hong Kong, and Singapore. This dynamic growth sustained export-oriented industrialization well into the 1990s, but was soon accompanied by the growth of other manufacturing, services as well as construction.

This is not to suggest that the fundamentals were all alright in Southeast Asia. Although high growth was sustained for almost a decade, during most of which fiscal balances were in order, monetary expansion was not excessive and inflation was generally under control, some other indices have been awry. The export-led growth of Southeast Asian economies since the late 1980s has been followed by a construction and property boom, fuelled by financial sectors favouring such 'short-termist' investments – involving loans with collateral, which bankers like – over more productive, but often, also more risky investments in manufacturing and agriculture. The exaggerated expansion of investment in such 'non-tradeables' has exacerbated current account trade deficits. Although widespread in East Asia for various reasons, the property–finance nexus was particularly strong in Thailand, which made it much more vulnerable to the inevitable bursting of the bubble.

Financial liberalization from the 1980s also saw major ramifications in the region, as foreign savings supplemented the already high domestic savings rates in the region to accelerate further the rate of capital accumulation, albeit in increasingly unproductive activities, owing to the foreign domination of most internationally competitive industries in the region. Consequently, several related macroeconomic concerns had emerged from the rapid growth of that decade by the mid-1990s:

First, the savings-investment gap, which was 5 per cent of GNP in 1997, lay behind the current account deficit,[1] which has exceeded RM12 billion since 1994. The gap had been bridged historically by heavy reliance on foreign direct investment (FDI). But high FDI and foreign debt have, in turn, caused growing investment income outflows abroad.[2] In recent years especially, the current account gap has been temporarily bridged by short-term capital inflows, as in 1993 and since 1995, with disastrous consequences later with the subsequent reversal of such flows. Many recent confidence restoration measures seek to induce such short-term inflows once again, but they cannot be relied upon to address the underlying problem in the medium to long term.[3]

Although always in the minority, foreign investment institutions 'made' the stock markets in the region, shifting their assets among securities markets as well as among different types of financial investment options all over the world. In the face of limited transparency, the regional nature of their presence, the nature of fund managers' incentives and remuneration, and the short-termism of their investment horizons, foreign financial institutions were much more prone to herd behaviour and contributed most to the regional spread of contagion.

Second, there was a recent explosion of private sector debt, especially from abroad, not least due to the efforts of 'debt-pushers' associated with the growth of 'private banking.'[4] The ratio of loans to GNP had risen rapidly in recent years. Meanwhile, commercial banks' foreign liabilities more than tripled between 1995 and 1997. This is partly why the standard insistence on raising domestic interest rates is quite misleading as much of the recent increase in corporate borrowings had come from abroad. This had exacerbated the impact of the current crisis, with triple pain caused by currency depreciation, stock market collapse, and rising interest rates.

Meanwhile, the *over-investment* of investible funds, especially from abroad, in 'non-tradeables' only made things worse, especially on the current account. Only a small proportion of commercial bank and other lending had gone to manufacturing, agriculture, mining, and other productive activities; the percentage is likely to be even smaller with foreign borrowings, most of which had been collateralized with assets such as real property and stock.[5] In other words, much of the inflow of foreign savings actually contributed to an asset price inflation, mainly involving real estate and share prices. In so far as such investments did not contribute to increased production of 'tradeables', they actually exacerbated the current account deficit,[6] rather than alleviated it – as they were thought to be doing. This, in turn, worsened the problem of 'currency mismatch' with borrowings in US dollars invested in activities not generating foreign exchange. In so far as a high proportion of these foreign borrowings were short-term in nature and were deployed to finance medium to long term projects, an additional 'term mismatch' problem also arose.

More generally, the foreign exchange risk of investments generally increased, raising the vulnerability of these economies to the maintenance of the quasi-pegs of their currencies to the US dollar,[7] which had, in turn, encouraged a great deal of unhedged borrowing involving an influential constituency with a strong stake in defending the peg regardless of its adverse consequences for the economy. Owing to foreign domination of export-oriented industries in Southeast Asia, unlike Northeast Asia, there was no strong domestic export-oriented industrial community to lobby for floating or depreciation of the Southeast Asian currencies despite the obvious adverse consequences of the peg for international cost competitiveness. Instead, after virtually pegging their currencies to the US dollar since the advent of flexible exchange rates, from the early 1990s and especially from the mid-1990s, most Southeast Asian central banks resisted downward adjustments in their exchange rates, which would have reduced, if not averted some of the more disruptive consequences of the recent currency collapses.[8]

According to the Bank of International Settlements (BIS) (*Asian Wall Street Journal*, 6 January 1998), well over half of the foreign borrowings from commercial banks were short-term in nature, i.e. coming due soon: Malaysia 56 per cent, Thailand 66 per cent, Indonesia 59 per cent, and South Korea 68 per cent. There is growing evidence of continued lending by continental European and Japanese banks to East Asian customers despite warnings by the BIS and others well before the crisis broke in July 1997 (Raghavan 1998).

Contrary to the claim that 'the market' will exact swift and painful punishment on governments and economies that do not have their macroeconomic house in order, the timing, nature, and consequences of the mid-1997 financial crisis in Southeast Asia underline the imperfect nature of financial markets. This has been reflected in the long delay in 'rectification'. For example, current account deficits were more serious in 1995 compared to 1997, but there was no rectification then, let alone punishment of the culprits, i.e. current account deficits in

Malaysia and some other neighbouring economies had reached all time highs, without any commensurate adverse effect.[9]

In the wake of the Mexican crisis in early 1995, even the International Monetary Fund (IMF) stepped back momentarily from its advocacy of virtually unfettered financial liberalization. Unfortunately, the short-termism of financial markets extends to human and institutional memories as well as to related policy making and advocacy. The recent crisis has also seen a market where the magnitude of 'overshooting' exceeds that of the 'correction' many times over. Further evidence of market-induced anarchy can be found in the 'herd' behaviour underlying the 'contagion' or 'domino' effects. While affected government and economies have been badly affected by the crisis since mid-1997, there is little evidence that the private sector culprits have suffered most as a consequence, i.e. the market is not only neither inefficient and slow, but also unjust.

Perceiving the Southeast Asian region as much more integrated than it actually is (e.g. in terms of trade links excluding Singapore, the regional entrepôt), the panicky investment decisions of fund managers based outside the region – e.g. in Wall Street or the City of London – have often been 'herd-like,'[10] causing a 'contagion' or 'domino' effect throughout the region. The very logic and magnitude of hedge fund operations[11] have tended to exacerbate these phenomena, with disastrous snowballing consequences for the region. Other international, regional and, increasingly, local currency speculators and hedgers have also been responsible, but mainly reacting in their own self-interest to perceived market trends, rather than as part of some grand conspiracy.

Policy lessons

There is little point in arguing that the crisis should not have happened since East Asian economic fundamentals were fine, even if that were true. In some instances such denial exacerbated the problem as authorities did not recognize and respond to the problem with any great sense of urgency. Unfortunately, as East Asia has painfully learnt, financial markets are driven by sentiments as much as by fundamentals. Hence, although much more serious current account deficits in 1995 did not result in crisis, it does not mean that an economy can maintain such deficits indefinitely without being vulnerable to speculative attack or loss of confidence.

One cannot, for example, liberalize the capital account, and then complain when short-term portfolio investors suddenly withdraw due to their whims and fancies. Even Chile, once the darling of the Chicago monetarists, makes it very difficult – and costly – to withdraw capital rapidly from its economy, and treats foreign direct investment very differently from portfolio investment. Such authorities try to distinguish between portfolio investments that are simply short-termist from, say, pension funds with a more medium-term orientation. After all, one cannot expect more birds to fly into rather than out of an open birdcage indefinitely since the basic premise of financial liberalization is 'easy come, easy go.'[12]

In recent years, some Southeast Asian economies became excessively reliant on such short-term capital inflows to bridge their current account deficits. This problem was exacerbated by excessive imports to make more non-exportables such as buildings and infrastructure. Ostensibly prudent financial institutions often preferred to lend for real property and stock purchases, and thus secure assets with rising values as collateral, rather than to provide credit for more productive ends.

While foreign banks were happy to lend US dollars at higher interest rates than available elsewhere, Southeast Asian businesses were keen to borrow at lower interest rates than available domestically. The costs of hedging – a hundred basis points or so for ringgit-dollar, a few hundred for baht-dollar or rupiah-dollar – now look cheap in hindsight. The existence of a well-developed swap market allows Southeast Asian companies to tap into foreign capital markets, at a not unreasonable cost, by swapping away the currency risk. Hence, the problem was ultimately one of greed: the combination of much lower foreign interest rates and seemingly fixed exchange rates caused borrowers to gamble and not prudently pay the cost for some insurance by hedging.

Hence, most such loans remained unhedged as Southeast Asian currencies seemed pegged to the US dollar since the 1970s despite the official fictions of exchange rates moving with the basket of currencies of major foreign trading partners. The boom in private banking in the region in recent years led to competitive lending reminiscent of the loans to Third World governments in the late 1970s (which built up to the debt crisis of the early 1980s). However, the new fiction in international policy-making circles was that such accumulation of private sector debt did not matter as long as public sector debt was reined in.

Meanwhile, portfolio investors moved into the newly emerging stock markets of Southeast Asia with encouragement from the International Finance Corporation, an arm of the World Bank. In Malaysia, for example, they came in a big way in 1993, only to withdraw even more suddenly in early 1994, leaving most retail stockholders in the lurch. But unfortunately, policy-makers seem to have short memories and did not learn the lessons from that experience as the new unsustainable build-up from 1995 sent stock prices soaring once again despite declining price-earnings ratios. The rest is history, but as a wise man once said, when history repeats itself, the first time it is tragedy, the second time farce.

Thus, the Southeast Asian currency and financial crises since mid-1997 have been partly due to financial liberalization and its consequent undermining of monetary and financial governance. The 'quasi-pegs' of the region's currencies to the US dollar and the encouragement of foreign capital inflows – into the recently opened-up stock markets as well as in the form of borrowings, often on a short-term basis[13] – to close the current account deficit, also ensured that foreign savings supplemented the already high domestic savings rate to raise investment rates in the region, contributing to a spiralling inflationary bubble of share and real property prices. The quasi-peg not only encouraged unhedged borrowing from abroad, but also became a target for currency speculators as regional currencies appreciated with the US dollar despite declining export competitiveness and growth.

Meanwhile, financial liberalization allowed lucrative opportunities for taking advantage of falling currencies, thus accelerating and exacerbating the collapse of regional currency and share markets. All this, together with unjudicious official responses, transformed the inevitable 'correction' of overvalued currencies in the region into a collapse of the currencies and the stock markets of the region as panic set in, exacerbated by 'herd' behaviour and 'contagion'.

Although the financial systems in the region are quite varied and hardly clones of the Japanese 'main bank' system, as often wrongly alleged, they have nevertheless become prone – owing to particular policy conjunctures – to the same financial–property 'bubble' phenomena, albeit for somewhat different reasons. Arguably, the more bank-based systems of Thailand, Korea and Indonesia had a stronger nexus of this sort compared to, say, Malaysia's much more stock market-oriented financial system. Rapid growth, on the basis of export-oriented industrialization from the late 1980s, gave rise to unregulated financial expansion, which contributed to a property boom and asset price bubbles, both in the more market-oriented or 'Anglo-Saxon' Malaysia as well as the more bank-oriented Thailand.

With the currency collapses, the assets acquired by short-term portfolio and other investors in the region depreciated correspondingly in value, precipitating an even greater sell-out and panic, causing herd behaviour and probably causing contagion to spread across national borders to the rest of the region. In Malaysia and perhaps elsewhere, further property market and stock market collapses seem imminent in view of uncoordinated over-building and the property-finance nexus. Thus, many have been and may still be hit by this 'triple whammy' from the currency, stock, and property markets.

The higher interest rates demanded by the financial community in 1998 added salt to the wound, but showed little success in attracting short-term capital inflows once again. But even when higher interest rates succeed in doing so, such flows can only be temporarily sustained and retained, at great and permanent cost to productive investments in the real economy. And if such inflows are eventually reversed in the precipitous manner experienced by Southeast Asia in the second half of 1997, much collateral damage will be experienced again.

As a consequence of these developments, Southeast Asia faced domestic policy reform challenges relating to four factors, namely greater exchange rate flexibility, the urgency of financial sector reform, as well as handling asset-price bubbles, and current account deficits. Before addressing the challenges on the domestic and international fronts, it is useful to summarize these four dimensions of the current crisis.

Without the advanced economies stabilizing exchange rates with regards to one another's currencies, the virtual or quasi-pegging of an economy's foreign exchange rate had become very dangerous, as the recent crisis demonstrated. Short-term capital inflows may temporarily supplement domestic savings, but the reversal of such flows can create severe disturbances. While such flows may be influenced by economic fundamentals in the long term, they are usually determined by speculative sentiments in the short term. Short-term exchange rate adjustments – with disruptive consequences for domestic prices and wages – are then deemed necessary to stem sudden outflows, but these, in turn, offer opportunities for currency speculators.

Financial sector reform has to be thought of, not only in terms of the liberalization insisted upon by international financial interests, but also the new prudential regulations needed to anticipate and respond to new challenges. While the problems caused by excessive as well as inappropriate regulation are often emphasized by advocates of liberalization, liberal banking policies can result in a weak domestic banking sector[14] unable to withstand competition from abroad, and even the collapse or costly bail-out of weak banks. For most developing economies, policies of 'financial restraint' are also still needed to 'direct' credit[15] to finance productive investments, especially in priority areas – instead of asset purchases or consumption. Recent trends involving greater capital account convertibility, innovative financial instruments, and the proliferation of off-shore financial centres and non-bank finance companies, as well as 'private banking' also pose new challenges for financial regulation in the face of diminished transparency.

Easy credit, partly due to capital inflows, resulted in meteoric rises in real property as well as share prices desired by most of those involved. Banking regulation to minimize such asset price inflation deserves the highest priority, and is always difficult to achieve in 'good times' without precipitating an asset price meltdown, but was easier to achieve right after the asset price bubble had burst.

As in many other fast growth situations, current account deficits came to be considered 'natural' in Southeast Asia in the 1990s before the crisis, as they supposedly simply reflected the excess of investments in the national economy over domestic savings; hence, they were not seen as a cause for major concern in certain policymaking circles. Since the debt crisis of the early and mid-1980s, the cutting of fiscal deficits gained top priority at the behest of the Bretton Woods institutions and others. Developments since the Mexican tequila meltdown of early 1995 suggest that the current account deficit was the Achilles heel of the Southeast Asian economies, eventually precipitating financial meltdowns beginning with the collapse of their currencies ('quasi-pegged' to the US dollar), inadvertently encouraging massive, often unhedged private borrowing from abroad.

The changed international financial system

Malaysian Prime Minister Mahathir Mohamad's criticisms[16] of the role of international currency speculation in precipitating the recent East Asian crisis as well as the IMF policy responses have largely been dismissed outside of Malaysia except for those who recognize his remarks as reflecting confused frustration in the face of a new phenomenon not satisfactorily explained by conventional economic analysis. Hence, dismissing Mahathir would be tantamount to throwing the baby out with the bath water, as Mahathir was trying to address a real problem, albeit incorrectly. After all, as many have already pointed out, the international financial system and its further liberalization have favoured those already dominant and privileged in the world economy, at the expense of the real economy and of 'late development' in the South.

Ironically, Mahathir's arch-nemesis, the international financier George Soros, has argued that the unregulated expansion of capitalism, especially finance capital, threatens to undermine its own future, i.e. that capitalism has to be saved from itself. While admitting that he himself has profited greatly from financial liberalization, Soros argued – in Keynesian mode – that excessive liberalization has been resulting in virtual anarchy, dangerous for the stability so necessary for the orderly capitalist growth and democratic development desired by his liberal vision of a Popperian 'open society'.

The prevailing system of flexible exchange rates was introduced over a quarter of a century ago, inaugurating a new international monetary regime with very mixed consequences. Hence, the current regime is relatively new, only beginning after US President Richard Nixon's 1971 unilateral withdrawal from the Bretton Woods' regime of fixed exchange rates – which had pegged the US dollar to gold at US$35 per ounce and the ringgit to the US dollar at RM3. Under the new regime, the volume of foreign exchange spot transactions had grown to more than 67 times the total value of the international trade in goods by 1995, or more than 40 times the value of all international trade (including 'invisibles' or services).[17] Viewed from a historical perspective then, such currency trading is hardly natural, inevitable, or even desirable. For most of human history, including that of capitalism, it has not been 'integral to global trade in goods and services', as claimed by then US Treasury Secretary Robert Rubin. In fact, as is well known, various critics have offered various alternatives to the present system such as returning to fixed exchange rates, the gold standard, and so on.

In a world economy where foreign exchange spot transactions are now worth more than 70 times the total value of international commodity trade transactions, the financial sector has become increasingly divorced from the real economy. With the recent proliferation of new financial instruments and markets, especially in Malaysia, the financial sector has an even greater potential to inflict damage on the real economy. Ever since Lord Keynes advocated 'throwing sand' into the financial system to check the potentially disastrous consequences of unfettered liberalization, Keynesians – and others – have been wary of the financial liberalization advocated by ideological neo-liberals and their often naïve allies.

Economics Nobel Laureate James Tobin has called for a tax on foreign exchange spot transactions to enable more independent national monetary policy, discourage speculative capital movements, and increase the relative weight of long-term economic fundamentals against more short-termist and speculative considerations. As a bonus, the tax collected would also more than adequately fund the United Nations system and programmes, not leaving it hostage to the whims of US leadership, as has long been the case. Another Nobel Laureate, Lawrence Klein, has mentioned two other options to be considered besides the Tobin tax, namely regional monetary arrangements as well as the introduction of 'circuit-breakers' into the system – a suggestion also made by the World Bank's Senior Vice President and Chief Economist, Joseph Stiglitz.

But the lobby for financial liberalization remains much stronger and far more influential, dominating most of the business media and the key financial institutions internationally, especially in the US. Acknowledging that money is not just another commodity, the *Wall Street Journal*, for example, continues to promote currency boards (instead of central banks) and the pegging of other currencies against the US dollar, while attacking most other international monetary alternatives, rarely acknowledging the advantages that dollar pegs have given to the US, such as having the rest of the world finance its huge deficits.

Consequences of international financial liberalization

An explosion of international financial flows followed the substitution of the Bretton Woods system of fixed exchange rates with a new system of flexible exchange rates. Strong speculative motives are generally ascribable to international capital flows. However, the loosening of fixed exchange rates was also associated with a loosening of capital controls, permitting many investors to diversify to their advantage. In any case, the trend picked up momentum from the 1980s, leading to a US$1250 billion daily foreign exchange market by 1997, and the proliferation of new financial instruments. Yet, many of the alleged benefits of financial liberalization have not been realized, as the following summary of recent findings by Eatwell (1997) shows.

a) Financial liberalization was expected to move resources from capital-rich to capital-poor countries,[18] when in fact, net flows of finance – and of real resources – have been very modest, and mainly toward the capital-rich.[19] Of course, most net flows to the 'capital-poor' were mainly to 'emerging markets' such as those in East Asia, which arguably contributed to asset price bubbles and, eventually, to financial panic and currency and stock market collapse.

b) While liberalization was expected to enhance opportunities for savers and lower costs to borrowers, savers have benefited most from higher real interest rates.[20]

c) The new financial derivatives – expected to improve risk management – have actually generated new systemic risks, especially vulnerable to sudden changes in sentiment.[21]

d) Improved macroeconomic performance – with greater investment
and growth expected from better allocative efficiency – has not
been realized; in fact, overall macroeconomic performance has been
worse than before liberalization.[22]

e) Financial liberalization has introduced a persistent deflationary bias
on economic policy as governments try to gain credibility to avert
destabilizing capital flows, instead of the 'healthy discipline' on governments expected to improve macroeconomic stability.

Financial markets seem to function in such a way as to impose their
own 'expectations' on the real economy, thus defining their own 'fundamentals' and logic, which in turn become self-fulfilling prophecies. In
other words, they do not just process information in order to efficiently
allocate resources. Since financial markets operate like beauty contests
and the real economy has no automatic tendency to converge to full-
employment growth, the presumed analytical assumptions of other
market participants become imposed on the economy.

The threat of instability in the now massive capital market forces both
government and private investors to pursue risk-averse strategies, resulting in low growth and employment creation. A deflationary bias in
government policy and the private sector emerges in response to the
costly risks of violating the rules of the game. This is exacerbated by the
high costs of debt due to high real interest rates owing to efforts to
maintain financial stability in a potentially volatile world. Thus, 'long
term price stability' supersedes a 'high and stable level of employment'
as the policy priority. Such a monetarily stable system, involving relatively slow growth and high unemployment, can last indefinitely.

A sophisticated liberalized financial system, prioritizing flexibility or
the possibility of easy exit, is necessarily fragile, as reflected in:

a) liquidity crises, reducing real output;

b) private sector risk aversion, encouraging short-termism;[23]

c) public sector risk aversion, resulting in a deflationary policy bias;

d) persistent pressure for ever greater flexibility, increasing the ease of
exit.

The benefits that the reduction of financial controls has brought to
'emerging markets' must be weighed against the increased instability

due to enhanced ease of exit. While increased flows of (real) foreign direct investment generally require agreement to unrestricted profit repatriation, this is quite different from the 'instant exit' conditions demanded by financial markets.[24]

There is considerable evidence that in the longer term, economic development has been associated with developmentalist states. The post-war Golden Age – which saw high levels of output and employment as well as short-run efficiency – was premised on active macroeconomic management under the Bretton Woods system. Post-war European reconstruction was achieved with tight capital controls. On the other hand, the recent rush to convertibility and capital control deregulation in Eastern Europe has resulted in Russia becoming a significant net capital exporter![25]

Some dangers associated with financial liberalization have now become quite evident, but most are not being sufficiently recognized, let alone debated and addressed. Most initiatives in this regard cannot be undertaken unilaterally without great cost, as market reactions to Malaysian Prime Minister Mahathir's critical remarks have made clear. The very few options available for unilateral initiatives need to be carefully considered, and only implemented, if deemed desirable. Selectively invoking instances of bad or incompetent policy making or implementation does not justify leaving things to liberalized markets that render systematic policy-making impossible. Instead, it emphasizes the importance of creating an environment and developing the capability for good and competent policy to be effective.

Many need to be actively pursued through multilateral initiatives, for which the government needs the support of neighbours and others. Given the power of the dominant ideology that infuses the prevailing international system, it is virtually impossible to assert control over the financial system without a fundamental change in priorities and thinking by the major governments involved. However, the currencies of a small number of major governments – the US, Japan, Germany, and the UK – were involved in over three-quarters of currency transactions in 1995. Hence, acting together, they have the capability to control capital flows, but of course, only if they abandon faith in the alleged superiority of neo-liberalism.

A crisis of a new type

It seems fair to say that no one fully anticipated the crisis in East Asia. There were, of course, sceptics who regarded the claims of an East Asian economic miracle as somewhat exaggerated, albeit for different reasons, for example because they had not achieved much productivity growth and would eventually run up against diminishing returns (Krugman 1994); others argued that the performances of the Southeast Asian newly industrializing countries were significantly inferior compared to Japan and the first-tier newly industrializing economies (Jomo *et al.* 1997).

It is now clear that the East Asian crisis differs from conventional currency crisis scenarios in at least several important ways (Krugman 1998a):[26]

a) the absence of the usual sources of currency stress, whether fiscal deficits or macroeconomic indiscipline;[27]
b) the governments did not have any incentive to abandon their pegged exchange rates, e.g. to reduce unemployment;
c) the pronounced boom-bust cycles in asset prices (real property and stock markets) *preceded* the currency crisis, especially in Thailand, where the crisis began;
d) financial intermediaries have been key players in all the economies involved;
e) the severity of the crisis in the absence of strong adverse shocks;
f) the rapid spread of the initial crisis in Thailand, even to economies with few links or similarities to the first victims.

Very importantly then, the traditional indices of vulnerability did not signal a crisis as the source of the problem was not to be found in the governments *per se* or in national income accounts. The (mainly private) financial intermediaries were 'not part of the governments visible liabilities until after the fact.' For Krugman (1998a) then, one cannot adequately make sense of the crisis in terms of conventional currency crisis models; for him, the crisis has mainly been about bad banking and its consequences, and only incidentally about currencies.[28]

Other issues also need to be taken into account for an adequate analysis of the East Asian crisis:

a) financial crises have very severe effects on growth because they disrupt the productive contribution of financial intermediation;
b) the East Asian crises have not only involved excessive investments, but also unwise investments;
c) the huge real currency depreciations are likely to cause large declines in output;

d) other kinds of market failure, e.g. herd behaviour, need to be taken into account.

While the analysis offered in this chapter is not inconsistent with Krugman's emphasis on asset price bubbles, excessive investments and other problems caused by moral hazard due to implicit government guarantees for weakly regulated financial intermediaries, a more adequate analysis must also account for various other phenomena including:

a) the implications of the growth in currency trading and speculation in the post-Bretton Woods international monetary system;
b) the reasons for the Southeast Asian monetary authorities to defend their quasi-pegs against the strengthening US dollar despite its obvious adverse consequences for export competitiveness and hence for growth;
c) the consequences of financial liberalization, including the creation of conditions which have contributed to the magnitude of the crises;
d) the role of herd behaviour in exacerbating the crises;
e) other factors accounting for the contagion effects.

A number of policy issues also deserve careful consideration, including the nature and implications of IMF 'rescue' programmes and the conditionalities imposed by the Fund, as well as of policies favoured by the international as distinct from the domestic financial communities, and others affected. The adverse consequences of financial disintermediation and grossly undervalued currencies for economic development also deserve special attention, especially as the crisis threatens the future of growth and structural change in the region, not only directly, but also as a consequence of policy responses. The contractionary policies favoured by the IMF, the international financial community as well as others, recently including Malaysia's financial authorities, may well throw out the baby of economic development with the bath water of financial crisis.

Southeast Asia's currency crisis

In late 1997, Manuel Montes (1998) published the most serious attempt to understand the crisis in Southeast Asia. He begins by considering the most oft-cited popular explanations, suggesting that the crisis stemmed from the banking sector due to imprudent expansion and diversification of domestic financial markets, fuelled by short-term private borrowings. Montes (1998: 3) suggests that this was especially true of Thailand, but less so for Indonesia, Malaysia, and the Philippines (in order of decreasing relevance), underlining the significance of the contagion effect: 'the differences raise questions about how sensitive the currency knockdown (and the associated divestment from these economies) are to economic fundamentals.'

In Kaminsky and Reinhart's (1996) study of 71 balance of payments (BoP) crises and 25 banking crises during the period 1970–95, there were only three banking crises associated with the 25 balance of payments crises during 1970–79. However, there were 22 banking crises that coincided with 46 payments crises over 1980–95, which they attribute to financial liberalization from the 1980s, with a private lending boom culminating in a banking crisis and then a currency crisis. Thus, Montes attributes the Southeast Asian currency crisis to the 'twin liberalizations' of domestic financial systems and opening of the capital account.

Montes argues that financial liberalization induced some new behaviour in the financial system, notably:

a) domestic financial institutions had greater flexibility in offering interest rates to secure funds domestically and in bidding for foreign funds;
b) they became less reliant on lending to the government;
c) regulations, such as credit allocation rules and ceilings, were reduced;
d) greater domestic competition has meant that ascendance depends on expanding lending portfolios, often at the expense of prudence.

Meanwhile, liberalizing the capital account has essentially guaranteed non-residents ease of exit as well as fewer limitations on nationals holding foreign assets, thus inadvertently facilitating capital flight.

Montes goes on to identify the following as key fundamentals of the affected Southeast Asian economies:

a) viability of domestic financial systems;[29]
b) domestic output and export responsiveness to nominal devaluations;[30]
c) sustainability of current account deficits;[31]
d) high savings rates and robust public finances.

Despite the sound fiscal situation before the crisis, the Southeast Asian economies are now expected to have even larger fiscal surpluses despite the need for greater public financing of physical infrastructure and social services. To restore confidence in their currencies, they are being asked to cut their current account deficits besides government spending, with ominous implications for economic recovery and sustainability.

Recognizing a limited but still significant scope for monetary independence in the Southeast Asian economies, Montes maintains that economic liberalization should not be allowed to frustrate the sound development of the financial system and improvements in the productivity of investment. He warns that sound macroeconomic fundamentals do not guarantee immunity from contagion and crisis. The scope for monetary independence partly depends on the soundness of macroeconomic management as well as political will. Favouring flexible exchange rates, he warns that capital controls and other efforts to prop up a currency under attack are ineffective and actually subsidize further speculative actions. International cooperation and coordination have often been the best response during such episodes, but are also important for effective prudential and regulatory initiatives as well as to reduce 'policy arbitrage'. He also advocates measures to insulate the domestic banking system from short-term volatility through regulatory measures and capital controls as well as stricter prudential regulation for the region.

International reform?

The challenge at the international level is formidable, especially with the vested interests underlying US as well as European positions on systemic reform. Yet, there have been many misgivings elsewhere too about the nature and volatility of the international financial system, with renewed attention to particular aspects with each new crisis. Southeast Asians need to work with others who are like-minded and to draw upon the rich critiques which have developed over the years in developing reform proposals which are likely to gain broad international support.

Incredibly, at the September 1997 Hong Kong annual meetings of the IMF and World Bank, the IMF's policy-making Interim Committee – which represents all 181 IMF member countries via 24 ministers – gave the IMF a mandate to alter its Articles of Association so that it would have additional 'jurisdiction' over the capital account as well as over the current account of members' balance of payments, which it has had for many decades.[32] In December 1997, the World Trade Organization also concluded its financial services agreement which basically commits member countries to scheduled accelerated liberalization of the trade in financial services. The *Wall Street Journal* noted that the agreement would primarily benefit the United States and Europe since it is most unlikely that the South is in a position to export financial services to the North. It is therefore likely that countries of the South will face even greater problems with their balance of payments as their services, and hence current account deficits worsen. Much of the nascent financial services which have emerged under protection in these countries is unlikely to survive international competition from transnational giants enjoying economies of scale and other advantages.

As recent press discussion of the IMF's record and capability suggests, there is growing international scepticism about the IMF's role in and prescriptions for the ongoing East Asian crisis. Perhaps partly out of force of habit in dealing with situations in Latin America, Africa, Eastern Europe, and elsewhere, where fiscal deficits have been part of the problem, the same prescription ('one size fits all') seems to underlie the recent IMF interventions in East Asia.

Many of its programmes are effectively contractionary in consequence, with little regard for the social and other adverse consequences of swallowing its medicine. Thus, what started off as a currency or financial crisis led, partly due to IMF-recommended policy responses, to economic slowdown, if not recession. For example, although all the affected East Asian economies had been running fiscal surpluses in recent years (except Indonesia which had a small deficit in 1996), the IMF forced all the governments to slash public expenditure and increase their budgetary surpluses.

There has been considerable doubt as to whether the IMF actually recognized the novel elements of the crisis and their implications ('old medicines for a new disease'), especially at the outset. The apparent failures of the IMF – to anticipate the current crisis in its generally glowing recent reports on the region, and also to stem, let alone reverse the situation despite interventions in Thailand, Indonesia, and Korea – have certainly not inspired much confidence. Nor has the fact that though the Philippines had long been under an IMF programme, it was not spared the contagion.[33]

The Fund does not seem to be sufficiently cognizant of the subjective elements contributing to the crisis, and seems to approach the crisis as if it were solely due to macroeconomic or other weaknesses. For instance, by closing down banks in Indonesia, the IMF undermined the remaining shreds of confidence there, inducing wholesale panic in the process. Also, while the IMF insists on greater transparency by the affected host government and those under its jurisdiction, it continues to operate under a shroud of secrecy itself.

The IMF's double standards, as reflected by its apparent priority for protecting the interests of foreign banks and governments, have also compromised its ostensible role as an impartial party working in the interests of the host economy. The burden of IMF programmes invariably falls on the domestic financial sector and, eventually, on the public at large – through the social costs of the public policy response, usually involving bail-outs of much of the financial sector if not the corporate sector more generally – who thus bear most of the costs of adjustment and reform, while commitments to foreign banks are invariably met, even though both foreign and domestic banks may have been equally irresponsible or imprudent in their lending practices.

As the Bank of International Settlements (BIS) noted in its January 1998 *Report on the Maturity and Nationality of International Bank Lending* (Raghavan 1998; Vadarajan, 1998), 'In spite of growing strains in Southeast Asia, overall bank lending to Asian developing countries showed no evidence of abating in the first half of 1997.' In the year from mid-1996 to mid-1997, South Korea received US$15 billion in new loans, while Indonesia received US$9 billion. Short-term lending continued to dominate, with 70 per cent of lending due within a year, while the share of lending to private non-bank borrowers rose to 45 per cent at the end of June 1997. The banks were also actively acquiring 'non-traditional assets' in the region, for example, in higher yielding local money markets and other debt securities. Most of this lending was by Japanese and continental European banks.

Thus, Western banks will emerge from the crisis not only relatively unscathed, but also relatively stronger. Some merchant banks and other financial institutions will also be able to make lucrative commissions from marketing sovereign debt as the short-term private borrowings – which precipitated the crisis – are converted into longer-term government-guaranteed bonds under the terms of the IMF programmes. Thus, the bail-out programmes are primarily for the foreign banks rather than the East Asian economies or people.

The limited willingness of the USA to contribute to the IMF bailout packages to Thailand, Indonesia, and South Korea – now exceeding a hundred billion US dollars – has also reflected new US priorities in the post-Cold War context. Despite its own unwillingness to commit more, the US administration also blocked Japanese and other regional initiatives to develop a regional facility for fear that it might enhance the Japanese role and leadership in the region and diminish the US's standing.

However, after the August 1998 global financial panic, the US administration seemed to take a leading role despite the limited exposure of US banks to the region. US concerns about a possible global financial meltdown, the US dollar's role as the leading reserve currency and the opportunities for US banks and other investors to take advantage of the situation seem to have influenced this change of stance.

Almost in tandem with financial liberalization, IMF intervention is generally recognized to undermine and limit national economic sovereignty.[34] Particularly damning is the clear abuse of imposed IMF conditionalities in the Korean aid package to resolve outstanding bilateral issues in favour of the US and Japanese interests (Chossudowsky 1998). Legislation and other new regulations enabling greater foreign ownership of, as well as increased market access to, the Korean economy – which have little to do with the crisis or its immediate causes – have been forced upon the Korean government. Even more damaging has been the further dismantling of many key institutional features which have made possible the Korean economic miracle since the 1960s. Meanwhile, Japanese banks have insisted that the Korean government guarantee repayment as a condition for rolling over Korean short-term debt.

More generally, throughout the region, there is a 'fire-sale' going on at bargain basement prices, with foreign investments taking up the best assets available for a song. If one accepts that the currency as well as more general financial crisis means that these assets are grossly under-priced by international standards, one cannot claim any welfare improvement (Krugman 1998b), given the likelihood that the new foreign owners need not be more efficient to be able to buy up these assets.

Conclusion

The currency and financial crises in Southeast Asia suggest that the region's economic miracle has been built on some shaky and unsustainable foundations. Recent growth in both Malaysia and Thailand has been increasingly heavily reliant on foreign resources, both capital and labour. Limited investments and inappropriate biases in human resource development have held back the development of greater industrial and technological capabilities throughout the region.[35] Southeast Asia's resource wealth and relatively cheap labour sustained production enclaves for export of agricultural, forest, mineral and, more recently, manufactured products, but much of the retained wealth generated was captured by business cronies of those in power, who contributed to growth by also re-investing captured resource and other rents in the 'protected' domestic economy in import-substituting industries, commerce, services, and privatized utilities and infrastructure.

Three closely related arguments involving liberalization and governance have been made (Jomo 1998). First, financial liberalization has undermined previously existing governance institutions and mechanisms without creating adequate alternatives in their place. Second, domestic governance arrangements, including those involving the financial system, have been shaped or abused by those with influence for their own advantage. Third, in some instances, especially in Thailand, Malaysia, and Indonesia, in the absence of adequate crisis response arrangements, official responses have been unduly influenced and compromised by vested interests as well as other considerations.

Thus, the roots of the crisis can usefully be summed up in terms of various challenges of governance, at both international and national levels. At the international level, governance issues have been raised by the transformations of financial, especially capital markets. Flexible exchange rates and other related developments have increased the scope for and activity in currency speculation. Increased international flows of investment funds have also contributed to currency volatility. Most of these funds are of a portfolio nature, and hence, are more liable to enhance volatility, while the share of foreign direct investments continues to decline.

Financial liberalization has also reduced monitoring and supervision of financial, including banking, operations and transactions, including those of a prudential nature. There has also been a significant increase in 'private banking' as well as increased banking transactions across borders with the proliferation of 'international off-shore financial centres' and other international banking facilities. The growing dollarization of the world economy, including international finance, has also skewed the nature of these developments in important ways.

Liberalization of financial services as well as of investment regulations, including liberalization of the capital account, have otherwise also reduced national oversight and management of financial flows, which created the conditions conducive to the recent Southeast Asian and South Korean crises. The scope for national macroeconomic – including monetary – management has been considerably reduced by various dimensions of financial liberalization. Options for developmentalist as well as rentier initiatives have been significantly reduced as a consequence.

The variety of regimes in East Asia do not allow easy generalizations for the entire region. It has been tempting for observers to contrast the economies and regimes that have experienced major crises since the second half of 1997, namely Thailand, the Philippines, Indonesia, Malaysia, and South Korea, with the other high performing East Asian economies which have not, namely Japan, Taiwan, Hong Kong, and Singapore, as well as China. There is no systematic evidence that the difference lies primarily in the extent of corruption, rent-seeking, government intervention, industrial policy, export-orientation, productivity growth, foreign direct investment or democracy. Although all the economies affected have liberalized their capital accounts, this may only be a necessary, but certainly not a sufficient condition for the crisis. The big difference seems to have been that the former have not had much foreign exchange in reserve unlike the latter, which have the highest reserves in the world, and hence were not vulnerable to currency attack.

The extent to which macroeconomic fundamentals were awry among the affected economies varied considerably and, by themselves, cannot explain the financial collapses, although they suggest their greater vulnerability to currency attack and the greater likelihood of panic. This crisis has underlined the significance of sentiments, and there is no convincing explanation for what happened, especially herd behaviour, which does not take account of market psychology. Hence, confidence restoration must necessarily be at the top of the agenda for any recovery programme, but this, in turn, raises the dilemma posed by the temptation of reviving confidence with an attractive, but potentially volatile set of arrangements, which can easily turn against the national economies concerned and their regimes' ambitions.

Previously hegemonic neo-liberal explanations of the East Asian miracle were effectively challenged from the late 1980s (White 1988, Amsden 1989, Wade 1990) and developed in sophistication (e.g. see Chang 1994) and nuance (Jomo *et al.* 1997) in the mid-1990s. The World Bank's (1993) influential response suggested that the political, bureaucratic, cultural, and institutional circumstances of the rise of Japan and the first-generation or first-tier East Asian newly industrializing economies of South Korea, Taiwan, Hong Kong, and Singapore were so exceptional as to be beyond emulation. Instead, it was suggested that other developing countries should seek to emulate the second-tier Southeast Asian newly industrializing countries (NICs) of Malaysia, Thailand, and Indonesia, which had, according to the World Bank, achieved rapid growth and industrialization after liberalizing in the mid-1980s.

In response, others have argued that the Southeast Asian NIC achievement has been much more modest than that of the first-tier East Asian NIEs in several important respects, and that the sustainability of their growth, industrialization and structural change was much more suspect as a consequence. Jomo *et al.* (1997) also suggested that the former's rapid export-oriented industrialization from the mid-1980s was partly due to a favourable conjuncture – involving Southeast Asian currency depreciation coinciding with Japanese and first-tier East Asian NIE currency appreciation and rising production, especially labour, costs – as well as liberalization of some existing regulations inimical to attracting such investments and their replacement with a new investment regime much more conducive to promoting export-oriented industrialization.

Many other features of the old regime have been retained, while 'rentrepreneurs' creatively utilized features of the new regulatory environment to advance and pursue their own interests. These features have all contributed to industrial organization and structure in these economies. Thus, while some regulations have undoubtedly enhanced growth and structural change, often by offering rents and incentives to encourage desired investments, others have also strengthened rentier abuse. While much of this may be analytically distinguishable, with the latter relatively easily isolated and checked through policy intervention, others may be much more difficult to unravel from developmentalist rents.

Simplistic perspectives and gross generalizations do not recognize and distinguish between developmentalist rents and rentier abuse. Policy reforms which fail to do so will encourage throwing out the developmentalist baby with the bath water of abuse, with disastrous consequences for developmentalist ambitions and projects. Of course, the willingness to check rentier abuses is ultimately determined by the regime's independence of such rentier interests, its consequent 'political will' and its capacity to bring about the necessary reforms.

Finally, as economic and business historians remind us, there have been important precursors to the recent crises in East Asia, even within the region. Unfortunately, the market – which is increasingly being left to its own devices – has neither a memory nor a capacity to develop natural immunity. It is therefore left to policy makers to build the necessary institutions and to design and redesign the needed institutional features of governance to ensure that tragedy does not become farce.

Notes

* This chapter is revised from the Introduction to Jomo (1998). I am grateful to Jan Kregel, Gerry Helleiner, Din Merican, and Warren Bailey for their useful critical feedback, but implicate none of them. There continues to be considerable debate over the principal causes and consequences of the recent currency and financial crises in Southeast Asia, particularly Malaysia. This essay is deliberately polemical as there is clearly no shared understanding of the various contentious issues involved. As far as possible, the language is not technical, in order to be accessible to as wide a readership as feasible. Since events are still unfolding, such reflections should be open to revision with the passage of time, events, and trends. Hence, criticisms and suggestions are especially appreciated.

1 Meanwhile, the 'financial analysts' have become so fixated with the current account deficit that this indicator, almost alone, has become the fetish of financial analysts, especially since the Mexican meltdown of early 1995. In earlier, different times, some economies sustained similar deficits for much longer, without comparable consequences. As noted in the immediate aftermath of the Mexican crisis of 1995, several Southeast Asian economies already had comparable current account deficits then despite, or rather because of rapid economic growth. Yet, as Fischer observed, the currency markets failed to adjust earlier in Southeast Asia.

2 Of course, the availability of cheap foreign funds – e.g. due to a low real interest rate – can help to close temporarily both domestic savings-investment as well as foreign exchange gaps, especially if well invested or deployed.

3 In this connection, it is interesting to note that the Chicago school-influenced Chilean government has maintained strict controls on the capital account. Portfolio investments in Chilean stock are permitted in the New York Stock Exchange, rather than in the Santiago stock market, while unlike foreign direct investment, portfolio capital inflows into Chile are subjected to conditions that inhibit easy exit.

4 In some countries, government-owned non-financial public enterprises (NFPEs) have been very much part of this supposedly private sector debt growth phenomenon.

5 There is also no evidence that the stock market boom in recent years has more effectively raised funds for productive investment; in fact, the converse seems more likely as financial intermediation has switched from commercial banks to the stock market in the last decade.

6 While the Southeast Asian economies have been running current account deficits, so has the US, especially with the region, except that it has different consequences given the actual and 'quasi' dollar pegs prevailing in much of the world today.

7 While the US economy was strengthening, the Southeast Asian economies were growing even faster until the 1997–98 debacle. Economic recovery since 1999 has been strongest in Malaysia and weakest in Indonesia.

8 In the mid-1990s, as the US dollar strengthened with the US economy, both the Japanese and the Germans allowed their currencies to depreciate against the US dollar, with relatively little disruption, in an effort to regain international competitiveness.

9   In a telling episode at the beginning of September 1997, IMF deputy head, Stanley Fischer pointed out that although the current account deficits in Southeast Asia had emerged quite some years ago, markets had failed to adjust – contrary to the predictions of conventional economic theory. (Instead of recognizing the failure of market mechanisms, US Federal Reserve Chair Alan Greenspan gently chided Fischer in response, as if expecting the IMF to 'remind' Wall Street of what it had forgotten.)

10 In the face of limited information and a novel, rapidly changing situation, such behaviour is often considered rational by market players, even if unfortunate.

11 Hedge funds may, however, go in different directions, for instance, when one fund's currency sell-off provokes another fund to snap up bargain equities, e.g. foreigners were often persistent net buyers of Japanese stocks throughout the bursting of the bubble there in the 1990s.

12 Financial liberalization means investors have a choice as to when they 'come and go', and, of course, the very existence of that choice may encourage them to stick around in certain circumstances.

13 Short-termism – encouraged by financial liberalization – has also accentuated the bias against longer term productive investments.

14 As in Chile in the early 1980s.

15 These can involve savers being encouraged with tax policies that do not punish them for putting money away. While banks should still make lending decisions based on economic criteria alone, systemic biases towards short-termism need to be mitigated. The government can prioritize and favour certain types of investments by subsidizing them through taxes or loan guarantees for those sectors or activities it deems important.

16 It has been very difficult for Malaysia to take the high moral ground on currency and other types of speculation credibly because of the well-known behaviour of Bank Negara in the 1980s. The Malaysian central bank was known to take very aggressive, short term speculative positions in the major currencies with a view to making a profit. This went on for several years until the Bank lost several tens of billions of ringgit in 1992 while betting on sterling, and then withdrew to tamer activities. There is a similar sense about the tin cartel in the early 1980s (Jomo 1990). Mahathir's comments are hence seen as insincere abroad in that he is seen to have directed the government to undertake speculative activities in the past and was able to do so because the international currency and commodity markets are so open. It has been difficult to gain sympathy about non-Malaysian speculators after having approved of such activities before.

17 Since trade-related currency trading is greatly exceeded by 'investment'-related currency trading, it is not surprising that the volume of currency trading is so large. One key question is how much of those investment-related trades are 'healthy', 'appropriate', or 'desirable', which is hard to determine. International investors want to hedge their personal income and wealth by spreading their investments across many countries and adjusting them quite frequently as conditions change, thus contributing to market volatility.

18 Recent results show that national savings tend to equate national investment, suggesting that flows of capital to 'the best possible use' are far from

universal and much smaller than simple theories predict. Lack of information or other risks and uncertainties tend to reduce cross border capital flows.

19 Eatwell suggests a negative correlation between dependence on 'foreign savings' and economic performance. This is true if we do not break down the nature of foreign savings. The numbers are strongly biased by the inclusion of short term money market flows, which may include efforts by governments to prop up their currencies with high interest rates which temporarily suck in money from overseas. Mexico, Brazil, and especially Venezuela typified this a few years ago. If only long term direct investment or equity investment was considered, a lot of poorly performing Latin American economies would be screened out. Southeast Asian countries, especially Singapore and Malaysia, would then rank high on both foreign savings (measured 'appropriately') and economic performance.

20 Currently, high interest rates represent a very unhappy situation for the region. They are intended, in part, to prop the currency up to maintain confidence but, perhaps more importantly, to allow local companies to pay off their foreign debts. The cost of this is slower growth. With lower interest rates and lower exchange rates, which help the economy grow and help consumers, mismanaged local companies would have to reorganize themselves, or otherwise lose their equity (which they deserve, in many cases, to forfeit). Foreign creditors who were stupid enough to lend dollars to mismanaged companies should see their bank loans and bonds defaulted on. Bankrupt local companies could be bailed out and re-capitalized, with 100 per cent equity ownership then going into mutual funds or pension funds distributed equally to the masses of ordinary citizens.

Liberalization is generally associated with higher interest rates. However, lower interest rates could have been due to a combination of pegged exchange rates, capital controls, and the deployment of funds inside such economies. Pegged exchange rates are enforced by capital controls that 'trap' a pool of savings inside an economy. The trapped savings are typically exploited by governments or banking cartels that may keep interest rates too low, even below inflation rates. The capital controls may thus force savers to accept low interest rates and stop them from getting a fairer return elsewhere. The cheap savings may get loaned to undeserving corporations or for other purposes, possibly at the direction of the government.

21 One could argue that some of this is the result of greed, stupidity, and lack of education or regulation. If used carefully, derivatives are ultimately insurance contracts.

22 There is evidence of a strong positive correlation between financial openness, foreign investment, GDP growth, and per capita income driven by the performance of the Asian countries.

23 Due to the separation of ownership and management of portfolio investments, though it may be in the interest of investors to 'buy and hold', it is difficult to write contracts to motivate pension managers, mutual funds, and other intermediaries to stay put.

24 Of course, liquidity is one of the features that induces otherwise risk averse investors to buy into a situation. Furthermore, in any transaction, there is a buyer for every seller.

25 Of course, capital flight is not an inevitable consequence of financial liberalization, but may reflect the fears and consequent hedging behaviour of locals.

26 Paul Krugman's (1998a) attempt at theoretical catch-up is particularly worthy of consideration in light of his own previous attempts at understanding related international economic phenomena as well as East Asian economic growth. As the crisis is still unfolding, such an attempt can hardly be definitive, especially since we do not even have the advantage of complete hindsight. Yet, as policy is very much being made on the hoof, his attempt to highlight certain relationships may well be illuminating. Hence, Krugman argues that:

> it is necessary to adopt an approach quite different from that of traditional currency crisis theory. Of course Asian economies did experience currency crises, and the usual channels of speculation were operative here as always. However, the currency crises were only part of a broader financial crisis, which had very little to do with currencies or even monetary issues *per se*. Nor did the crisis have much to do with traditional fiscal issues. Instead, to make sense of what went wrong we need to focus on two issues normally neglected in currency crisis analysis: the role of financial intermediaries (and of the moral hazard associated with such intermediaries when they are poorly regulated), and the prices of real assets such as capital and land.

27 None of the fundamentals usually emphasized seem to have been important in the affected economies: all the governments had fiscal surpluses and none were involved in excessive monetary expansion, while inflation rates were generally low.

28 Krugman (1998a) argues: 'The boom-bust cycle created by financial excess preceded the currency crises because the financial crisis was the real driver of the whole process, with the currency fluctuations more a symptom than a cause. And the ability of the crisis to spread without big exogenous shocks or strong economic linkages can be explained by the fact that the afflicted Asian economies were...highly vulnerable to self-fulfilling pessimism, which could and did generate a downward spiral of asset deflation and disintermediation.'

29 Montes emphasizes that sentiments can either favourably or unfavourably influence fundamentals and the health of financial systems; in particular, the collapse of the Southeast Asian currencies due to sentiments would adversely affect the viability of investments made in different exchange rate conditions, which could in turn further exacerbate the domestic banking crisis.

30 Montes argues that the rural-based economies of Southeast Asia have been better able to carry out real devaluations from nominal changes in currency value, while their export sectors have not been too tied down by supply side inflexibilities to respond to real devaluations. After asserting that stock markets have served to share risks among asset owners rather than raise financing, he argues that except for financial system weaknesses, Southeast Asian real sectors have been relatively immune from the recent asset market frenzy.

31 Montes points out that equity and portfolio investments overtook direct investment, loans and trade credit in providing external financing in the 1990s. He cites Reisen's warning (Montes 1998: 34) that offers of foreign financing should be resisted if they would 'cause unsustainable currency appreciation, excessive risk-taking in the banking system, and a sharp drop in private savings.' Hence, in a market-sentiment driven world, currencies become too strong with offers of strong external financing and too weak when capital withdraws.

32 I am grateful to Anthony Rowley for confirming these details with Kunio Saito, director of the IMF's new Tokyo regional representative office on 17 December 1997.

The executive board of the Fund is currently holding a series of meetings to discuss the detailed implementation of this mandate and will report again to the Interim Committee on the *modus operandi* at the spring meeting. Thereafter, individual member governments have to ratify the change, but a simple majority will be sufficient. In other words, a unanimous vote is not needed to approve the change in the Fund's articles.

However, other colleagues – including Professor Gerald Helleiner of the University of Toronto and Dr Yilmaz Akyuz of UNCTAD – suggest that the situation is not as dire as the above account suggests because the approval process is much more complicated.

33 Arguably, the Philippines currency has not taken quite as hard a hit, in part because their (colonial-inherited) banking and accounting standards are considered relatively better, but also because short-term capital inflows have been relatively less, given the recentness of its economic recovery.

34 However, invoking 'national economic sovereignty' may become very dubious when it is clearly hijacked by special interests.

35 While the low productivity growth critique popularized by Krugman (1994) may be theoretically and methodologically faulted, there is little doubt that East Asian growth has generally been boosted by high savings and investment rates. While this might give the impression of 'all perspiration, no inspiration', as suggested by total factor productivity (TFP) critics, the dominance of FDI in the internationally competitive export-oriented industries suggests the transfer or import of 'inspiration' embodied in new plant and equipment as well as the necessary technological learning to get the jobs done.

9
Keynesian Economics: a Note on its Relevance and Limitations in the Face of Globalization

Jayati Ghosh

Now that the twentieth century is over, we can say with some degree of confidence that John Maynard Keynes was its most influential economist. His *General Theory of Employment, Interest and Money*, first published in 1936, revolutionized the discipline of economics and has dominated attitudes towards economic policy ever since. The parallel development of the basic ideas by the Polish economist Michal Kalecki, operating with a Marxist perspective on the capitalist economy, is worth noting (See Kalecki 1939, 1971).

In the first three decades after the publication of the *General Theory*, governments and economic analysts were heavily influenced by Keynes' ideas, or at least a version of them; and macroeconomic management in both industrial and developing countries was dominated by the implications of these ideas in terms of the state's role in maintaining effective demand through fiscal and monetary policy.

The subsequent thirty years witnessed the reaction to this. Keynesian economics – especially in terms of the policy implications that had been derived – was seen as not just outmoded but wrong, based on aggregations and assumptions about economic behaviour that were unjustified. The mainstream economics profession tended to swing to the opposite side of the pendulum, reaffirming slightly revised versions of the old monetarist ideas that the Keynesian revolution was supposed to have definitively swept away. A Keynes' student Lorrie Tarshis put it recently, 'though almost no one now reads his book, almost everyone claims to know what it contains, and incidentally, why it is wrong' (Tarshis 1987).

This chapter considers briefly some of the most essential ideas of Keynes, and how the interpretation of these ideas has changed over time in different forms of Keynesian economics. It notes how the essential ideas retain their relevance, and how ignoring them can lead to very negative consequences. The discussion next turns to the reasons, especially the political economy factors that have led to the changing perceptions regarding the validity of these ideas. Finally, the discussion suggests what Keynesian policies would imply in the current international economic context, what are their limitations and what are the possibilities for adaptation.

The economics of Keynes

The basic idea underlying the Keynesian approach is the principle of effective demand. Effective demand is simply the aggregate income or sales which entrepreneurs expect to receive from their current production. Keynes' innovation was to consider the role this plays not just in the production of individual goods, but for the economy as a whole. He put forward the proposition that the equality between savings and investment in any one period is ensured not by changes in the interest rate as was generally believed, but by changes in the aggregate level of output or economic activity.

The argument can be briefly stated as follows: When employment increases, aggregate real income increases. Then consumption increases too, but not as much as income (that is, there is a marginal propensity to consume in the society, which is less than unity). So, if employers were to produce goods to meet only the consumption equivalent to the whole of the increased income, they would make a loss. This means that to justify any given amount of employment, there must also be current investment, for without this employers would not receive profits sufficient to make them offer the given amount of employment. The current investment, in turn, depends upon the inducement to invest, which depends upon the relation between interest rates and expected returns on investment (or what Keynes called the marginal efficiency of capital).

The anticipation of future demand is thus critical in determining the level of investment, and it is this that dictates the aggregate level of employment and therefore economic activity. Since saving is the excess of income over consumption, it follows that saving is then determined as a residual, which must be equal to investment. Keynes highlighted the critical role of expectations about the future in determining current levels of investment and therefore total employment. While the received wisdom of the time believed that 'supply creates its own demand', Keynes reversed the causation to infer that effective demand brings forth aggregate supply.

This then leads to the central argument of the theory, that of the possibility of an unemployment equilibrium. Keynes showed that there is no automatic tendency in a capitalist market economy, which ensures that the level of aggregate output is that which corresponds to full employment. Indeed, the effective demand associated with full employment is just a special case, realized only when there is a certain relationship between the marginal propensity to consume and the inducement to invest. This follows, since it is not conditions of supply that create the demand, rather supply is determined by aggregate demand which is reflected in both investment decisions as well as the propensity to consume.

Once there is a level of aggregate output that is below the full employment level, there is no automatic mechanism within a capitalist economy that can raise the level of economic activity. Investors' low expectations about markets tend to be confirmed by their low sales proceeds, and this reduces their inducement to invest in the next period as well. If this is so, then once the economy is in such an unemployment equilibrium, then it can only be raised from it by something outside the system *per se*. This brings in the critical role of the state in increasing effective demand through its own expenditures, and therefore acting as macro-manager in ensuring full employment. Keynes spoke of the need for 'the socialization of investment' in order to achieve full employment.

Related to this idea of investment determining output and therefore saving, is the concept of the multiplier, which was originally developed by Robert Kahn (1931, 1933), but is very much part of the Keynesian tradition. This is the idea that an increase in investment induces further increases in consumption, income and saving. The initial expenditure adds to purchasing power, which then demands more goods, and so on. Thus the final effect of any initial outlay will depend on the propensity to consume of the society. The higher this is, the higher will be the multiplier effects of investment on income.

It should be clear that all this is dependent on the idea that there are no supply bottlenecks in the system, and that excess capacity in the productive sector allows for expansion and for the multiplier process to work itself through. This has been seen as limiting the applicability of this argument in developing countries where in some specific sector (say agriculture) production cannot be easily increased and becomes a bottleneck.

Of course, this argument relates to the real economy, but it is naturally crucially affected by the perception of the role of money, and this was another of Keynes' major innovations. His notion of liquidity preference is an important part of the broad argument, and remains a significant factor in disputing the conclusions of monetarist theory today. According to Keynes, there are three reasons why money is held. The first is the 'transactions' motive, on the part of households and other economic agents for their ordinary economic transactions. This demand is a stable function of the level of income or economic activity. Second is the holding of money for 'precautionary' purposes, that is, against the possibility that some unexpected payment may have to be made or that some expected receipts may not materialize. Finally, there is the 'speculative' motive, which occurs because of possibilities of changes in the interest rate, and is therefore critically dependent upon expectations.

The theory of liquidity preference was intended to describe the market mechanism through which changes in the interest rate occur, rather than its absolute level. The speculative motive played an important role in this, not only because of its quantitative significance, but also because of its high degree of volatility. What is important is the essentially unstable nature of the speculative demand for money, which is affected by expectations regarding interest rate changes, and therefore by expected variations in the capital value of financial assets.

The significance of this idea in the current world economic context must be emphasized. Not only does it provide a powerful insight into the functioning of money and financial markets, but it also offers several compelling reasons to be sceptical of the monetarist arguments which currently hold sway over so many of our policy makers across the world. First, it becomes impossible to define money in a way that will lead to universal agreement, and distinguish it clearly from other liquid assets, 'quasi-moneys' and 'near-moneys'. So establishing the quantity of money in an economic system is near impossible. Second, the idea of liquidity preference emphasizes that the demand for money cannot be a stable function of real income, because it contains at least one highly unstable element, the speculative demand. Third, and following from these, it can be argued that the supply of money does not operate automatically as a significant brake on the possibilities of portfolio reshuffling by financial players, even though it can dramatically affect real economic decisions. The relevance of this argument to economies like those in Southeast Asia today should be obvious.

Keynesian economics

Keynesian economics has followed a trajectory rather different from that explored by Keynes himself. There have been two broad strands. One sought to integrate Keynes with the basic neo-classical tradition, and became the dominant mainstream opinion, especially in Western academia. The other, which was possibly more reflective of Kalecki's influence, has emphasized the impossibility of achieving socially desirable outcomes through capitalist market processes.

The attempt to integrate Keynes with the basic neo-classical model began fairly early after the publication of the General Theory, and found its clearest and most famous expression in the 'neo-classical synthesis' of John Hicks (1937). The purpose was to show that, far from being a general theory, Keynes' argument referred to a special case of the broader neo-classical analysis. The basic idea was that the notion of equilibrium in which all markets (including that for labour) clear, was still an accurate description of the economic system. However, the forces that ensured this full employment market-clearing outcome could be frustrated by rigidities and imperfections, and also took a long time to work themselves through.

Thus, Keynesian unemployment was attributed to rigid money wages, and supposedly confined to short-run rigidities that inhibited the operations of labour markets. Similarly, liquidity preference was treated as a theory determining the level of the rate of interest, rather than changes in it. This completely bypassed Keynes' emphasis on the inherent instability of the demand for money because of the uncertain character of expectations about the future level of the interest rate, and made it a stable function.

The neo-classical synthesis accepted that the economy could, for certain periods of time, experience sustained unemployment due to the inadequacy of overall effective demand. Therefore there was a role for government to reinforce and speed up the processes by which the economy could find its way back to long-run full-employment equilibrium. Once at that point, the traditional neo-classical theory of resource allocation would be relevant once again.

This approach caused the label of 'Keynesian' in industrial countries to be put on policies of macro-management that eschewed micro-economic intervention by the state and did not incorporate any comprehensive 'socialization of investment' as envisaged by Keynes. Economic management by government became a search for appropriate mixes of monetary and fiscal policies, with the relative weight of each being based on assumptions of the responsiveness of investment and money demand to the interest rate, which in turn depended upon the degree of faith in the market mechanism.

All this was furthered by the advocacy of the 'Phillips Curve' – the idea (not to be found in Keynes' own writing) that there is an inverse relation between the rate of inflation and the rate of unemployment. Essentially, the macro-economic conclusions were grafted onto micro-economic foundations that had the same theoretical basis as the neo-classical approach. This made it quite vulnerable to counter-attack, especially when the stagflation of the 1970s blew the Phillips Curve sky-high, and when aggregate demand management policies in industrial countries proved to be incapable of meeting the tasks of economic restructuring and maintaining competitiveness.

This period also brought out another weakness of this type of economic management, subsequently highlighted by the 'rational expectations' school. That is, that the continued use of Keynesian aggregate demand management policies will lead economic agents to predict such policies and discount for them in their own actions, so that they will become ineffective because they will not stimulate greater economic activity.

This entire approach was seen to be an illegitimate use of Keynes' ideas by a (minority) Keynesian tradition, giving rise to the term 'Bastard Keynesianism' as first coined by Joan Robinson in 1962, (see Robinson 1969). From this perspective, the basic insight of Keynes was that markets do not necessarily function efficiently and to the common good, and that the neo-classical theory of resource allocation is not a good guide to understanding either the functioning of capitalist economies or working out appropriate policies for them. The work of Kalecki (1933–70) has been particularly influential in this context, especially in some developing countries that tried to incorporate some notions of the socialization of investment, of planning and of micro-economic management by the state.

The political economy of Keynesian economics and its relevance today

It is now commonplace to argue that the dethroning and even discrediting of Keynesian economics has been closely related to the rise to dominance of finance, both nationally and internationally. The latter is of course a complex process calling for explanation in its own right. But there is no doubt that the growing political and economic power of finance has indeed played a role in three major ways: first, by rendering Keynesian policies far more difficult to engage in on a purely national level; second, by creating domestic conditions allowing for greater social tolerance of high levels of unemployment and greater intolerance of inflation; and finally, by constraining even the possibility of concerted expansions across the world.

Keynesian economics was really developed for closed economies. The possibility of external trade did not alter the basic results or insights, although it did bring in the option of using external markets to compensate for insufficient domestic demand. It also forced recognition of the fact that expansionary domestic policies designed to bring about full employment could cause external deficits that would have to be met somehow.

However, international capital mobility created an entirely new set of problems for such policies. Any attempt at domestic expansion could now bring about not only a trade deficit, but also a flight of capital and consequent pressure on the currency, forcing a retreat from such policies. The experience of the Mitterand Government in France in the 1980s was the first glaring example of this in industrial countries; for developing countries, of course, it had long been a well-known fact of life. But having tasted blood in this way, it was not to be expected that financial markets would give up the possibility of being able to control and influence economic policy making through such movements. Indeed, the world of the 1990s, which is now showing the effects of successive waves of financial deregulation and liberalization across first developed and then developing and formerly socialist countries, bears testimony to the power of finance in determining economic policy.

This may be the single most important reason for the downfall of the Keynesian strategy, at least in its neo-classical synthesis form. As long as financial markets remain open and capital can move across borders in response to policy changes or expectations, there are clear limitations to the use of Keynesian policies to attain full or near-full employment.

However, even Global Keynesianism, or the idea of co-ordinated economic expansion that will not cause punitive capital flight in any single country, faces constraints. These also became evident in the 1970s, in the form of the inflationary barrier posed by the effects of such capitalist expansion on wages and commodity prices. Thus, concerted expansion will increase demand for labour and for goods produced by primary product exporters, leading to an increase in bargaining power. Consequently, if any attempt by these groups to raise their income share is resisted, the result will be inflation. Not only can this be destabilising, it is complete anathema to finance. It is this feature, which essentially amounts to a fight over distributive shares of income both across regions and between economic classes within regions, which is responsible for the current unemployment equilibrium in the world economy as a whole.

But while Bastard Keynesianism may indeed be dead, this does not mean that the economic ideas of Keynes are no longer relevant. In fact, each of the basic principles of Keynes' economic thought outlined above – the principle of effective demand, the possibility of unemployment equilibrium, the working of the multiplier, the role of the state, and the concept of liquidity preference and monetary instability – remain as important as ever.

The trouble is not just that policy makers have abandoned the old Keynesian ways of attempting demand management. The real problem is more that the implications of these basic insights seem to have been forgotten, to be obscured by the miasma of half-truths forced upon us by financial institutions and market analysts. The task before us today is to translate these insights into practical policy alternatives that we can demand from all of our governments.

Bibliography

Akhtar H. K. (1994). 'The Impact of Uruguay Round on World Economy', paper presented at the Tenth Annual General Meeting, Pakistan Society of Development Economists, Islamabad, Pakistan, 2–5 April.

Akyuz, Y. (1991). *Financial Liberalization in Developing Countries: A Neo-Keynesian Approach*, UNCTAD Discussion Paper, No. 36, March.

Akyuz, Y. (1993a). *Financial Liberalization: The Key Issues*, UNCTAD Discussion Paper, No. 56, March.

Akyuz, Y. (1993b). 'Financial Liberalisation: The Key Issues', in Yilmaz Akyuz and Gunther Held (eds), *Finance and the Real Economy*, Santiago: United Nations University.

Akyuz, Y. and A. Cornford (1994). 'Regimes for International Capital Movements and Some Proposals for Reform', UNCTAD Discussion Papers No. 83, Geneva: UNCTAD.

Akyuz, Y. and D. J. Kotte (1991). *Financial Policies in Developing Countries: Issues and Experience*, UNCTAD Discussion Paper, No. 40, August.

Alaigal (1995). 'The Privatization of the Government Medical Store', *Aliran*, 15(10): 11–16.

Allen, F. (1993). 'Stock Markets and Resource Allocation', in C. Mayer and X. Vives (eds), *Capital Markets and Financial Intermediation*, Cambridge: Cambridge University Press.

Allen, F. and D. Gale (1995). 'A Welfare Comparison of Intermediaries and Financial Markets in Germany and the US', *European Economic Review*, 39: 179–209.

Amsden, A. (1989). *Asia's Next Giant: South Korea and Late Industrialisation*, New York: Oxford University Press.

Amsden, A. and T. Hikino (1994). 'Project Execution Capability, Organisational Know-how, and Conglomerate Corporate Growth in Late Industrialisation', *Industrial and Corporate Change*, 3.

Amsden, A. H. and Euh Yoon-Dae (1990). 'South Korea's 1980s Financial Reforms: Goodbye Financial Repression (maybe), Hello New Institutional Restraints', *World Development*, 21(3).

Arestis, P. and P. Demetriades (1997). 'Financial Development and Economic Growth: Assessing the Evidence', *Economic Journal*, 111.

Asian Wall Street Journal, 6 January 1998.

Aslam, M. (1993). 'Tariff Reductions and Trade Performance: A Case of Malaysia', M.Ec. dissertation, University of Malaya, Kuala Lumpur.

Aslam, M. (1997). 'Perdagangan: Polisi dan Isu', in Mohamed Aslam (ed.), *Pembangunan Ekonomi Malaysia: Pengalaman, Isu dan Cabaran*, Kuala Lumpur: Jabatan Penerbitan Universiti Malaya.

Asquith, P. and D. Mullins (1983). 'Equity Issues and Stock Price Dilution,' unpublished paper, Harvard Business School, November.

Athukorala, P. (1993). 'Manufactured Exports from Developing Countries and Their Terms of Trade: A Re-examination of the Sarkar-Singer Results', *World Development*, 21, May: 1607–13.

Athukorala, P. and J. Menon (1996). 'Foreign Investment and Industrialization in Malaysia: Exports, Employment and Spillovers', *Asian Economic Journal*, 10(1).

Atje, R. and B. Jovanovic (1993). 'Stock Markets and Development', *European Economic Review*, 37: 632–40.

Bairoch, P. (1982). 'International Industrialization Levels from 1750 to 1980', *Journal of European Economic History*, 11: 269–310.

Bairoch, P. (1993). *Economics and World History*, Brighton: Wheatsheaf.

Bairoch, P. and R. Kozul-Wright (1996). 'Globalisation Myths: Some Historical Reflections on Integration, Industrialization and Growth in the World Economy', Geneva: *UNCTAD Discussion Papers*, No. 13, March.

Bank Negara Malaysia (1994). *Annual Report 1993*, Kuala Lumpur.

Bank Negara Malaysia (1996a). *Annual Report 1995*, Kuala Lumpur.

Bank Negara Malaysia (1996b). *Annual Report of the Director General of Insurance 1995*, Kuala Lumpur.

Bank Negara Malaysia (1999). *Annual Report 1998*, Kuala Lumpur.

Bank of International Settlements (BIS). *Survey of Foreign Exchange Market Activity*, Basle, various issues.

Barberis, P. and T. May (1993). *Government, Industry and Political Economy*, Buckingham: Open University Press.

Baumol, W. J. (1965). *The Stock Market and Economic Efficiency*, New York: Fordham University Press.

Bello, Walden (1997). 'Addicted to Capital: The Ten-year High and Present-day Withdrawal Trauma of Southeast Asia's Economies', *Issues and Letters*, Philippine Center for Policy Studies, September–December.

Bello, Walden, Nicola Bullard and Kamal Malhotra (eds) (2000). *Global Finance: New Thinking on Regulating Speculative Capital*, London: Zed Books.

Benston, G. J. (1994). 'Universal Banking', *Journal of Economic Perspectives*, 8(3), Summer: 121–43.

Bhaduri, A. and D. Nayyar (1996). *The Intelligent Persons's Guide to Liberalisation*, New Delhi: Penguin Books.

Bhagwati, J. (1994). 'Free Trade: Old and New Challenges', *Economic Journal*, 108.

Bhide, A. (1993). 'The Hidden Cost of Stock Market Liquidity', *Journal of Financial Economics*, 34: 31–51.

Boltho, A. and A. Glyn (1995). 'Can Macroeconomic Policies Raise Employment?' *International Labour Review*, 134(4–5): 451–70.

Business Times, various issues.

Campbell, T. and W. Kracaw (1980). 'Information Production, Market Signalling and the Theory of Intermediation', *Journal of Finance*, 35: 863–82.

Chakravarty, S. and A. Singh (1988). 'The Desirable Forms of Economic Openness in the South', mimeo, WIDER, Helsinki.

Chang Ha-Joon (1994). *The Political Economy of Industrial Policy*, London: Macmillan Press – now Palgrave.

Chin Kok Fay with Jomo K. S. (1996). 'Industrial Financing Options: Lessons for Malaysia', paper prepared for the International Conference on 'Globalisation and Development: Lessons for the Malaysian Economy', 12–13 August, Faculty of Economics and Administration, University of Malaya, Kuala Lumpur.

Cho, Y. J. (1986). 'Inefficiencies from Financial Liberalization in the Absence of Well-Functioning Equity Markets', *Journal of Money, Credit and Banking*, 18(2), May: 191–9.

Cho, Y. J. (1989). 'Finance and Development: The Korean Approach', *Oxford Review of Economic Policy*, 5(4): 88–102.

Cho, Y. J. and D. Khatkhate (1989). 'Financial Liberalisation: Issues and Evidence', *Economic and Political Weekly*, 24(20), May.

Chossudowsky, Michel (1998). 'The IMF Korea Bailout', *Third World Resurgence*, 89, January.

Chowdhury, A. and I. Islam (1993). *The Newly Industrialising Economies of East Asia*, London: Routledge.

Claassen, E. (1992). 'Financial Liberalization and Its Impact on Domestic Stabilization Policies: Singapore and Malaysia', *Weltwirtschaftliches Archiv*, 114: 136–67.

Claessens, S. (1995). 'The Emergence of Equity Investment in Developing Countries: Overview', *The World Bank Economic Review*, 9(1), January: 1–18.

Claessens, Stijn and Thomas Glaessner (1997). *Are Financial Sector Weaknesses Undermining the East Asian Miracle?*, Washington, DC: IBRD/World Bank.

Cline, W. (1982). 'Can the East Asian Model be Generalized?', *World Development*, 10: 81–90.

Coakley, J. and L. Harris (1983). *The City of Capital: London's Role as a Financial Centre*, Oxford: Basil Blackwell.

Corea, G. (undated). *GATT: The Uruguay Round*, Colombo: Dr N. M. Perera Memorial Centre.

Correa, C. M. (1995). 'The Uruguay Round: The Social Costs of the New Patent Rules', *Third World Economics*, 117, 16–31 July: 19–20.

Daim Zainuddin (1997). 'I Was Taken By Surprise', *Asiaweek*, 7 November.

Daly, Herman and John Cobb (1989). *Toward the Common Good*, Boston: Beacon.

Dam, K. W. (1982). *The Rules of the Game: Reforms and Evolution in the International Monetary System*, Chicago: University of Chicago Press.

D'Arista, Jane and Tom Slesinger (1998). 'Reforming the Privatized International Monetary System', *FOMC Alert*, Vol. 2, No. 7–8, December, Financial Markets Center, P.O. Box 334, Philomont, VA 20131, USA:<www.fmcenter.org>

Das, B. L. (1997). *WTO Agreements: Deficiencies, Imbalances and Required Changes*, Penang: Third World Network.

Davis, E. P. (1992). *Debt, Financial Fragility and Systemic Risk*, Oxford: Clarendon Press.

Davis, E. P. (1995). *Pension Funds: Retirement-Income Security and Capital Markets, An International Perspective*, Oxford: Clarendon Press.

de Cecco, M. (1993). 'New Forms of Financial Regulation and the Evolution of Financial Firms', in P. Gourevitch and P. Guerrieri (eds), *New Challenges to International Cooperation*, San Diego: University of California Press.

Dembinski, Paul H. and Alan Schoenenberger (1998). 'The Safe Landing of the Financial Balloon Is Not Impossible', *Finance & the Common Good* Autumn, Geneva.

Demiriguc-Kunt, A. and R. Levine (1995). 'Stock Market Development and Financial Intermediaries', paper presented at the World Bank Conference on 'Stock Markets, Corporate Finance and Economic Growth', 16–17 February.

Dertouzos, M. L., R. K. Lester and R. M. Solow (1990). *Made in America: Regaining the Productive Edge*, New York: Harper Perennial.

Diamond, D. (1984). 'Financial Intermediation and Delegated Monitoring', *Review of Economic Studies*, 51: 393–414.

Dore, R. (1985). 'Financial Structure and the Long-term View', *Policy Studies*, July: 10–29.

Drake, P. J. (1980). *Money, Finance and Development*, Oxford: Martin Robertson.

Dunning, J. H. (1983). 'Changes in the Level and Structure of International Production: The Last One Hundred Years', in M. Casson (ed.), *The Growth of International Business*, London: Allen and Unwin, pp. 84–139.

Eatwell, J. (1995). 'Disguised Unemployment: The G7 Experience', *UNCTAD Review 1995*.

Eatwell, John (1997). *International Financial Liberalisation: The Impact on World Development*, Discussion Paper Series, Office of Development Studies, United Nations Development Programme, New York, May.

Economic Commission for Europe (1996). *Economic Survey 1995–1996*, Belgium: ECE.

Eduardo, Fernandez-Arias and P. J. Montiel (1996). 'The Surge in Capital Inflows to Developing Countries: An Analytical Overview', *The World Bank Economic Review*, 10(1), January: 51–80.

Eichengreen, B. (1996). 'International Lending in the Long-run: Motives for Management', paper presented at the Conference on 'The Future of Emerging Market Capital Flows', New York University, 23–24 May.

Eichengreen, Barry (1999). *Toward a New International Financial Architecture*, Washington, DC: Institute for International Economics.

El-Erian, M. A. and M. S. Kumar (1995). 'Emerging Equity Markets in Middle Eastern Countries', paper presented at the World Bank Conference on 'Stock Markets, Corporate Finance and Economic Growth', 16–17 February.

Epstein, Joshua M. and Robert Axtell, (1996). *Growing Artificial Societies*, the 2050 Project of Brookings Institution, The Santa Fe Institute, and the World Resources Institute: MIT Press.

Euh, Yoon-Dae and J. Baker (1990). *The Korean Banking System and Foreign Influence*, London: Routledge.

Faini, R., F. Clavijo and A. Senhadji-Semlani (1990). 'The Fallacy of the Composition Argument: Does Demand Matter for LDC Manufactured Exports?', Discussion Paper No. 499, CEPR, December.

Fama, E. (1985). 'What's Different about Banks?' *Journal of Monetary Economics*, 15: 29–39.

Favaro, E. and P. T. Spiller (1991). 'Uruguay', in D. Papageurgiou, M. Michaely and A. M. Choksi (eds), *Liberalizing Foreign Trade*, Vol. 1, Cambridge, MA: Basil Blackwell, 321–407.

Feldman, R. A. and M. S. Kumar (1994). 'Emerging Equity Markets: Growth, Benefits and Policy Concerns', IMF paper on Policy Analysis and Assessment, March.

Felix, D. (1995). *Financial Globalization versus Free Trade: The Case for the Tobin Tax*, UNCTAD Discussion Paper No. 108, Geneva.

Fischer, S. (1995). 'Comment on J. D. Sachs and A. Warner, "Economic Reform and the Process of Global Integration"', *Brookings Paper on Economic Activity*, 1: 100–5.

Fischer, Stanley (1997). 'IMF – The Right Stuff', *Financial Times*, 17 December.

Freeman, C. (1989). 'New Technology and Catching Up', *European Journal of Development Research*, 1(1): 85–99.

Fukuyama, F. (1989). 'The End of History', *The National Interest*, 16: 3–18.

Georgescu-Roegen, Nicholas (1971). *The Entropy Law and The Economic Process*, Cambridge, MA: Harvard University Press.

Glyn, A., A. Hughes, A. Lipietz and A. Singh (1990), 'The Rise and Fall of the Golden Age', in S. Marglin and J. Schor (eds), *The Golden Age of Capitalism*, Oxford: Clarendon Press, 39–125.

Gomez, E. T. and Jomo K. S. (1997). *Malaysia's Political Economy: Politics, Patronage and Profits*, Cambridge: Cambridge University Press, 2nd edition, 1999.

Greenwald, B., J. E. Stiglitz and A. Weiss (1984). 'Information Imperfections in the Capital Market and Macroeconomic Fluctuations', *American Economic Review*, 74(2): 194–9.

Gurley, J. and E. Shaw (1960). *Money in a Theory of Finance*, Washington, DC: The Brookings Institution.

Hamilton, C. and J. Whalley (1995). 'Evaluating the Impact of the Uruguay Round Results on Developing Countries', *The World Economy*, 18(1).

Harmsen, R. (1995). 'Regional Trading Arrangements', in *International Trade Policies: The Uruguay Round and Beyond, World Economic and Financial Surveys*, Washington DC: International Monetary Fund.

Harrison, G., T. Rutherford and D. Tarr (1995). 'Quantifying the Outcome of the Uruguay Round', *Finance and Development*, December: 38–41.

Hellmann, T., K. Murdock and J. Stiglitz (1994). 'Addressing Moral Hazard in Banking: Deposit Rate Control vs. Capital Requirements', mimeo, Stanford University.

Hellmann, T., K. Murdock and J. Stiglitz (1995). 'Financial Restraint: Towards a New Paradigm', mimeo, Stanford University.

Helwig, M. (1991). 'Banking, Financial Intermediation and Corporate Finance', in A. Giovannini and C. Mayer (eds) *European Financial Integration*, Cambridge: Cambridge University Press.

Henderson (1971). 'Toward Managing Social Conflict', *Harvard Business Review*, Vol. 49, No. 3 (May–June).

Henderson, H. (1973). 'Ecologists Versus Economists', *Harvard Business Review*, Vol. 51, No. 4 (July–August).

Henderson, H. (1978/96). *Creating Alternative Futures: The End of Economics*, New York: Putnam's Sons, reprint, (1996) Hartford CT: Kumarian Press.

Henderson H. (1981/88). *The Politics of the Solar Age*, Garden City, NY: Anchor Press/Doubleday.

Henderson, H. (1988). 'The Breaking Point', *Australian Financial Review*, pp. 1–9, 4 December.

Henderson, H. (1990). 'Green' Taxes, *Christian Science Monitor*, 6 July.

Henderson, H. (1995). *Paradigms in Progress: Life Beyond Economics*, San Francisco: Berrett Koehler Publishers.

Henderson, H. (1996/97). *Building a Win–Win World*, San Francisco: Berrett Koehler.

Henderson, H. (1966). 'What's Next in the Great Debate About Measuring Wealth and Progress?' *Challenge*, Vol. 39, No. 6, Nov–Dec.

Henderson, H. (1999). *Beyond Globalization: Shaping a Sustainable Global Economy*, West Hartford, CT: Kumarian.

Henderson, H. and Alan F. Kay (1996). 'Introducing Competition to Global Currency Markets', *Futures*, Vol. 28, May.

Henderson H. and Alan F. Kay (1999). 'FXTRS^{sm}, A Foreign Exchange System for Central Banks', *Futures*, Vol. 31, October.

Henderson, H., Harlan Cleveland and Inge Kaul (eds) (1995). 'The UN: Policy and Financing Alternatives', *Futures*, Special Issue. London: Elsevier Scientific; US edn, (1996) 'Global Commission to Fund the UN', Washington, DC.

Hicks, R. John (1937). 'Mr. Keynes and the "Classics": A Suggested Interpretation', *Economterica*, Vol 5, April, pp. 147–59.

Hobsbawm, E. (1987). *The Age of Empire*, London: Weidenfeld and Nicolson.

Hoshi, Takeo, Anil Kashyap and David Scharfstein (1991). 'Corporate Structure, Liquidity and Investment: Evidence from Japanese Industrial Groups', *Quarterly Journal of Economics*, 106, February: 33–60.

Huntington, Samuel (1993). 'Clash of Civilizations', *Foreign Affairs*, Summer, Vol. 72, No. 3.

International Monetary Fund. *Annual Report* and *World Economic Outlook*, Washington, DC, various issues.

Islam, S. (1996). 'Yearning to be Free', *Far Eastern Economic Review*, 2 May: 76.

Iwan J. Azis (1997). 'Currency Crisis in Southeast Asia: The Bubble Finally Bursts', paper presented at the 45th Annual Conference on the Economic Outlook, organized by Research Seminar in Quantitative Economics (RSQE), University of Michigan, USA, 20–21 November.

Jackson, J. H. (1995). 'The World Trade Organisation: Watershed Innovation or Cautious', *The World Economy*, 18: 11–31.

James, C. (1987). 'Some Evidence on the Uniqueness of Bank Loans', *Journal of Financial Economics*, 16: 217–36.

Jomo K. S. (1990). *Undermining Tin: The Decline of Malaysian Pre-eminence*, Sydney: Transnational Corporation Research Project.

Jomo K. S. (ed.) (1998). *Tigers in Trouble: Financial Governance, Liberalisation and Crises in East Asia*, London: Zed Books.

Jomo K. S. *et al.* (1997). *Southeast Asia's Misunderstood Miracle: Industrial Policy and Economic Development in Thailand, Malaysia and Indonesia*, Boulder, CO: Westview.

Kahn, Richard (1972). *Selected Essays on Employment and Growth*, Cambridge: Cambridge University Press.

Kahn, Robert F. (1931). 'The Relation of Home Investment to Unemployment', *Economic Journal*, June: 173–98.

Kahn, Robert F. (1933). 'Public Works and Inflation', *Journal of the American Statistical Association*, Supplement: 168–73.

Kalecki, Michal (1939). *Essays in the Theory of Economic Fluctuations*, London: G. Allen & Unwin.

Kalecki, Michal (1971). *Selected Essays on the Dynamics of the Capitalist Economy, 1933–1970*, Cambridge: Cambridge University Press.

Kaminsky, G. and C. M. Reinhart (1996). 'The Twin Crises: The Causes of Banking and Balance-of-Payments', Working Paper No. 17, Center for International Economics, University of Maryland at College Park.

Keayla, B. K. (1994). 'Final Dunkel Act, New Patent Regime: Myth and Reality', *Frontline*, 6 May: 14–16.

Keynes, J. M. (1921). *The Economic Consequences of the Peace*, London: Macmillan Press – now Palgrave.

Keynes, J. M. (1936). *The General Theory of Employment, Interest and Money*, New York: Harcourt Brace; (1937) London: Macmillan Press – now Palgrave.

Khor K. P. (1983). *The Malaysian Economy: Structures and Dependence*, Kuala Lumpur: Marican & Sons.

Khor K. P. (1994). 'The South at the End of the Uruguay Round', *Third World Resurgence*, 45: 35–8.

Khor K. P. (1995). 'Countering the North's New Foreign Investment Treaty', *Third World Resurgence*, 64: 10–13.

Kim, J. and L. J. Lau (1994). 'The Sources of Economic Growth', *Journal of the Japanese and International Economies*, 8: 235–71.

Kindelberger, C. A. (1992). 'Why Did the Golden Age Last So Long?', in F. Cairncross and A. Cairncross (eds), *The Legacy of the Golden Age, the 1960s and Their Economic Consequences*, London: Routledge.

King, R. G. and R. Levine (1993). 'Financial Intermediation and Economic Development', in Colin Mayer and Xavier Vives (eds), *Capital Markets and Financial Intermediation*, Cambridge: Cambridge University Press.

Kitchen, R. L. (1986). *Finance for the Developing Countries*, Chichester: John Wiley.

Kojima, K. (1995). 'An International Perspective on Japanese Corporate Finance', RIEB Kobe University Discussion Paper, No. 45, March.

Konan, D. E., S. J. La Croix, J. A. Roumassett and J. Heinrich (1995). 'Intellectual Property Rights in the Asian–Pacific Region: Problems, Patterns and Policy', *Asian–Pacific Economic Literature*, 9(2): 13–35.

Kregel, J. (1994). 'Capital Flows: Globalisation of Production and Financing Development', *UNCTAD Review*, pp. 23–38.

Kreinin, M. E. (1995). 'The Uruguay Round and the Future of Trade Policy', in M.E. Kreinin (ed.), *Contemporary Issues in Commercial Policy*, Oxford: Pergamon: 83–90.

Krugman, Paul (1994). 'The Myth of Asia's Miracle', *Foreign Affairs*, November–December.

Krugman, Paul (1995). 'Dutch Tulips and Emerging Markets', *Foreign Affairs*, 74(4): 28–44.

Krugman, Paul (1997a). 'Bahtulism', *Slate Magazine*, 14 August.

Krugman, Paul (1997b). 'What ever happened to the Asian miracle?', *Fortune*, 18 August.

Krugman, Paul (1997c). 'Currency Crises', prepared for NBER conference, October.

Krugman, Paul (1998a). 'What happened to Asia?', prepared for a conference in Japan, January.

Krugman, Paul (1998b). 'Firesale FDI', Available from: URL: http://web.mit.edu/krugman/www/disinter.html

Kumar, P. C. (1994). 'Inefficiencies from Financial Liberalization in the Absence of Well-Functioning Equity Markets: A Comment', *Journal of Money, Credit and Banking*, 26(2), May: 341–4.

Lamberton, Donald M. (ed.) (1971). *The Economies of Information and Knowledge*, Harmondsworth: Penguin Books.

Lawrence, R. Z. (1993). 'Future for the World Trading System and Their Implications for Developing Countries', in M. R. Agosni and D. Tussie (eds), *Trade and Growth, New Dilemmas in Trade Policy*, London: Macmillan Press – now Palgrave, pp. 43–68.

Lee, K., M. H. Pesaran and R. P. Smith (1996). 'Growth and Convergence: A Multicountry Empirical Analysis of the Solow Growth Model', Department of Applied Economics Working Paper, Amalgamated Series 9531, University of Cambridge, Cambridge.

Leland, H. and D. Pyle (1977). 'Information Asymmetries, Financial Structure and Financial Intermediaries', *Journal of Finance*, 32: 371–87.

Levine, R. and S. Zervos (1995). 'Policy, Stock Market Development and Economic Growth', paper presented at the World Bank Conference on 'Stock Markets, Corporate Finance and Economic Growth', 16–17 February.

Lewis, M. K. (1991). 'Theory and Practice of the Banking Firm', in C. J. Green and D. T. Llewellyn (eds) *Surveys in Monetary Economics*, 2nd edition, Oxford: Blackwell.

Lewis, W. A. (1977). *The Evolution of the International Economic Order*, Princeton: Princeton University Press.

Lewis, W. A. (1978). *Growth and Fluctuations: 1870–1913*, London: Allen and Unwin.

Long, Simon (1997). 'The Limits to Golf: Regional Implications of the Southeast Asian Currency Depreciations of 1997', paper presented at the IISS/CSIS Conference on 'Political Change and Regional Security in Southeast Asia', Bali, 7–10 December.

Lucas, R. (1988). 'On the Mechanics of Economic Development', *Journal of Monetary Economics*, 22, July: 3–42.

McKinnon, R. I. (1973). *Money and Capital in Economic Development*, Washington, DC: Brookings Institution.

Maddison, A. (1982). *Phases of Capitalist Development*, Oxford: Oxford University Press.

Maddison, A. (1989). *The World Economy in the Twentieth Century*, Paris: OECD Development Centre.

Maddison, A. (1991). *Dynamic Forces in Capitalist Development*, New York: Oxford University Press.

Maizels, A. (1963). *Industrial Growth and World Trade*, Cambridge: Cambridge University Press.

Malaysia (1991). *Sixth Malaysian Plan, 1991–1995*, Kuala Lumpur: Percetakan Nasional Malaysia.

Malaysia (1996). *Seventh Malaysian Plan, 1996–2000*, Kuala Lumpur: Percetakan Nasional Malaysia.

Malhotra, Kamal (1996). 'Globalisation, Trade and Financial Integration: The Case of Thailand', paper presented at the Social Research Institute, Chulalongkorn University, Bangkok.

Malhotra, Kamal (1997). 'Celebration of "Miracle" Turns Into Damage Control by IMF', *Focus on the Global South*, 3 October.

Marsh, P. (1990). 'Short Termism on Trial', Institutional Fund Managers' Association, London.

Martin, W. (1993). 'The Fallacy of Composition and Developing Country Exports of Manufactures', *World Economy*, 16: 159–72.

Matthews, R. C. O. and A. Bowen (1988). 'Keynesian and Other Explanations of Post-war Macroeconomic Trends', in W. Eltis and P. Sinclair (eds), *Keynes and General Policy: The Relevance of the General Theory after Fifty Years*, London: Macmillan Press – now Palgrave.

Mayer, C. (1988). 'New Issues in Corporate Finance', *European Economic Review*, 32, June: 1167–89.

Mayer, C. (1989). 'Myths of the West: Lessons from Developed Countries for Development Finance', Working Paper WPS301, Washington, DC: World Bank.

Mayer, C. (1990). 'Financial Systems, Corporate Finance and Economic Development', in R. Glen Hubbard (ed.), *Asymmetric Information, Corporate Finance, and Investment*, Chicago: University of Chicago Press.

Mayya, M. R. (1993). *Reflections on the Changing Scenario of the Indian Stock Market*, Bombay: The A. D. Shroff Memorial Trust.

Meeks, G. and G. Whittington (1975). 'Giant Companies in the United Kingdom 1948–69', *Economic Journal*, 86.

Minford, P., J. Riley and E. Nowell (1995). 'The Elixir of Growth: Trade, Non-Traded Goods and Development', Discussion Paper No. 1165, CEPR, May.

Ministry of International Trade and Industry, Japan (1995). *White Paper on International Trade, 1994*, Singapore: McGraw Hill.

Ministry of International Trade and Industry, Malaysia (MITI) (1994). *Malaysia International Trade and Industry Report, 1993*, Kuala Lumpur.

Ministry of International Trade and Industry, Malaysia (MITI) (1995). *Malaysia International Trade and Industry Report, 1994*, Kuala Lumpur.

Mitchell, Ralph A. and Neil Shafer (1984). *Depression Scrip of the United States*, Iola, Wis: Krause Publications.

Moggridge, D. (1980). *The Collected Writings of John Maynard Keynes*, Vol. 25, Cambridge: Cambridge University Press.

Møller, J. Ørstrom (1995). *The Future European Model* Westport, CT: Praeger/Greenwood.

Montes, Manuel F. (1998). *The Currency Crisis in Southeast Asia*, Singapore: Institute of Southeast Asian Studies (ISEAS).

Morgenstern, O. (1959). *International Financial Transactions and Business Cycles*, Princeton: Princeton University Press.

Morgenthau, R. (District Attorney, New York) (1998). 'On the Trail of Global Capital', *New York Times*, 9 November, p. 125.

Mullin, J. (1993). 'Emerging Equity Markets in the Global Economy', *Federal Reserve Bank of New York Quarterly Review*, Summer: 54–83.

Nagaraj, R. (1994). 'Development of India's Capital Market: Implications and Issues', mimeo, Centre for International Studies, Princeton University, Princeton.

Nayyar, D. (1989). 'Towards a Possible Multilateral Framework for Trade in Services: Some Issues and Concepts', in *Technology, Trade Policy and the Uruguay Round*, New York: United Nations.

Nayyar, D. (1993). 'National and International Approaches to Intellectual Property Rights', in M. B. Wallerstein *et al.* (eds), *Global Dimensions of Intellectual Property Rights in Science and Technology*, Washington, DC: National Academy of Sciences, pp. 162–8.

Nayyar, D. (1994). *Migration, Remittances and Capital Flows*, Delhi: Oxford University Press.

Nayyar, D. (1995a). 'Globalisation: The Past in Our Present', Presidential Address to the Indian Economic Association, Chandigarh, 28 December, reprinted in *Indian Economic Journal*, January–March 1996: 1–18.

Nayyar, D. (1997). 'Themes in Trade and Industrialization' in Deepak Nayyar (ed.), *Trade and Industrialization*, Delhi: Oxford University Press.

OECD (1992). *National Accounts, 1992*, Paris: OECD.

OECD (1994). *Economic Outlook*, No. 55, Paris: OECD.

OECD (1995). *Historical Statistics*, Paris: OECD.

Oman, C. (1994). *Globalisation and Regionalisation: The Challenge for Developing Countries*, Paris: OECD Development Centre.

Pagano, M. (1993a). 'Financial Markets and Growth: An Overview', *European Economic Review*, 37: 613–22.

Pagano, M. (1993b). 'The Flotation of Companies on the Stock Market', *European Economic Review*, 37: 1101–25.

Panic, M. (1992). *European Monetary Union: Lessons from the Classical Gold Standard*, London: Macmillan Press – now Palgrave.

Panic, M. (1995). 'The Bretton Woods System: Concept and Practice', in J. Michie and J. G. Smith (eds), *Managing the Global Economy*, Oxford: Oxford University Press.

Park, Y. C. (1994). 'Concepts and Issues' in H. T. Patrick and Y. C. Park (eds), *The Financial Development of Japan, Korea and Taiwan: Growth, Repression and Liberalisation*, New York: Oxford University Press.

Patrick, H. (1994). 'The Relevance of Japanese Finance and Its Main Bank System', in M. Aoki and H. Patrick (eds), *The Japanese Main Bank System: Its Relevance for Developing and Transforming Economies*, Oxford: Oxford University Press.

Porter, M. E. (1992). 'Capital Disadvantage: America's Failing Capital Investment System', *Harvard Business Review*, September–October: 65–82.

Poterba, M. and L. H. Summers (1988). 'Mean Reversion in Stock Prices: Evidence and Implications', *Journal of Financial Economics*, 22: 27–59.

Prebisch, R. (1950). *The Economic Development of Latin America and Its Principle Problems*, New York: United Nations.

Pryor, Richard J. *et al.*, 'Aspen Model', Sandia National Labs, New Mexico, USA.

Quah, D. (1993). 'Empirical Cross-section Dynamics in Economic Growth', *European Economic Review*, 37: 426–434.

Raghavan, C. (1991). *Recolonisation: GATT, the Uruguay Round and the Third World*. Penang: Third World Network.

Raghavan, C. (1996). *The Role of Multilateral Organisations in the Globalisation Process*. Penang: Third World Network.

Raghavan, C. (1998). 'BIS Banks Kept Shovelling Funds to Asia, Despite Warnings', *Third World Economics*, 16–31 January.

Rasiah, R. (1995). *Foreign Capital and Industrialization in Malaysia*, London: Macmillan Press – now Palgrave.

Robinson, Joan (1962). 'Review of H. G. Johnson's *Money, Trade and Economic Growth*', *Economic Journal*, Vol. 72, September, pp. 690–2.

Robinson, Joan (1969). *Introduction to the Theory of Employment*, 2nd edn, London: Macmillan Press – now Palgrave.

Rodrik, D. (1994). 'The Rush to Free Trade in the Developing World: Why So Late? Why Now? Will It Last?', in S. Haggard and S. B. Webb (eds), *Voting for Reform: The Politics of Adjustment in New Democracies*, New York: Oxford University Press.

Roemer, P. (1989). 'Capital Accumulation and the Theory of Long-run Growth', in R. Barro (ed.), *Modern Business Cycle Theory*, Cambridge, MA: Harvard University Press.

Rowthorn, R. E. (1995). 'A Simulation Model of North-South Trade', *UNCTAD Review 1995*, New York and Geneva: United Nations.

Sachs, J. D. (1997). 'Secretive Workings of the IMF Call for Reassessment', *New Straits Times*, 23 December.

Sachs, Jeffrey, (1998). 'Global Capitalism Making It Work', invited essay, *The Economist*, 12 September, pp. 23–5.

Sachs, J. D. and J. Warner (1995). 'Economic Reform and the Process of Global Integration', *Brookings Papers on Economic Activity*, 1: 1–95.

Sarkar, P. and H. W. Singer (1991). 'Manufactured Exports of Developing Countries and Their Terms of Trade Since 1965', *World Development*, 19, April: 333–40.

Sarkar, P. and H. W. Singer (1993). 'Manufacture-Manufacture Terms of Trade Deterioration: A Reply', *World Development*, 21, May: 1617–20.

Schultz, S. (1993). 'Services Sector in Uruguay Round', *Intereconomics*, Sept/Oct.

Schumpeter, J. (1939). *Business Cycles*, New York: McGraw-Hill.

Sen, S. R. (1994). 'From GATT to WTO', *Economic and Political Weekly*, 24(43), 22 October: 2802–3.

Shahin, M. (1996). *From Marrakesh to Singapore: The WTO and Developing Countries*, Penang: Third World Network.

Sharpe, S. A. (1990). 'Asymmetric Information, Bank Lending, and Implicit Contracts: A Stylized Model of Customer Relationships', *Journal of Finance*, 45(4), September: 1069–87.

Shaw, E. S. (1973). *Financial Deepening in Economic Development*, New York: Oxford University Press.

Singer, H. W. (1950). 'The Distribution of Gains Between Investing Countries and Borrowing Countries', *American Economic Review*, 40(2): 473–85.

Singh, A. (1990). 'The Institution of a Stock Market in a Socialist Economy: Notes on Chinese Economic Reform', in P. Nolan and Dong Fueng (eds), *The Chinese Economy and Its Future*, Cambridge: Polity Press.

Singh, A. (1992a). 'Corporate Take-overs', in J. Eatwell, M. Milgate and P. Newman (eds), *The New Palgrave Dictionary of Money and Finance*, London: Macmillan Press – now Palgrave.

Singh, A. (1992b). 'The Stock Market and Economic Development: Should Developing Countries Encourage Stock Markets?', UNCTAD Discussion Paper, No. 49, October.

Singh, A. (1993). 'The Stock Market and Economic Development: Should Developing Countries Encourage Stock Markets?', *UNCTAD Review*, No. 4.

Singh, A. (1994a). 'Openness and the Market Friendly Approach to Development: Learning the Right Lessons from Development Experience', *World Development*, 22(12): 1811–24.

Singh, A. (1994b). 'Industrial Policy in Europe and Industrial Development in the Third World', in P. Bianchi, K. Cowling and R. Sugden (eds), *Europe's Economic Challenge: Analyses of Industrial Strategy and Agenda for the 1990s*, London: Routledge.

Singh, A. (1995a). 'Competitive Markets and Economic Development: A Commentary on World Bank Analyses', *International Papers in Political Economy*, 2(1).

Singh, A. (1995b). 'Institutional Requirements for Full Employment in Advanced Economies', *International Labour Review*, 134(4–5): 471–96.

Singh, A. (1995c). 'The Causes of Fast Economic Growth in East Asia', *UNCTAD Review 1995*, pp. 91–128.

Singh, A. (1996). *Savings, Investment and the Corporation in the East Asian Miracle*, UNCTAD Discussion Paper on East Asian Development: Lessons for a New Global Environment, Study No. 9, Geneva.

Singh, A. (1997a). 'Financial Liberalisation, the Stock Market and Economic Development', *Economic Journal*, 111.

Singh, A. (1997b). 'Liberalisation and Globalisation: An Unhealthy Euphoria', in J. Michie and J. Grieve Smith (eds), *Employment and Economic Performance*, Oxford: Oxford University Press.

Singh, A. and A. Zammit (1995). 'Employment and Unemployment, North and South', in J. Michie and J. G. Smith (eds), *Managing the Global Economy*, Oxford: Oxford University Press.

Singh, A. and J. Hamid (1992). *Corporate Financial Structures in Developing Countries*, International Finance Corporation Technical Paper No. 1, Washington, DC: World Bank.

Smeets, M. (1995). 'Tariff Issues in the Uruguay Round: Features and Remaining Issues', *Journal of World Trade Law*, 29(3).

Smith, R. C. and I. Walter (1996). 'Rethinking Emerging Market Equities', paper presented at the Conference on the 'Future of Emerging Market Capital Flows', 23–24 May, New York University.

Soete, Luc and Baster Weel (1999). 'Cybertax', *Futures*, Vol. 30, No. 9, pp. 853–71.

Somel, C. (1992). 'Finance for Growth: Lessons from Japan', UNCTAD Discussion Paper, No. 44, Geneva: UNCTAD.

Soros, George (1997). 'Avoiding a Breakdown', *Financial Times*, 31 December.

Soros, George (1998). 'Toward a Global Open Society', *The Atlantic Monthly*, 281(1): 20–32, January.

Soros, George (1998b). *The Crisis of Global Capitalism*, New York: Public Affairs.

South Centre (1995). *The Uruguay Round and the South: A Critical Analysis*, Geneva: South Centre.

South Commission (1990). *Challenge to the South* Oxford: Oxford University Press.

Stalker, P. (1994). *The Work of Strangers: A Survey of International Labour Migration*, Geneva: International Labour Office.

Steinherr, A. and C. Huveneer (1990). 'Universal Banks: The Prototype of Successful Banks in the Integrated European Market? A View Inspired by German Experience', Research Report No. 2, CEPS Financial Markets Unit, Centre for European Policy Studies, Brussels.

Stiglitz, J. E. (1985). 'Credit Markets and the Control of Capital', *Journal of Money, Credit and Banking*, 17(2), May: 133–52.

Stiglitz, J. E. (1994). 'The Role of the State in Financial Markets', Proceedings of the World Bank Annual Conference on Development Economics 1993, Washington, DC: World Bank.

Summers, V. and L. Summers, (1989). 'When Financial Markets Work Too Well: A Cautious Case for a Financial Transaction Tax', *Journal of Financial Services*, No. 3.

Tarshis, Lorrie (1987). 'The Keynesian Revolution', in *The New Palgrave Dictionary of Economics*, London: Macmillan Press – now Palgrave.

Taylor, L. (1996). 'Globalisation, the Bretton Woods Institutions and Economic Policy in the Developing World', mimeo, New School of Social Research, New York, April.

The Economist (1989). London, 9 September.

The Economist (1994). 'A Survey of the Global Economy', London, 1 October.

The Economist (1995). 'A Survey of the World Economy', London, 7 October.

Third World Network, *Third World Resurgence*, various issues.

Tinker, H. (1974). *A New System of Slavery: The Export of Indian Labour Overseas, 1830–1920*, Oxford: Oxford University Press.

Tirole, J. (1991). 'Privatisation in Eastern Europe: Incentives and the Economics of Transition', in O. J. Blanchard and S. S. Fischer (eds), *NBER Macroeconomics Annual 1991*, Cambridge, MA: MIT Press.

Tobin, J. (1984). 'On the Efficiency of the Financial System', *Lloyds Bank Review*, July: 1–15.

ul Haq, Mahbub, Inge Kaul and Isabelle Grunberg (eds) (1996). *The Tobin Tax: Coping with Financial Volatility*, Oxford: Oxford University Press.

United Nations Centre on Transnational Corporations (UNCTC) and UNCTAD. *World Investment Report*, New York and Geneva, various issues.

United Nations Conference on Trade and Development (UNCTAD). *Handbook of International Trade and Development Statistics*, Geneva, various issues.

United Nations Conference on Trade and Development (UNCTAD). *Trade and Development Report*, various issues.

United Nations Development Program (1995). *Human Development Report, 1995*, New York: Oxford University Press.

United Nations. *Transnational Corporations in World Development*, various surveys.

United Nations. *Yearbook of International Trade Statistics*, various issues.

United Nations. *Yearbook of National Accounts Statistics*, various issues.

Vadarajan (1998). *Times of India*, 30–31 January.

Von Urff, W. (1995). 'The Result of the Uruguay Round Concerning Agriculture and Their Consequences', *Economics*, 51.

Wade, R. (1990). *Governing the Market*, Princeton, NJ: Princeton University Press.

Wain, Barry (1997). 'Let's Not Bury Asian Values', *Asian Wall Street Journal*, 5–6 December.

Weiss, Linda (1998). *The Myth of the Powerless State*, Ithaca NY: Cornell University Press.

White, G. (ed.) (1998). *Developmental States in East Asia*, London: Macmillan Press – now Palgrave.

WIDER (1990). *Foreign Portfolio Investment in Emerging Equity Markets*, Study Group Series No. 5, Helsinki: World Institute for Development Economics Research of the United Nations University.

Woo-Cumings, Meredith (1997). 'Bailing Out or Sinking In?: The IMF and the Korean Financial Crisis', paper presented at the Economic Strategy Institute, 2 December.

Wood, A. (1994). *North–South Trade, Employment and Inequality: Changing Fortunes in a Skill-Driven World*, Oxford: Clarendon Press.

World Bank (1993). *The East Asian Miracle*, New York: Oxford University Press.

World Bank. *World Development Report*, Washington, DC, various issues.

Young, A. (1995). 'The Tyranny of the Numbers: Confronting the Realities of the East Asian Growth Experience', NBER Working Paper No. 4860, Washington: National Bureau of Economic Research.

Zysman, J., (1983). *Government, Markets and Growth: Financial Systems and the Politics of Industrial Change*, Oxford: Martin Robertson.

Index